NOLO *Your Legal Companion*

OUR MISSION
Make the law as simple as possible, saving you time, money and headaches.

Whether you have a simple question or a complex problem, turn to us at:

NOLO.COM
Your all-in-one legal resource
Need quick information about wills, patents, adoptions, starting a business—or anything else that's affected by the law? **Nolo.com** is packed with free articles, legal updates, resources and a complete catalog of our books and software.

NOLO NOW
Make your legal documents online
Creating a legal document has never been easier or more cost-effective! Featuring Nolo's Online Will, as well as online forms for LLC formation, incorporation, divorce, name change—and many more! Check it out at **http://nolonow.nolo.com**.

NOLO'S LAWYER DIRECTORY
Meet your new attorney
If you want advice from a qualified attorney, turn to Nolo's Lawyer Directory—the only directory that lets you see hundreds of in-depth attorney profiles so you can pick the one that's right for you. Find it at **http://lawyers.nolo.com**.

ALWAYS UP TO DATE
Sign up for NOLO'S LEGAL UPDATER
Old law is bad law. We'll email you when we publish an updated edition of this book—sign up for this free service at nolo.com/legalupdater.

Find the latest updates at NOLO.COM
Recognizing that the law can change even before you use this book, we post legal updates during the life of this edition at **nolo.com/updates**.

Is this edition the newest? ASK US!
To make sure that this is the most recent available, just give us a call at **800-728-3555**.

(Please note that we cannot offer legal advice.)

Please note

We believe accurate, plain-English legal information should help you solve many of your own legal problems. But this text is not a substitute for personalized advice from a knowledgeable lawyer. If you want the help of a trained professional—and we'll always point out situations in which we think that's a good idea— consult an attorney licensed to practice in your state.

1st edition

Patent Savvy
for Managers

by Attorney Kirk Teska

NOLO

FIRST EDITION	OCTOBER 2007
Editor	RICHARD STIM
Cover design	SUSAN WIGHT
Book design	TERRI HEARSH
Proofreading	JOE SADUSKY
Index	BAYSIDE INDEXING SERVICE
Printing	DELTA PRINTING SOLUTIONS, INC.

Teska, Kirk, 1962-
  Patent savvy for managers : spot & protect valuable innovations in your
company / by Kirk Teska. --.1st ed.
      p. cm.
  ISBN-13: 978-1-4133-0694-1 (pbk.)
  ISBN-10: 1-4133-0694-2 (pbk.)
  1. Patent laws and legislation--United States--Popular works. 2. Patents--United
States--Popular works. I. Title.
KF3114.6.T47 2007
346.7304'86--dc22

                              2007013012

For information on bulk purchases or corporate premium sales, please contact the Special
Sales Department. For academic sales or textbook adoptions, ask for Academic Sales. Call
800-955-4775 or write to Nolo, 950 Parker Street, Berkeley, CA 94710.

Dedication

To Lora, my wife.

Acknowledgments

This work would not have been possible without the input of many people who have shaped the way I think, write, and talk about patents. Here, unfortunately I can acknowledge only a small subset of that group—those who directly provided input to my original manuscript and the many versions of this work between then and publication.

First, my wife Lora, who many times reviewed, edited, and constructively criticized my original manuscript, my editor's revisions thereto, and my revisions to his edits. Although Lora is a boring patent attorney like me, she gets the intersection of patents, technology, and business.

Second, my editor, Rich Stim. Rich patiently educated me about the publishing process (I thought the editor just proofread the manuscript) and he alone transformed my manuscript into a tighter, more readable, and better organized commercial product. A fair amount of the resulting book is entirely Rich's and/or originated from a previous book of his. Rich, at just the right times, provided both encouragement and criticism.

My partner of 16 years, Joe Iandiorio, himself a prolific writer, was one of the key people who shaped the way I think, write, and talk about patents. At times, I would like to think I've surpassed him, but I know in my heart of hearts that's impossible. Some of the key ideas in this book originated with Joe.

Thanks too to my secretary of many years, Olga Kadish. I still initially write everything longhand. Olga deciphered my cryptic scribblings and worked on numerous edits to each chapter of this book. Like me, Olga spent the better part of the last two years on this book.

Finally, thanks to everyone at Nolo. They alone saw the need for a book at the intersection of patents, technology, and business.

Table of Contents

Your Legal Companion 1

1 No Guarantees ... and Other Patent Principles 5

Patent Principles 7

Patent Myths 10

Comparing Lifecycles: Patent and Product 11

A Word on Patent Management 16

2 Does Four Include Three? Case Studies You Can Understand 19

Gillette v. Schick: Does Four Include Three? 21

John Deere v. Toro: Control Means What? 31

Amazon.com v. Barnes & Noble: You Can't Have It Both Ways 37

The Case of the Unintelligible Dog Chew Patent 43

3 Anything Under the Sun (Made by Man): What's Patentable? 49

What's Patentable? 50

Key Standards: New and Unobvious 52

Reinventing the Wheel: Improvements and New Uses 64

Should You Patent It? 67

4 The Claim Game: How to Read a Patent 83

Anatomy of a Patent 85

The Claim Game 105

What a Patent Doesn't Tell You 125

5 What to Do When Your Candy Bar Melts: Capturing Patents 129

Patent Policies and Ownership 132

Trade Secret Considerations 136

Documentation 139

Patent Committees 148

6 The Long and Winding Road to "Patent Pending" 153

Playing the Claim Game: Part Two 155

To Search or Not to Search? 158

Things to Keep in Mind About Patent Searching 160

The Patentability Study 165

The Patent Application 167

The Provisional Patent Application 177

7 The Good Shepherd: Patent Prosecution and Management 181

Hurry Up and Wait 182

Dealing With Rejection 184

How Much Should You Say During Prosecution? 185

How Costs Mount Up During Prosecution 187

Post-Prosecution Activity 190

Management and Tracking 192

8 The Worldwide Patent Party 197

The One-Year Rule: How It Affects Foreign Patent Filing 198

How Do You File Outside the U.S.? 199

Where and When Should You File? 201

Foreign Patent Budgeting: The Robot 206

The *Running Tab*: What a Typical U.S. and
Foreign Filing Might Cost 211

9 Live and Let Die:
The Exhausting Effects of Patent Litigation 213

The Battle Over the BlackBerry 216

The Claim Game: Part Three 218

The BlackBerry: From Application to Trial 220

The BlackBerry: Judgment and Reexamination 222

Post-Trial: The Never-ending Story 223

What Did NTP Do Right? 230

What Did RIM Do Wrong? 231

Common Lessons for All Litigation 231

What to Expect in Patent Litigation 232

10 Caveat Emptor: Buying and Licensing Patents 235

Determining Patent Value 237

Do You *Really* Need the Patent? 239

Assignment or License? 244

Licensing a Patent 247

Buying a Patent 256

G Patent Glossary 259

I Index 271

Your Legal Companion

Patents are boring.

I can understand how you might think that. The first patent law course I took in law school was the most boring course I had ... *and I was studying to be a patent attorney*. Adding to that misconception is the fact that many patent attorneys are also boring. We're hybrids, part attorney, part engineer, and we usually get little respect from either camp (and often pick up the worst traits of both). Perhaps you've sat slack-jawed in a meeting with a patent attorney. Then you know what I'm talking about.

But the truth is that patents are not boring at all. Actually, they're fascinating. Patents are at the intersection of two topics the general public finds interesting: the law and technology.

My wife and I are patent attorneys, and we find patents exciting. So do many professionals in medicine, science, investments, research, production, sales and marketing, design, testing, fabrication, business, engineering, and manufacturing. Just about everyone in the business world shares the excitement of patents—once they *understand* patents and how they can both benefit and adversely affect a company.

It would be a rare case if anyone who's spent considerable time in a business had not yet come across a patent issue. These issues reach into even the most mundane and low-tech businesses. For example, I was at a court hearing some time ago involving a patent dispute over a plastic holder that comes with a floral bouquet sold by a florist.

Unfortunately, you can't make informed business decisions about patents unless you can understand the language. It's what I call an "information asymmetry" that exists between patent attorneys and people in the business world, and it's the biggest problem in dealing with patents. How can you learn the strange nomenclature—for example, terms such as "provisional patent application," "means plus function," and "file wrapper"?

For most businesses, being patent literate is not a luxury, it's a necessity. Patents are everywhere, and business owners and managers ignore patents at their peril. If you are charged with a patent violation, you can be sure the people on the other side of the fence will be patent literate.

The fact is that anybody can understand patents. Over the last 15 years, I've educated scientists, engineers, business managers, corporate attorneys, venture capitalists, and others about the business realities of patents. And that's one of the reasons I wrote this book—I had trouble finding a cogent quick-read reference exploring patents and the patent system that would suit businesspeople, engineers, and project managers—the very audience who needs to understand patents the most.

My goal in writing this book is to help businesspeople—whether engineers, managers, scientists, or CEOs—spot patentable innovations, protect them through the patent review process, and preserve them through tracking and vigilance. Although I explain how the law works, this is not a legal tome, nor is it intended as a do-it-yourself kit for independent inventors.

Here are some things I'm *not* trying to do here: I'm not trying to make you a patent expert or a patent professional; I'm not trying to show you how to prepare, file, or prosecute a patent application; and I'm not trying to show you how to draft and review a patent license, patent assignment, or other legal documents. I advise that most of this legal heavy-lifting be done by a patent attorney, a patent agent, or your company's general counsel. With that mind, this book will:

- explain patent principles, review patent lifecycles, and expose patent myths
- provide numerous (easy to understand) case studies
- describe what's patentable
- show you how to read a patent
- explain procedures for capturing patentable ideas
- walk you through the steps from patent review to filing a patent application
- help you analyze whether foreign patent protection is worth the expense

- review the basics of patent litigation and analyze a patent lawsuit
- explain the principles of buying, selling, and licensing patents
- show you methods to manage and track patents.

If I provide you with a basic understanding of patents, how to manage the associated risks associated with patents, and how to contain patent costs, then I will have succeeded. You will be patent savvy.

Great! Let's embark on a short patent course that hopefully will make your job easier, your employer more secure, and your business more prosperous.

No Guarantees ...
and Other Patent Principles

Patent Principles 7

Patent Myths..10

Comparing Lifecycles: Patent and Product 11

A Word on Patent Management..16

As I write this, it's possible that you or your company may be developing a technology, process, or device that will give you an edge over competitors or even transform the marketplace. But it's also possible that through mismanagement, short-sightedness, or a lack of funds the ability to monopolize that innovation (or an improvement) will slip through your company's hands. That possibility is not as unusual as you may think.

> *"My father invented the burglar alarm which, unfortunately, was stolen from him."*
>
> —VICTOR BORGE

It's also possible that your company may be on an equally wrong-headed course of patenting everything despite the fact that most of these technologies have little chance of earning back the hundreds of thousands spent for patent filings and prosecution. Hopefully, this book will help you avoid both courses of action—alerting you how to protect what you've got, and avoiding the cost of dubious patents.

"Patent"—the word connotes idea, invention, ingenuity, innovation, improvement protection, asset, expense, mystery, land mine, hurdle, or frustration. But the connotation that I'd like you to make when you think of patents is *business*. That's because the relationship between patents and business is inseparable. And by thinking of patents as a business proposition, you can see them in terms of costs and benefits, not simply as a hybrid of technology and law. After all, patents are one of the most valuable assets in U.S. commerce, operating almost as a discrete form of currency. Businesses create them, buy and sell them, barter with them, fight over them, and often die because of them.

In fact, it could be argued that American's success as a global marketplace leader is based on its patent system. Bill Gates has said that Microsoft, at any given time, is only two years away from failure. His basic message is that all companies have to innovate to survive. Since innovation inevitably begets competition and since the only the reliable way to protect innovation against competition is by patents, it is essential that everyone involved in the innovation business be patent savvy.

Whatever level of interest you have in patents, there is no denying their importance in commerce. In its 230-year history, the United States Patent Office (better known as the U.S. Patent and Trademark Office or USPTO) has issued over seven million U.S. patents—No. 7,000,000 was granted to DuPont in 2006 for biodegradable, cotton-like fibers useful in textiles. Thousands of patents are also the subject of litigation each year—for example, 2,720 patent cases were filed in 2005. (No doubt you've read about some of this litigation.) And every day millions of dollars pass hands among U.S. companies as valuable patents are bought, sold, and licensed.

And always, there are more patents on their way. Over 300,000 patent applications are filed annually in the U.S., and about half those applications become patents. In one week while I was writing this book, Patent Office examiners considered patent applications for a system for estimating the cost of fishing gear, a method for managing property cleaning services, and a system for prepurchasing air flight miles.

So, let's start our journey by exploring some patent principles and myths.

Patent Principles

Here are ten patent principles that I'll explore in this book:

- **Patents offer no guarantees.** Patents, although prevalent and important, offer no absolute guarantees. Often, it cannot be reliably predicted whether your patent will have economic value—that is, whether or not your product will sell well because of its patented features. It's also often difficult to predict how a competitor might engineer a viable competing product. And sometimes it's tough to determine whether someone with a prior patent will have a case against you should you sell your patented product—even if a search is conducted before your patent application is filed. Don't let this rule of "no guarantees" scare you away from patents. After all, at the beginning of any product innovation, nobody knows for certain whether a new product will really sell, what it will really cost, or whether it can be successfully engineered and manufactured at a reasonable cost. The unpredictability of patents is really a reflection of the unpredictability of commerce.

- **Many (maybe even most) patents do not provide any real value.** The number-one reason for this is patent claims—the patent's boundaries—which are sometimes too detailed with too many requirements. When no effort is made to predict how a competitor might engineer a competing product, or when care is not taken with the prosecution of the patent application, the resulting patent can be rendered useless because of even a single word in a patent. Other times, the patented invention itself is narrow, in light of the state of the art at the time the invention was made. So, just having a patent is not always enough.

- **Some patents have unintended consequences.** Even a worthless patent, by sheer virtue of its existence, may stop a competitor in its tracks if the competitor believes that the patent prevents him from competing. Also, patents which are unintelligible, clearly invalid, and/or seemingly irrelevant sometimes thwart competition by competitors simply because it's not worth the fight, or because it's cheaper to settle than to litigate.

- **The Patent Office, like any organization, makes mistakes.** Unintelligible and invalid patents do issue. Fortunately, there are mechanisms to correct the mistakes, like a reexamination at the Patent Office or an invalidity defense raised in court.

- **There is no room for knee-jerk reactions in patent-related decisions.** Patents are expensive, and patent litigation is even more expensive. Companies must thoughtfully consider their patent decisions and not apply conventional wisdom or "go with their gut." Those who fail to heed this advice will wish they had patented more or that they had taken someone else's patents more seriously.

- **A patent alone does not make you money.** Inventors and business-people sometimes believe that the money will come rolling in if only they had a patent. Patent-savvy people, though, know a patent is just a document. Innovative products and services make you money. If those products and services are properly patented, you might make more money. Or, if you own a valuable patent covering technology that someone else wants or has implemented in their product or service, they might pay you for your patent either by choice or as a result of litigation. Therefore, without a product or service, without a licensing program, or without litigation, no payments are made to the patent owner just because he holds a patent. Like the engineering and technology underlying a product, patents are a necessary but not a sufficient condition for product success.

- **Some products sell just fine without being patented.** This is a corollary to the previous principle: A patent is not a condition precedent to good sales figures; innovation and quality is. I would venture to guess that many of the products on the shelves of a typical box store are not patented. Therefore, not having a patent is not the end of the world. Some products sell well because they are the first of their kind, are of good quality, and have a distinguishable design, or for a myriad of other reasons. I often get asked if a given invention is worthwhile. That's the wrong question to ask a patent attorney. The "Pet Rock" sold well. I never would have believed people would pay for bottled water. Only your company can properly judge the marketability of a new product.

- **There are no shortcuts to patent protection.** In Chapter 6, I explain the inherent challenges with the provisional patent application—a simple document that will preserve your rights at the Patent Office for one year. I also explain that if inventors don't spend sufficient time with the patent attorney, the result can be that you pay a high cost for a patent with a low value. The same is true if a company fails to document its steps in the patent review process. In short, you can't cut corners when looking to protect company innovations.

- **All things patent are costly.** Through this book, I have included a running total for your patent costs from the time an innovation is identified, through the patent review and the filing of a patent, then through patent prosecution and foreign filing and post-issuance activities. As you can imagine, acquiring a U.S. patent is expensive (foreign patents are even more expensive), and the cost of patent litigation is … well, astronomical.

- **All things patent must be managed or else the first nine principles have no real import.** Without patent management, a lot can go wrong—for example, people rely too heavily on patents for competitive advantage, patents of low value are procured, business opportunities are missed, mistakes by the Patent Office are left uncorrected, and wrong decisions are made regarding your own or a competitor's patent. In short, a company sometimes pays a high price for failing to properly manage its patents.

Patent Myths

Considering the crucial part patents play in American commerce, it's a wonder, then, that there are so many inaccuracies in the business world concerning patents. Below are some of the myths that will be debunked in this book:

- You must conduct a patent search before filing a patent application.
- You can file a worldwide patent.
- There is a patent application form you can fill out.
- Patents can be reliably searched on the Internet.
- You can still get a patent so long as a prior patent doesn't disclose your idea in the patent claims.
- You can't patent software, financial tools, or business methods.
- A competitor cannot copy your product because you have patents pending.
- The most important thing is to file the patent early; you can always add things to it later.
- You can predict with confidence exactly what a patent will cost.
- The marketing department has no business in the management of patents.
- A patent application need be understood only by those skilled in the art.

- Patents are primarily for revolutionary ideas.
- Your patent will sail through the Patent Office.
- Having a patent will stop poachers.
- The company with the most patents wins.
- If you can't get a patent, you can always use trade secret (or copyright or trademark) law to protect this product.
- Everything you need to know about a patent is on the title page.
- Having a patent means you are free to sell your product.
- A competitor can't patent an improvement or a new use for your patented product.
- Engineers don't need to deal with patent claims; that's the patent attorney's job.
- If you didn't know about another patent when you created an innovation, you're not infringing.
- Most patents have commercial value.
- You have to wait until you get the patent before you can sell a product.
- A patent is good for forever.
- Most infringers will stop copying when notified by an attorney.
- You can extend the term of a patent.
- You can file provisional patent applications in foreign countries.
- A provisional patent application allows you to stop a competitor from making the product.
- Patents are boring.

Hopefully, I'll bust the last "myth" within one or two chapters.

Comparing Lifecycles: Patent and Product

Before we review several case studies and patent management principles, it's a good idea to review the lifecycle of a patent. The flowchart below illustrates the nine steps in the lifecycle of a patent. This cycle takes 20-25 years to complete. The lifecycle does not include foreign patent protection (typically initiated within a year after the U.S. patent application is filed) and also does not include the potential for patent litigation, which can seriously affect the lifecycle. I'll also provide basic management tasks.

- **Invention.** This is the innovation process, sometimes known as the "Eureka" moment that results in something new and nonobvious. Your company's goal at this point is to recognize that the innovation may be protected under patent law and to treat it accordingly—for example, to preserve confidentiality and to avoid sales or public disclosure until a full patent review has been conducted. Later we'll learn that to be patentable, the invention doesn't really have to be the subject of a "Eureka" moment or even be remarkable. In fact, many patents cover new functionality or features added to an existing product or device.

- **Invention Capture.** This is the procedure for recording the idea, innovation, or improvement, for example, by the use of inventor notebooks. Your company must maintain accurate documentation for a variety of reasons, the most important of which is to confirm the dates of conception and the dates when the innovation was successfully tested. As between two companies fighting over the patent rights to the same invention, one way that conception of an invention is proven in court is those inventor notebooks—bound tablets with places on each page for the date, an inventor's signature, and witness signatures. Later I'll teach you an easy way to capture inventions.

- **Determining Whether to Seek a Patent.** This is the process whereby your company's patent review committee, those managing a project, or a "tiger team" meets to evaluate whether it's worth proceeding with a patent filing. Don't worry if your company doesn't have a patent review committee. Later, I'll discuss how to create one.

- **Patent Application Drafting.** Once the decision is made to seek a patent, the drafting process begins with an "interview" between the inventor or inventors and your patent attorney, followed by the drafting of the application. Subsequently, company

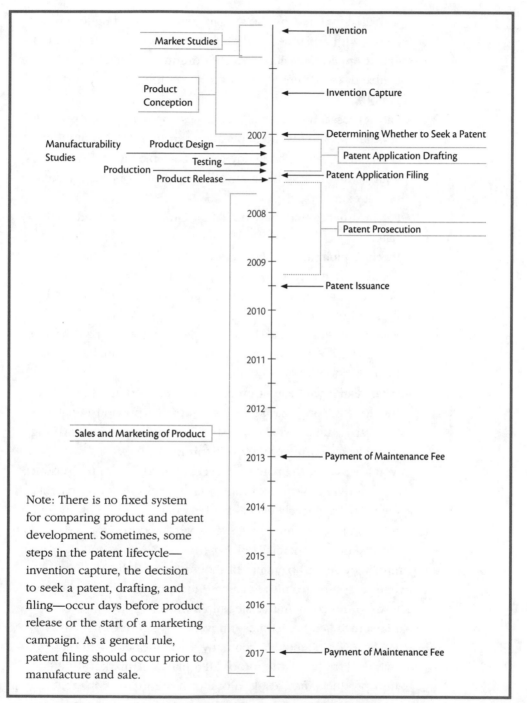

Comparison of Product and Patent Development

managers will review the application prior to filing to ensure a patent with a planned and definite purpose is being pursued.

- **Patent Application Filing.** Once it's drafted, the patent application is filed at the Patent Office, kicking off the "patent pending" period.
- **Patent Prosecution.** This is the process by which your patent attorney shepherds the application through the Patent Office, overcoming or resolving any examiner objections. If necessary, your company may be involved in resolving objections from the patent examiner.
- **Patent Issuance.** Victory. The Patent Office has granted your patent.
- **Patent Exploitation and Preservation.** With patent in hand, your company seeks revenue for its patent through either sales or licensing and, at the same time, diligently protects its turf by fighting infringers.
- **Payment of Maintenance Fees.** In order to keep the patent alive (or "maintain" the patent), your company must make periodic payments to the Patent Office.
- **Patent Expiration.** Patent protection has ended and the public is free to use, copy, and sell your company's previously patented innovation unless you've pursued additional patents covering new ideas—and kept the cycle turning.

As you are aware, the patent lifecycle coincides with the product lifecycle. When we review the product lifecycle in regard to patents, many key product lifecycle events fall between the point of invention and patent application filing. That's for a very good reason. Fewer than 5% of patents are commercialized. So, there's no sense going through the patent lifecycle and payment of thousands of dollars in fees unless the revenue resulting from the patented technology justifies the cost.

Below are the comparative steps in a product's development.

- **Market Studies.** Sometimes innovation is spurred by market studies. For example, a company sees an opening in the marketplace for a waterproof MP3 player. A market study for new products may result in one or more innovations that trigger the patent lifecycle. Hopefully, your company will not incur substantial patent costs until marketing determines whether the market is weak or strong. Also, the resulting patent or patents hopefully protect the relevant market share expected.

- **Conception.** Product conception is not always the same as the invention of the patentable technology. Turning a discovery or creative idea into a product that can be sold is often a long process. For example, ten years passed between the date Stephanie Kwolek discovered the aramid fiber and when Dow Chemical first used it in Kevlar bullet-resistant vests.
- **Design.** The design of the product also runs parallel with the patent's development. The design enhances the functionality and marketability of the patented technology and also influences the cost of goods. The design may also affect the drafting of the patent application, as design elements may trigger new functionality. Finally, an industrial design may give rise to a separate design patent.
- **Manufacturability Studies.** The information obtained from manufacturability studies influences the decision to patent—there's no sense patenting an item that will be too expensive to produce. At the same time, a manufacturability study may determine that costs can be cut by changing, substituting, or removing some features, which, in turn, affects patentability.
- **Testing.** Here is a situation where patents and products may overlap. Testing for functionality, safety, and appeal can all affect the decision to patent, as well as trigger design changes that affect the drafting of the patent.
- **Production.** A company may prefer to wait to go into production until a patent has been filed or gets the okay from a patent attorney.
- **Product Release.** As with production, the release of the product may be tied to its patent status. Keep in mind that you cannot stop infringers of your patent until after the patent issues. Product release also starts the clock running regarding what can be patented.
- **Sales and Marketing.** In the case of patented products, this period usually begins in the period following patent filing (or

in some cases, after issuance) and continues until the patent expires. Many products continue to be successfully marketed after a patent expires, relying instead on brand recognition and trademark protection of their name and logo.

- **Product Improvement.** Here, new features are included in the product or new functionality is added. And, just as the product development cycle begins anew, so too does the patent lifecycle where additional patents are pursued for the new features or functionality.

Sometimes, some of the steps in the patent lifecycle—for example, invention capture, the decision to seek a patent, drafting, and filing— all occur just a few days before product release or the start of a marketing campaign. Other times, it all happens too soon, before the design is baselined, for example, and the resulting patent doesn't end up covering the product sold.

There's no perfect fixed process. And, we'll learn later why at least filing should occur before production or marketing and why, if the decision to patent takes too long or is not made until it is too late, no patent can ever be obtained. Like any project, mismanagement of a patent project can result in missed opportunities.

A Word on Patent Management

The gurus tell us that effective project management includes, among other things, lifecycle definition, organization of a team, establishing a budget and cost controls, resource allocation, quality, reliability and maintainability, documentation and reporting, system integration, scheduling, organizing, forecasting, configuration control, and procurement and manufacturing controls.

I view a company's overall efforts at patenting as one large program and each individual patent within that program as a discrete "micro-project." To manage the program and each of its individual projects, one needs to understand the cost-benefit analysis associated with patents, and that the value of a patent is measured by its claims which define scope.

To best track the cost-benefit analysis, I've included several tables alerting you to the costs you are likely to incur in each stage of the process.

Throughout this book, I'll also explain the tools used to manage patents—for example, the patent lifecycle, patent committees, patent searches, patentability studies, the patent application, and patent prosecution. Using these tools will enable you to put in place and employ effective project management techniques for these costly, time-consuming, and often unpredictable documents we call patents.

Does Four Include Three?
Case Studies You Can Understand

Gillette v. Schick: Does Four Include Three? 21

John Deere v. Toro: Control Means What?..31

Amazon.com v. Barnes & Noble: You Can't Have It Both Ways.................37

The Case of the Unintelligible Dog Chew Patent..43

Ever take part in an exercise where you have to write instructions to perform some fairly simple task and then someone else has to follow your written instructions, often with comical results? The lesson is that one person's "precise" instructions may be confusingly imprecise to another.

The same can be said for patents. A patent is supposed to define an invention and describe where competitors may not tread. Writing a patent is somewhat like describing the boundaries of a piece of real estate:

> *"Microsoft patents ones, zeros"*
>
> —HEADLINE IN THE MARCH 25, 1998 ISSUE OF THE SATIRE NEWSPAPER *THE ONION*

You must clearly express what you're claiming title to so that you can later explain what constitutes a trespass of the property.

In the case of patents—where technology is the subject matter—finding suitable words can be difficult, and your choice of words even more difficult to construe. As the United States Supreme Court stated in 1892, a patent constitutes "one of the most difficult legal instruments to draw with accuracy." Over a century later, in 2002, The Supreme Court revisited the issue, stating:

> Unfortunately, the nature of language makes it impossible to capture the essence of a thing in a patent application ... A verbal portrayal of an invention is usually an afterthought written to satisfy the requirements of patent law. This conversion of machine to words allows for unintended idea gaps which cannot be satisfactorily filled. Often an invention is novel and words do not exist to describe it. The dictionary does not always keep abreast of the inventor. It cannot. Things are not made for the sake of words but words for things .... The language in the patent claims may not capture every nuance of the invention or describe with complete precision the range of its novelty.

To both of these quotes, patent attorneys like me say, "Amen."

In computer software, a single typo in a program thousands of lines long can render the program useless. The same is true of patents:

A single bad word might render a patent ineffective at protecting against a competitor's entry into a lucrative market.

In patent cases, for example, courts have struggled with the "nature of language" and had to decide if the word "or" in a patent meant A *and/or* B or meant only A *or* B (but not A *and* B).

One patent case from a few years back revolved around the word "member": Does that mean only a single part, or could "member" also be a multi-component structure? Does the word "portion" invoke the idea being separate, or could the "portion" be integrated with other component parts? Does "groove" mean only a long narrow channel, or could it also mean a slight depression? Does "board" mean only a sawed piece of lumber or, instead, any long and narrow "member" made of any relatively rigid material? A lot of time and money is often spent trying to make sense of these patent language "imprecisions."

As we'll see below, even in cases involving fairly simple technology like razor blades, ambiguous patent words (or, in the Gillette case, numbers) can breed controversy.

Gillette v. Schick: Does Four Include Three?

BOTTOM LINE: *A patent should be broad enough to block competitors from marketing even less-than-optimal versions of your invention.*

RULE: *Adding something to a patented invention is typically still considered an infringement even though it creates something different.*

CAVEAT: *Litigating patents can sometimes be a crapshoot.*

It's hard not to crack a smile when lawyers and engineers begin talking in open court about closer shaves, nicks and cuts, and skin irritation. But that was the testimony presented when Gillette sought a preliminary injunction against Schick in a Boston courtroom in 2003. The issue: whether Schick's four-bladed Quattro razor infringed Gillette's patent for its three-bladed Mach3 razor. At stake was Schick's ability to continue to market the Quattro razor.

How did this patent battle develop? Gillette, after many years of research and development and several setbacks, finally arrived at a working three-blade razor, which was commercialized as the Mach3 razor in 1998. The patent for the Mach3 issued in April of 2001. Then, to one-up Gillette, Schick introduced the Quattro razor with four blades.

Gillette believed Shick's Quattro four-bladed razor infringed Gillette's patent, and Schick, of course, disagreed. Schick asserted a number of arguments, many of them common defenses to charges of patent infringement, such as:

- Gillette's patent should never have been awarded in the first place or was otherwise unenforceable because Gillette, when it applied for the Mach3 razor patent, neglected to inform the Patent Office about the real state of the art in razor technology. In other words, Gillette was guilty of misconduct that would render the Gillette patent unenforceable.

- Had the Patent Office known the details regarding Gillette's own prior Sensor razor, the Patent Office would never have issued Gillette's patent for the Mach3. In other words, Gillette's patent was invalid.

- Gillette's patent clearly pertained only to razors with three blades, and therefore the Quattro four-bladed razor did not violate the Gillette patent. In other words, Schick did not infringe the Gillette patent.

The judge who would decide if Gillette deserved a preliminary injunction in the face of Schick's defenses was the Honorable Patti Saris. No stranger to patent litigation, she had previously presided over important patent cases involving Bose, Genentech, and State Street Bank.

One of the judge's tasks in this trial—and the focus of much attention within the industry—was to resolve a simple question: Did Gillette's patent on a three-bladed razor enable the company to stop Schick from selling a four-bladed razor?

Based on common sense, you might conclude that in counting to four, you pass three. Therefore, four of something always includes three of that thing. So, wouldn't Schick's four-bladed razor have to include the three-bladed technology patented by Gillette?

The razor that started the fight: Gillette's three-bladed Mach3.

How many blades does it take for a close shave? Schick's response to the Mach3 has four.

What's a Preliminary Injunction?

In a patent infringement lawsuit, a court can order all infringing activity be halted immediately (a preliminary injunction) rather than wait for the end of a trial (a permanent injunction). It's an extraordinary remedy, and two primary factors are used when a court determines whether to grant a preliminary injunction: (1) Is the patent owner likely to succeed in the lawsuit? (2) Will the patent owner suffer irreparable harm if the injunction is not granted? Irreparable harm is harm of such commercial magnitude that it cannot be repaired by a payment of money damages.

The Companies

Gillette (officially known as Global Gillette) was acquired by Proctor & Gamble in 2005. Gillette has annual sales of approximately $10 billion, and a market capitalization of $40 billion. Besides its razor divisions, the company owns several brands including Oral-B, Duracell, and Braun. The company was founded by King Gillette, a frustrated anti-capitalist who invented the double-edged safety razor after a friend suggested that he create a product that the public would use and throw away. He patented the double-edged razor blade in 1904. His most innovative marketing idea was to give away razors, knowing that consumers would then have to buy his blades. King Gillette was a strong believer in patents and never shied away from a patent battle, a business approach that eventually made Gillette the leading name in shaving products. He died in 1932, still a fervent anti-capitalist. Continuing his throw-away mentality, Gillette became the first company to sell fully disposable razors—the Good News brand—in 1971. Currently Gillette is estimated to control 70 percent of the non-electric razor business.

Schick (originally the Schick Dry Shaver Company) was founded in 1921 by Jacob Schick, an inventor who patented the first electric "dry shaver." The company was acquired by Warner-Lambert in 1970, and in 1993 Warner-Lambert also purchased Wilkinson Sword and merged the two companies as Schick-Wilkinson Sword. The company was subsequently acquired by Pfizer and in 2003, Pfizer sold Schick-Wilkinson Sword to Energizer for $930 million. Currently Schick is estimated to control 25 percent of the non-electric razor business.

In order to stop sales of the Schick Quattro razor before a full jury trial could be held on the merits, Gillette had to prove two things: first, that Gillette was likely to secure a finding of patent infringement at trial and second, irreparable harm would be suffered by Gillette.

To decide whether Gillette was likely to win at trial, Judge Saris had to determine the likelihood that Schick's razor infringed Gillette's patent and also determine whether the Gillette patent would stand up

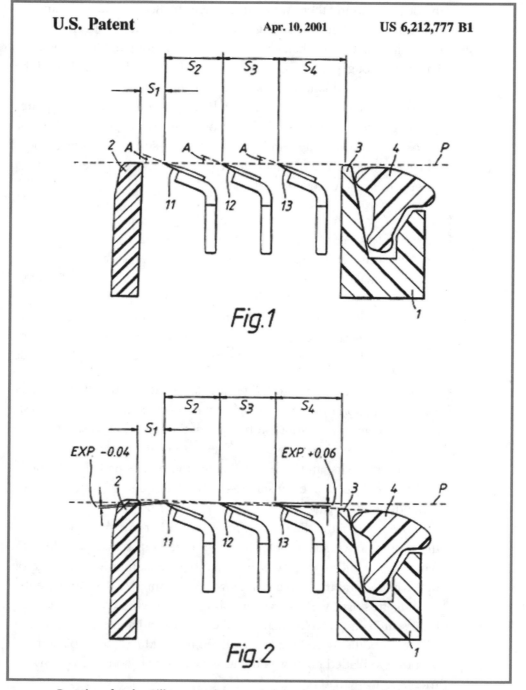

Drawings for the Gillette Mach3 patent show the three-bladed configuration.

in court. Assuming there was infringement by Schick and assuming that Gillette's patent was strong and could withstand an attack, the remaining issue was whether Gillette would be irreparably harmed. That was a tough question by itself, given that Schick probably had the resources to pay financial damages to Gillette.

At its heart, the case was really a battle of words—specifically the meaning of terms such as "blade," "progressive blade geometry," "blade exposure," "guard," "cap," and "skin contacting surfaces." To give you an idea of the "nature of language problem" in this case, here is an excerpt from the Gillette patent:

> A safety razor blade unit comprising a guard, a cap, and a group of first, second, and third blades with parallel sharpened edges located between the guard and cap, the first blade defining a blade edge nearest the guard having a negative exposure not less than -0.2 mm, and the third blade defining a blade edge nearest the cap having a positive exposure of not greater than +0.2 mm, said second blade defining a blade edge having an exposure not less than the exposure of the first blade and not greater than the exposure of the third blade.

The first hearing before Judge Saris lasted about three hours. Given that the six attorneys representing each side, billed at a rate of at least $300 per hour, this hearing probably cost the parties at least $10,000. That figure is eclipsed, however, by the cost of the more than fifty motions, affidavits, and other documents the parties had already filed in the case despite its early stages—a fact that Judge Saris noted with some disappointment.

After prohibiting the parties from any further briefing, she gave them strict time limits: Gillette had one three-hour session in which to have three witnesses testify, Schick had one session in which to put on one witness, and then both parties would summarize their arguments.

Gillette's first witness was Dr. John Terry, a retired Vice President of Research and Development at Gillette who had an active role in the invention of the Mach3 razor. His stated that adding a third blade to a prior two-bladed razor was not as easy as it may sound. Many had tried and many had failed.

Gillette's second witness was William Trotta, a long-time Gillette mechanical engineer, who oversaw the evaluation and testing of Schick's Quattro razor in order for Gillette to determine if the Quattro infringed Gillette's patent. It was during the examination of this witness by both Gillette and Schick that Judge Saris began asking questions about the specific language of Gillette's patent and the various components of the competing razors.

Next, the testimony and questioning turned more complex. If, according to Gillette's patent, the primary blade has a negative "exposure" (exposure defines how close the blade is to the skin), the middle blade has a neutral exposure, and the third blade has a positive exposure, how negative is negative and how positive is positive? Had Schick's four-bladed razor followed this pattern—negative, neutral, positive—with a minor twist by making its two middle blades neutral?

Gillette's last witness testified about the commercial success of the Mach3 razor and claimed that an injunction against Schick was warranted for one very simple reason: Once people switch from the Mach3 razor to the Quattro, they may never come back. Gillette asserted that this was the harm that could not be repaired.

In January of 2004, months after Gillette filed the lawsuit, Judge Saris arrived at her decision.

Judge Saris found that rather than just reciting "a plurality" or "a number" of blades or "at least three blades," Gillette's patent specifically recited a *group* of first, second, and third blades, each progressively positioned further outward from the blade below it to overcome undesirable drag forces on the skin. The Gillette patent further speaks of *a* second blade. The Quattro razor, in contrast, has a group of four blades or, depending on how you look at it, two "second" blades.

One problem for Schick, at this point, had to do with an important maxim of patent law: *Additions* to a patented device typically still constitute patent infringement. In other words, to *not* infringe, you generally have to take something away from what is specified in the patent and/or replace it with something else. When attempting to not infringe a patent, it's best to think subtraction, not addition. Schick didn't simply *replace* one component of Gillette's patented razor system with something else. Instead, Schick *added* something—namely a fourth blade.

So, the Gillette case was more accurately about whether *a* second blade between a first and a third blade, as stated in Gillette's patent, encompasses the two "second" blades of Schick's razor.

Judge Saris noted that Gillette's patent included approximately thirty references to three blades and not a single reference to a fourth blade. That fact in particular hurt Gillette when Judge Saris ultimately ruled that Gillette's patent did not cover Schick's four-bladed Quattro razor.

She denied Gillette's request for the preliminary injunction.

The Quattro would remain on the market, at least until a full trial was held, and potentially forever if her decision withstood an appeal. For the time being, Schick had beat the odds: Patent owners—like Gillette in this case—win much more often than they lose.

Schick's victory, though, was short-lived. Gillette, predictably unhappy with Judge Saris' ruling, appealed to a higher authority: the Court of Appeals for the Federal Circuit, or simply "the Federal Circuit."

In April 2005, the Federal Circuit, in a 2-1 decision, ruled that Judge Saris was wrong in construing Gillette's patent as precluding the addition of a fourth blade, or, more accurately, two "second" blades. Two of the three appellate justices agreed with Gillette that a reference in the patent to a "plurality" of blades meant that there could be more than three. (The third appellate justice disagreed and said that since Gillette's patent refers in the singular form to "a" or "the" second blade, there was no patent coverage for two second blades.)

Also influencing the appellate ruling was a Gillette European patent in which Schick had taken the unfortunate position that Gillette's patent covered more than just three blades. The Federal Circuit ruled:

It may be that a four-bladed safety razor is a less preferred form of the invention (or "embodiment" in patent-speak). A four-bladed razor costs more to build, requires more parts, and adds more frictional drag compared to the three-bladed version. Nevertheless, a person applying for a patent typically drafts an application that is broad enough to cover less preferred embodiments as well as more preferred embodiments, precisely to block competitors from marketing less than optimal versions of the claimed invention.

What Is the Federal Circuit?

There are nine "regular" federal court of appeals spread across the United States. The First Circuit, for example, is on the East Coast in Boston and the Ninth Circuit is in California. Under each appellate court are a number of district or trial courts where cases are initially decided. The First Circuit Court of Appeals, for example, is the appellate court for Boston's Federal District Court where Judge Saris presides. But most patent cases are decided by a special appellate court called the Federal Circuit. The Federal Circuit was created by Congress in 1982 to provide more uniformity in patent law. The Federal Circuit, for example, if an appeal is taken:

- reviews all district court decisions regarding what a patent means
- reviews whether or not a patent is infringed
- reviews whether or not a patent is valid
- reviews decisions of the U.S. Patent Office when an examiner refuses to grant a patent.

Lest you think that all the Federal Circuit judges are technology specialists, note that fewer than half of the 16 judges have a degree in science or engineering. If a party loses at the Federal Circuit, an appeal can be taken to the U.S. Supreme court, but it's rare that the Supreme Court decides to hear patent cases. At best, the Supreme Court decides only one or two patent cases each year.

This dispute highlights the fact that a patent must anticipate not just the best version of an invention envisioned but also less preferable designs as well. And we also see that ambiguous language in a patent can lead to expensive and narrowly decided lawsuits, causing risk, expense, and uncertainty for business.

From a manager's perspective, the case poses big headaches.

As a manager at Schick, for example, your common-sense tendency might be to think that creating a four-bladed razor is unlikely to infringe a patent for a three-bladed razor. You might also be frustrated by the uncertainty. Knowing what does and what does *not* infringe Gillette's patent is probably impossible. However, a savvy manager should also know that adding something to a patented invention is typically still an infringement, even though it creates something different.

As a manager of the research department at Gillette, you may also be confused. Should you have used the word "three" in the patent? This single word in Gillette's multipage patent seemed to be at the root of Gillette's initial problems. Does the use of the number "three" protect against less optimal (or low-end) versions of the invention?

Like the game of poker, the world of patents relies on rules, skill, and chance. It's important to know the rules and to employ skilled engineers and patent experts. But even so, patent lawsuits are often a crapshoot. Trying to predict ahead of time whether or not a judge will see it your way versus adopting your competitor's position can be as big a gamble as predicting expected market share for a new product. Remember that in the end two judges—Judge Saris and an appellate judge—sided with Schick, but two different judges—both appellate judges—sided with Gillette. Gillette won because its two judges' opinions mattered more than Schick's two judges!

As commonly happens even in patent lawsuits, Gillette and Schick reportedly settled in February of 2006. But consider the money, time, and other resources Gillette spent in order to gain a ruling that four does indeed include three. As an aside, Gillette, in September of 2005, introduced the Fusion *five*-bladed razor, allegedly protected by more than 70 patents. Apparently, Gillette sees the strength in numbers— both in blades and in patents. With 70 percent of the global razor market, Gillette's strategy seems to have worked. King Gillette would have been proud.

John Deere v. Toro: Control Means What?

BOTTOM LINE: *A patent should be broad enough to block competitors from marketing versions of your invention that perform the same function but carry it out in a different way.*

RULE: *Sometimes, replacing a minor component in a patented system with something else can be enough to escape patent infringement even when the component and the replacement perform the same function.*

CAVEAT: *Patent litigation is not always fair; some companies are lucky.*

Are you familiar with lawn thatch? It's the layer of dead organic material that deprives the lawn of oxygen. Without oxygen, the organic life below the surface will die and your lawn will starve.

Manufacturers like Deere & Company and the Toro Company are concerned about this lawn thatch and the related problem of soil compaction—a condition that limits irrigation and makes it difficult for your grass to root. The solution: soil aeration.

Soil aeration penetrates lawn thatch, improves soil drainage, and encourages all kinds of organic life—worms and things like that—that bring in much-needed oxygen.

There are two popular methods for aerating lawns: (1) You can use a device to spike the lawn and punch holes in your soil—for example, by using footwear with spikes, or (2) you can pull out plugs of soil.

The Toro Company's innovative approach to aerating golf courses and the like was based on three soil-aerating patents it procured. The Toro machine, looking a little like a specially configured lawnmower, uses water pressure and a series of nozzles to fracture the lawn under the machine, injecting slugs of water into the soil to aerate it.

Two of Toro's patents specifically describe a mechanical cam-based system which opens and closes a valve to deliver the pressurized water to the nozzles to create the aerating water jet slugs.

The Companies

The **Toro Company** was founded in 1914 as a manufacturer of tractor engines. The company later expanded to provide commercial lawn mowers, sprinklers, and related lawn supplies. Toro was the first company to offer consumer power lawn mowers (1935), rear-engine riding mowers (1959), consumer snow throwers (1962), and electric lawnmowers (1968). The company generates earnings of approximately $1.6 billion a year.

The **John Deere Company** (officially known as Deere & Co.) generates earnings of approximately $1.4 billion a year and is the leading producer of farm equipment in the world, as well as a major producer of construction and forestry equipment and lawn care products. The company was founded by the blacksmith John Deere who, in 1837, developed the world's first commercially successful, self-scouring steel plow, a breakthrough that is considered to have enabled the farming and settlement of the midwestern United States. But Deere's genius as an entrepreneur was that he did something no other blacksmith had previously considered. He manufactured his plows before customers had ordered them, thereby having them available for sale. His company Deere and Company, later led by his sons, acquired various farm equipment and tractor companies. We'll learn later about "obviousness" in patent law. Indeed, it was a 1966 John Deere patent infringement lawsuit at the Supreme Court that framed "obviousness."

Toro's aerator is shown in the three figures below reproduced from Toro's patents.

Toro's patents explain how slugs or jets of a liquid such as water, a liquid fertilizer, or a weed killer exit the nozzles marked as 71 in Figure 5 to penetrate the turf and soil to reduce compaction and promote turf growth. To create the slugs of water, the valve controlling the delivery of the liquid to the nozzles has to open and close very quickly. To control the valve, Toro implemented the mechanical cam-based system shown in cross-section view in Figure 3.

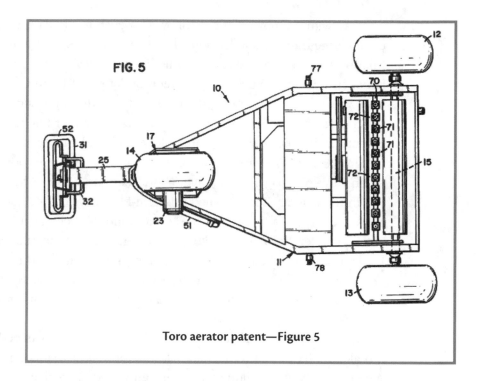

Toro aerator patent—Figure 5

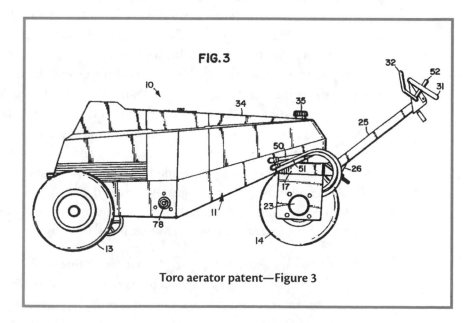

Toro aerator patent—Figure 3

Stay with me now; you can follow this even if you have no engineering training. Outlet port 91 in Figure 11 leads to the nozzles. Inlet port 64 leads to the source of liquid pressurized by a pump (to between 2,300 and 5,000 psi). Between outlet port 91 and inlet port 64 is valve 67, which is opened and closed quickly to produce the water slugs, which penetrate the soil to aerate it. According to the Toro patents, slide mechanism 93, cam follower 94, and cam 95 cooperate to control valve 67. Water flows from inlet port 64 to outlet port 91 when valve 67 is opened. If valve 67 is closed, no water flows.

In the patents, Toro deemed this cam-based system for controlling the valve a type of "control means" or a "control mechanism."

Soon after, Toro's competitor John Deere entered the market with its own aerating machine, also using pressurized water and nozzles. One important difference was that Deere employed an electrically operated solenoid to control the valve that delivered the water to the nozzles.

Every mechanism requires a control, whether it is a gas pedal, a brake, an iPod, or a refrigerator. How important is that control when it comes to patenting a device? Can you avoid a claim of patent infringement if you duplicate a patented process but use a different means of controlling that mechanism? If so, how different must the control mechanism be to escape infringement?

Toro filed a patent infringement suit against Deere claiming that a cam (as specified in the Toro patents), and a solenoid (as used in the Deer aerating machine) both performed the same function: operating a valve and controlling the flow of water to the nozzles. A cam-based system and a solenoid are both just different species of a control means or mechanism specified in the Toro patents. Cams and solenoids can be used interchangeably, asserted Toro.

The Federal Circuit disagreed and ruled against Toro. According to the court, cams and solenoids *don't* work the same way:

> The cam system uses a metal "cam follower" that travels up the slope of the cam, lifting a valve stem to open the liquid valve. The solenoid system uses electricity to create a magnetic force that pulls open the liquid valve.

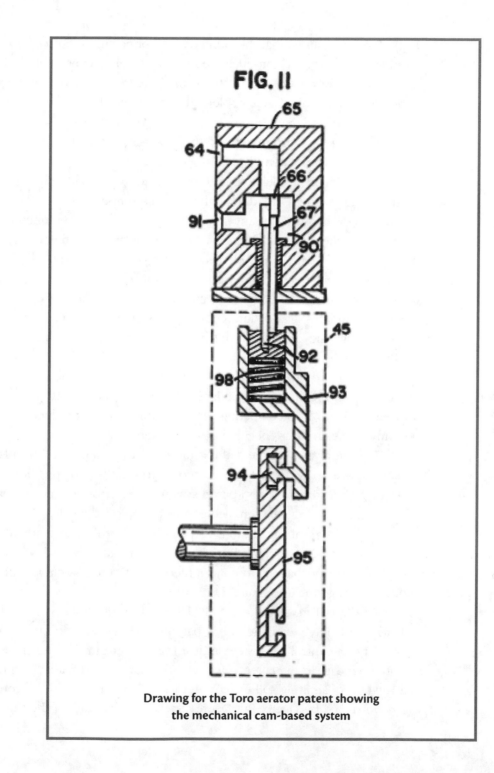

FIG. 11

Drawing for the Toro aerator patent showing
the mechanical cam-based system

The court stated that the cam system, connecting the pressurized fluid to the nozzles to produce the slugs of water, was not a stand-in for any type of control means; the cam system was an essential *part* of the "control means." Deere's solenoid-based control system was not the same as or even equivalent to Toro's cam-type control system.

A manager at Toro might find this analysis difficult to comprehend. After all, the Toro patents merely specified that a "control means" or "control mechanism" delivered the pressurized water to the nozzles. The patents seemed broad enough to block competitors from marketing versions of the invention that perform the same function but use a different control means. And from a "macro" engineering perspective, Deere's solenoid was clearly a type of "control means," the same as a mechanical cam-based system.

But patent law often takes a "micro" view, which in this case is that a solenoid is legally different from a mechanical cam-based system even though they both achieve the same end result: controlling a valve.

Stated more broadly, the downside associated with the macro "means"- or "mechanism"-type language in a patent is that it is often harder to stop competing products unless those products are configured exactly as specified in your patent.

There is always a potential for imprecision in language, but this seems like a no-win situation for Toro. If Toro had used specific language referring to a cam-based system to describe the mechanism that controls the valve, then Deere, which employed a solenoid, would clearly not have infringed the Toro patents. When Toro instead used "control means" and "control mechanism" in an attempt to describe *any* possible mechanism to control the valve, Deere's solenoid still didn't infringe the Toro patents.

How was Toro to protect itself? Hindsight is 20/20 but, perhaps Toro should have explained in its patents that the invention included any type of control subsystem and/or that a control mechanism was not a mandate in the patents. In fact, Toro had a third patent covering a method of aerating soil using water jets. That patent, said the court, *was* infringed by Deere. But Deere attacked the validity of the third patent, asserting it failed to cover anything new. That issue is still not resolved.

A manager at Deere & Company may see the court's decision as a matter of common sense. Toro's device was built around a cam control; Deere's device was not. Replacing even a minor component in a patented system with something else may be enough to escape patent infringement even when the component and the replacement perform the same function. In this case, Deere's adherence to this principle paid off.

At the very least, the Gillette and Toro cases prove that since patents are written in words and since words can often be ambiguous, what any given patent protects can be debated. You can add precision and lose the ambiguity, but only at the expense of a patent that does not adequately protect against competition. On the other hand, even loose words like "means" and "mechanism" can sometimes be problematic. Again, the world of patents is guided by rules and chance, and there's no *sure* thing.

Amazon.com v. Barnes & Noble: You Can't Have It Both Ways

BOTTOM LINE: *Patents are for "everything under the sun made by man" and that includes software, Internet ideas, and even business methods.*

RULE: *You can't have it both ways: A patent will not be construed one way to find infringement and a different way to uphold its validity.*

CAVEAT: *The accused infringer in an important patent lawsuit will try to invalidate the patent. The success rate is approximately 33%.*

Everybody hates waiting in a long checkout line. Even in cyberspace, the time period between a purchasing decision and the purchase can make or break a merchant. So, after discovering that a large percentage of online customers abandon their virtual shopping carts before checkout, Amazon.com's president, Jeff Bezos, conceived of a way to solve that problem: Amazon would eliminate the checkout process entirely.

Bezos streamlined online ordering by providing the ability to click on an item and purchase it without the item having to be placed in the shopping cart and without the need for the consumer to input additional confirmation information at checkout.

How does the Amazon website know how to charge you for the purchased product and mail it to you? Simple. If you've been to the website before, a record of your credit card information and your address is stored and can be retrieved. A computer simply uses that stored record to order the product, bill you for it, and have it sent to your home or office. Bezos patented his "1-click" invention (to the chagrin of many) based on previous cases which held that "anything under the sun made by man" is patentable—so-called business methods included.

(Turn 1-Click On)

Click the button to start a patent battle.

As you're probably aware, Amazon's "1-click" feature was a hit, and it didn't take long before there was competition in the form of Barnes & Noble's online "Express Lane" feature—basically "1-click" under a different name.

Amazon moved quickly. Less than a month after Amazon's 1-click patent issued on September 28, 1999, Amazon.com sued Barnes & Noble over its use of the competing Express Lane online ordering feature.

Amazon, like Gillette in our earlier case study, moved for a preliminary injunction. A five-day hearing was held in November, 1999 before a federal judge in Washington state. At issue was the meaning of the language used in Amazon's patent but also, more important, whether Amazon's patent was valid.

When Is an Invention Obvious?

Obviousness refers to the ability of the invention to produce results that were not anticipated by the prior art (prior technology in the field). To be patentable, an invention must be nonobvious to a person "skilled in the art". For example, an invention involving video technology would need to be considered nonobvious to a video engineer thoroughly familiar with prior art in the video field.

The initial determination of whether an innovation or improvement is (was) nonobvious is made by a Patent Office examiner in the course of deciding whether a patent should issue.

The patent examiner generally approaches this task by examining similar technology that existed as of the date of invention (known as "prior art" references).

However, once a patent issues, the patent may be attacked (usually in court) on the ground that the patent examiner made a mistake on the question of nonobviousness. In this situation—for example, as happened in the Amazon/Barnes and Noble dispute—both sides will typically produce experts who provide opposing opinions ("Yes, it was obvious"; "No, it absolutely wasn't").

The inventor will also attempt to prove that the invention was not obvious because the invention enjoyed commercial success or solved an unperceived need. In Chapter 3, I'll provide more details on the standards used when determining obviousness.

The Companies

Amazon.com, which originated as an online book seller, was one of the few dot.com era companies to survive the dot.com bust. Its founder, Jeff Bezos, was *TIME* magazine's 1999 "Person of the Year." Barnes and Noble was a large "brick and mortar" chain of book stores that Bezos felt "isn't doing any innovation at all on the web—all they do is copy Amazon feature for feature, sometimes down to the exact wording."

In the face of the controversy surrounding Amazon's 1-click patent (some felt it was evidence of the Patent Office's incompetence; others felt such a simple idea should not be patentable), Bezos asserted he patented 1-click to survive. Amazon, he said, had no intention of pursuing small, independent developers who were using 1-click purchasing on their sites. "We're just going after the big guys who are going after us, the guys who are not innovating themselves but just copying us and working to crush us."

The 1-click idea is trivial to duplicate, but Bezos' position is that that is not the point. Amazon spent thousands of hours and millions of dollars to develop the system.

The real invention, said Bezos, was reframing the online purchasing problem when everyone else was locked into the mindset of the shopping cart metaphor. Still, Bezos does agree the U.S. patent system is in need of some reform. And yet, Bezos still continues to patent business methods: In 2006, Amazon patented its "movers and shakers" feature for ranking book sakes. Also, Amazon has been sued for patent infringement numerous times. In 2007, Amazon was sued by IBM for infringing patents purportedly covering the basics of Internet shopping.

Barnes & Noble is a Fortune 500 Company with over 800 bookstores nationwide. Barnes & Noble allegedly pioneered the concept of a "book superstore" with a large selection of titles and reading and coffee-drinking areas. The Barnes & Noble website BarnesandNoble.com was launched in 1997.

In its attack on Amazon's patent, Barnes & Noble asserted that single-action ordering was known in the industry or was at least obvious. At the hearing, the Judge considered several earlier shopping cart systems including Netscape's "merchant system," Compuserve's "trend" service, and several other technologies that existed before Amazon filed its patent application.

Barnes & Nobles' initial attempt at invalidating the 1-click patent was not successful. The trial court in this case determined there was insufficient evidence that single-action ordering was used previously. Further, since the industry considered Amazon's 1-click purchasing feature highly innovative, the judge found insufficient merit in Barnes & Noble's patent invalidity arguments. In other words, if the idea was so obvious, why hadn't merchants adopted it before?

(Note: Approximately one-third of all litigated patents *are* invalidated, either because a company accused of violating a patent successfully proves the patented invention is not new or because the patent in question has defects that render it void.)

For its next defense, Barnes & Noble argued that its Express Lane feature did not infringe the Amazon patent because an Express Lane customer visiting the Barnes & Noble website was required to take more than one action to order a product. The Judge found this position untenable in part because Barnes & Noble's website itself described the Express Lane option as "one-click ordering."

The court issued the injunction because infringement on the part of Barnes & Noble seemed clear and harm to Amazon was presumed.

Based on that December 4, 1999 ruling, Barnes & Noble would have to modify its Express Lane feature and require online shoppers to take an additional action to confirm orders. Amazon, on the other hand, had to post a $10 million bond in case Amazon did not win the trial—remember, this was a preliminary injunction hearing, a procedure that precedes the trial. The $10 million would be used to compensate Barnes & Noble in the event it eventually won at trial. For the time being, Amazon had won.

Barnes & Noble appealed the preliminary injunction decision to the Federal Circuit and, this time, Amazon lost. In a relatively technical decision, the Federal Circuit found that the trial judge had used inconsistent standards: one standard to determine infringement, and a different standard to determine patent validity. That was a mistake: You can't have it both ways. The language of a given patent might be inexact, but it can mean only one thing. If that language means the patent is infringed by the competitor's product—great. But watch out if that same language also means the patent is invalid based on the state of the art that existed before the patent application was filed. Here's how it worked in the Amazon case.

If Amazon's patent is construed to mean that one mouse click is all it takes to purchase the item *whenever* information is displayed about that item, then Barnes & Noble's Express Lane feature doesn't infringe the patent. That's because product information is provided on Barnes & Noble's menu page without the ability to click and purchase the product.

But, if Amazon's patent is construed to mean that *sometimes* when product information is displayed one-click purchasing is possible, then Barnes & Noble does infringe, because other web pages of the Barnes & Noble site do include the ability to one-click a product order.

The problem is, under this construction where Barnes & Noble does infringe, there are prior systems that seemingly featured the exact same thing. That put Amazon's patent in jeopardy. In the view of the Federal Circuit, that fact raised a substantial question regarding the validity of Amazon's patent—enough for Barnes & Noble not to be subject to an injunction pending a full trial. So, in round two, it was Barnes & Nobel that prevailed. Again, this still is not a trial—all of these issues arose during the preliminary injunction procedure.

The case never proceeded to trial. Amazon and Barnes & Noble reportedly settled a year after that ruling. The Amazon one-click patent is still valid, and there haven't been any published reports of Amazon's attempts to enforce it.

You as a manager may want any competitive and infringing activity stopped ASAP. But, in any patent infringement lawsuit, the competitor has the opportunity to challenge the patent, and all that is required is a reasonable *chance* of a successful challenge in order to overcome a preliminary injunction. You might not be able to stop infringement without incurring high costs and patiently awaiting a trial and then an appeal. You also have to understand that a competitor faced with a patent lawsuit will often challenge your patent. Look at the extremes Barnes & Noble went to invalidate Amazon's patent. Managers need to understand that if a competitor is sued for infringing a patent, the competitor will likely challenge the patent, raising both the cost and the stakes of the litigation. It's one thing to lose a patent infringement battle; it's quite another to lose a patent.

In the Gillette case study, Schick, too, raised an invalidity defense to Gillette's patent. Since, after the appeal, the law of the case was that Gillette's patent encompasses a razor with two "second" blades, if Schick could have shown a prior razor with that configuration, Gillette's patent might have been found by the court or a jury to be invalid.

Thus, owning a patent is clearly not the end game. You have to take steps to ensure the patent has no "defective" wording and that somewhere, sometime, someone didn't document something that places the validity of the patent in question. The patent has to be construed so that it covers the competing product but not construed so that it also covers old technology.

Another point: Without a patent, generally nothing can be done if a competitor adopts your technology. Bezos understood that anything under the sun made by man is patentable and that if 1-click wasn't patented, it could be copied without recourse. Unfortunately, there is no sure-fire way to prevent a challenge to your patent. Alas, as we've seen before, there is no sure thing when it comes to patents.

The Case of the Unintelligible Dog Chew Patent

BOTTOM LINE: *Sometimes, imprecise or even confusing language in a patent proves beneficial.*

RULE: *Patents are presumed to be valid.*

CAVEAT: *Patent litigation is very expensive. Sometimes, it's cheaper and less risky to change than to fight.*

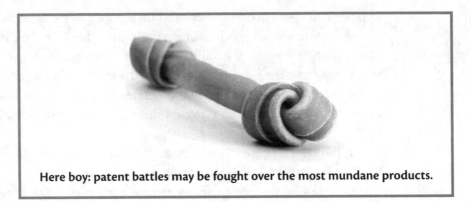

Here boy: patent battles may be fought over the most mundane products.

Okay, perhaps your business is not exactly on par with Gillette, John Deere, or Amazon. Even so, patents sometimes affect even smaller non-high tech firms, as the following case study explains.

My client sold a line of pet products, including dog chews. A competitor of my client sent us a patent and demanded we stop selling our competing dog chew toy product. And, we did. The reason, however, may surprise you.

Here is an excerpt from the patent:

> An edible dental care article, fit to be eaten as food, for cleaning the teeth and massaging the gums of pets during consumption of said edible dental care article comprising at least one of a processed casing material, made from an extract of at least one of a vegetable material and an animal material, and a natural casing material, comprising at least one of an animal gut and an animal skin, wherein said processed casing material is formed in one of a thread-like manner, a string-like manner, and a thin-tube-like manner, and wherein said natural casing material is selected from a group of natural casing materials formed in a thread-like manner, a string-like manner, and a thin-tube-like manner; wherein said at least one of the processed casing material and the natural casing material is twisted into a rope-like member of a prescribed shape and size, and wherein constituent parts of the twisted rope-like member are fixed by fastening means so as to retain a rope-like shape.

What? You can't understand it either?

Exactly.

I couldn't understand the patent, my client couldn't understand it, and I don't think a judge or a jury would have been able to understand it. Still, the patent existed. That is, Patent Office Examiners—employees of the United States Federal Government—reviewed this patent, supposedly checked it to make sure it documented something new and unobvious, and checked to ensure that the excerpt recited above was sufficiently clear and definite pursuant to federal patent law. After conducting those checks, the Federal Government issued the patent. And now the patent was presumed by law to be valid.

The Companies

Unlike the previous case studies, the companies involved in this case are smaller privately held businesses with less revenue to spend on patent litigation. I must keep the name of my client confidential, but suffice it to say that my client sells dog chews and also a wide variety of other pet- related products: dog houses, clothing, shampoos, and the like. The patent owner's business focuses primarily on dog chews available at stores and also online (at Amazon.com, for example).

I thought then (and still believe today) I could convince a judge and a jury that despite the government's blessing, the patent in question was unintelligible and thus void, but that effort would have involved a certain degree of uncertainty and would have cost money—a lot of money. A patent infringement lawsuit, if taken all the way through a jury trial, can cost millions of dollars. That was a lot more money than my client's product was worth.

So, here's a patent, that because it couldn't be understood, resulted in a product being taken off the market without the patent owner ever having to go to court or spend a substantial amount of money. This is a case where imprecise patent language *protected* the patent owner because the cost of challenging the patent wasn't worth the benefit of being able to continue to sell the allegedly infringing product, given the risk associated with losing. This same scenario plays out every day with patents owned by so called "patent trolls."

What's a Patent Troll?

"Patent troll" is a derogatory term used to describe a patent owner who sues for patent infringement but who does not make or sell any products using the patented technology.

Engineers may believe a given patent is ridiculous, absurd, clearly invalid, and so on. Managers need to understand that the patent is still presumed to be valid. It sometimes hurts to yield or pay a royalty for such patents, but it's often times less expensive and less risky to yield or pay than to fight.

Managers need to understand, then, that although most any patent *can* be challenged, sometimes the cost and risk associated with the challenge isn't worth the ultimate return. Of course, that's not always true. For Barnes & Noble, the cost of the challenge to Amazon's 1-click patent seems to have outweighed the risk Barnes & Noble's challenge would fail.

This case, and even the Gillette, Amazon, and Toro cases, might be viewed as extreme, to be sure. Managers need to understand there are many other cases where patent holders successfully litigate their patents in court in the face of weak challenges and, conversely, many cases where nonsensical and clearly invalid patents are struck down. Mostly, the system works.

Nevertheless, these particular case studies prove that merely having a patent is not the end game. Patent litigation is sometimes a crapshoot and always expensive. The words of your patent may not always mean what you think they do. And, it's almost always the case that your patent will be challenged.

But sometimes the cost of the challenge isn't worth the return. Consider that, as an accused infringer,

- You'll spend $1 million or more on a patent challenge.
- Statistically, infringers have only a 33% chance of winning.
- All that you will gain is the ability to keep selling a product that might never generate $1 million in profit.

In this case, it doesn't take an economist to know that the challenge is not worth it. My client in the dog chew case did not believe it had done anything wrong, but the product was taken off the market because that was the correct business decision. In summary, the case study demonstrates that even an unintelligible patent can result in a product being taken off the market.

We see now that patents sometimes work in strange and mysterious ways. For example, like many patent attorneys, I have advised clients numerous times that if they made product X, it might infringe patent Y. My client then decided *not* to market product X. As a result, a patent prevented competition without any court action and without the patent owner even knowing it!

Keep in mind as well that only a few patents are litigated. So, in cases where a patent provides a roadblock to competition *without* litigation, then the patent is well worth its cost. Perhaps that's why there are now over 7 million patents.

Our next task, then, is to gain an understanding of what exactly is patentable and, more important, since almost anything is patentable, how patents can differ in scope and value. After that, we'll learn how to read patents and gain a quick understanding of the scope and value of any patent you might be interested in. Then we'll discuss how to obtain patents of value.

Anything Under the Sun (Made by Man): What's Patentable?

What's Patentable?...50

Key Standards: New and Unobvious...52

    What's *New*?...52

    What Is Unobvious?..55

    Finding Patents Within Patents...62

Reinventing the Wheel: Improvements and New Uses 64

    Improvement Patents..64

    Incorporating New Technologies in Old Products...............................65

    New Twists on Old Ideas..67

Should You Patent It?...67

    What's It Cost?..71

    Will This Patent Stop Competitors? 72

    Patentability and Patent Scope 73

    Other Factors...77

    Patent Value as a Defense or Deterrent 77

    A Cost-Benefit Formula 78

Managers cannot be expected to decide what is patentable under the law—that's the job of a patent attorney. The manager's job is like the sailor in the crow's nest—to survey the horizon and report potential sightings. Commonly the manager does this by flagging innovations, improvements, and new features and functions that deserve further scrutiny by a company's attorneys (or by its marketing department). In this manner, a manager acts to preserve patent rights.

> *"I invented the cordless extension cord."*
>
> —STEVEN WRIGHT

Even though you, as manager, may not ultimately decide what is patentable by your company, your opinion may be required in the patent decision process. For that reason, this chapter is devoted to determining what can be patented and how patentability decisions are made.

I'll explain some general principles that can help you, and you will see later in this chapter that the major challenge really isn't identifying what's patentable; it's identifying whether the resulting patent will provide real protection and value.

What's Patentable?

BOTTOM LINE: *Almost anything can be patented.*

RULE: *To be patentable, an innovation doesn't have to be the subject of a "Eureka" moment or even particularly remarkable or newsworthy.*

CAVEAT: *A patent with real value can be harder to come by.*

So, how can you tell what's patentable? The good news is that almost *everything* that is useful and new is patentable. In the words of the Supreme Court, you can patent "anything under the sun made by man." So, as a general rule, assume new innovations are patentable, at least until a determination is made by patent counsel that that they are not.

Is Cubic Zirconium Useful?

Usefulness, also called utility, is a fairly low standard for most ideas. In one notable example, Juicy Whip, Inc. had a patent for a beverage dispenser that deceived customers into thinking the beverage was drawn out of a display reservoir, when actually the beverage came from two hidden dispensers: one for the syrup concentrate and one for the water mixed with the concentrate.

When Juicy Whip sued a competitor for patent infringement, the trial court invalidated Juicy Whip's patent on the grounds it lacked utility because the product patented was deceptive. The Federal Circuit, however, upheld the patent, stating that "it is not at all unusual for a product to be designed to appear to viewers to be something it is not." Cubic Zirconium, for example, is specifically designed to simulate diamond and thus exhibits "usefulness." Even if the use is considered deceptive, the court wrote, "that is not by itself sufficient to render the invention unpatentable."

Usefulness and utility, however, do sometimes prevent patenting things like perpetual motion machines and even some biological discoveries (especially if the utility stated is not specific enough).

Keep in mind that here we're talking about the most common type of patent: utility patents. There are also design patents for the appearance of useful products and plant patents (See "Design and Plant Patents," below). I discuss these other types of patents briefly at the end of this chapter. The basic rules for utility patents are as follows:

- You can get a patent for anything that is useful, new, and not obvious to others in the field of invention. (How can you tell what's new and not obvious? We'll explain that below.).
- Conversely, you *can't* get a patent if your innovation is old, obvious, or not useful. Also, under U.S. patent law, you must abide by the "one-year rule," which provides that a patent application must be filed within one year after the invention is

first sold, offered for sale, or commercially or publicly used or described. (What's that mean exactly? For a brief explanation, see "The Clock Is Ticking," below.)

Key Standards: New and Unobvious

In order for an innovation to be patentable, it must be new and not obvious to those in the field. Below we discuss these standards in more detail.

What's *New*?

There's a misconception among many engineers and managers that patentable technology must be remarkable, revolutionary, or the result of a so-called "Eureka" moment. This misconception is often more common among highly educated folks, for example, like some PhDs I know who often have the opinion that "it's all been done before." Truth is, to be patentable, a product or method just has to be different in some way from what came before.

The "been done before" attitude reminds me of the head of the Patent Office way back in 1899, who supposedly said, "Everything that can be invented has been invented." If the development of a product, even a new version of an old product, took a team of five engineers six months and they tell me there is nothing really novel in the product, I often wonder how they were spending their time. Of course, there is *something* different—otherwise there would be no need to engage in an engineering effort at all. To be patentable, it just has to be different in some way.

Novelty or "newness" is a fairly easy objective determination: You ask the question, "Does the product include something, some feature, some capability, some function never before seen in that type of product?" In other words, is it somehow distinguishable from the products that preceded it? These previous innovations are referred to as "prior art." Prior art is used to gauge two patent standards, novelty and nonobviousness.

The Clock Is Ticking

Earlier I mentioned that an inventor who fails to file within one year of when they publish, publicly use, publicly disclose (in person, at a trade show, or via a published paper or article for example,) or offer to sell (or sell) an invention cannot get a patent, because the Patent Office no longer considers that invention new or novel. As you can see, that conforms to the description of "prior art". In other words, if you let the public see your invention more than a year before you file, you lose your ability to get a patent. Stated another way, you have one year to file a patent application after a sale or disclosure event. (Keep in mind this only applies for U.S. patents; in Chapter 8, I discuss how you must file a foreign patent *before any* public use or sale).

The Patent Office won't generally know that you didn't comply with the one-year rule. So it is possible to obtain a patent if more than one year has passed since public disclosure. But that patent can be voided if you attempt to enforce it, making it a worthless exercise. Your adversary will surely dig into the facts surrounding the first sale, offer for sale, and public disclosure of the patented product.

This principle, that no patent can be granted if filed more than one year after public disclosure, is true even if the patentable technology is deep within the product—for example, a new circuit amongst many in one chip of an electronic device. If the product was sold more than one year before a patent application for the new circuit was filed, then no patent.

To give you an example of how important the filing date can be, consider the problems 3M encountered when it developed a method for perforating carbonless paper. In July 1989, 3M arranged to manufacture 10,000 forms using their newly developed laser-perforated sheets and distributed the forms for use within 3M. The company filed for a patent more than a year later, on August 17, 1990. Unfortunately, 3M's patent was later invalidated when the company revealed during a court case that its invention had been "in public use" more than one year prior to the date it filed its patent application.

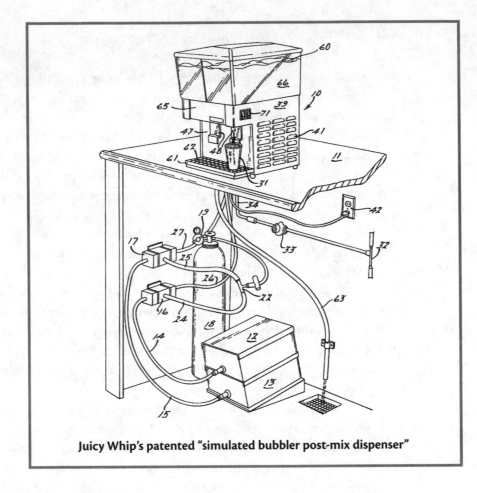

Juicy Whip's patented "simulated bubbler post-mix dispenser"

Prior art includes:
- any invention in public use or on sale in the United States for more than one year before the filing date of your patent application
- anything that was publicly known or used by others in the United States before the date of invention
- anything that was made or built in the United States by another person before the date of invention
- any work that was the subject of a prior patent, issued more than one year before the filing date of your patent or any time before the date you created the invention, or

- any work that was published more than one year before the filing date of your patent or any time before your date of invention.

What Is Unobvious?

Determining unobviousness—the term used (along with "nonobviousness") to describe innovations that are not obvious—is a thornier issue than determining what is new, since it necessarily involves a subjective determination. As Judge Learned Hand (considered by many experts to be the finest patent judge in history) once pointed out, the difficulty with this standard is so that many devices seem obvious *after* they have been discovered.

Over forty years ago, in a case involving the John Deere company (a different case from the one I discussed in Chapter 2), the Supreme Court established a method for courts to determine whether an invention is obvious. Judges are to determine whether a person of ordinary skill in the field of the invention would consider the differences between the prior art and the invention obvious. So, if the invention is an aerator, a person of ordinary skill in the field is probably a mechanical engineer involved with turf equipment. Other factors that may indicate that an invention is not obvious are if:

- The inventor does what others said could not be done.
- The invention enjoys commercial success.
- The invention has been praised within the field.
- Others tried and failed to achieve the same result.

Even with these standards, however, determinations of obviousness still confound the courts. That's because the "test" for whether something is obvious is, "Is it obvious?" Such a test does not lead to predictable results, to the chagrin of businesspeople. Let me present two controversial inventions and their patents, to illustrate some of the issues in play.

The first example is the Furminator pet-grooming tool (U.S. Patent Nos. 6,782,846 and 7,077,076). The blade of the Furminator is, as admitted in the patent, an Oster A5 blade, long used in Sunbeam Corp.'s electric hair clippers. Pet groomers often used that same blade, taken out of the clipper, to remove shed hair, but the blade was difficult to hold by itself. So the Furminator patents cover the clipper blade positioned in an "elongate handle portion."

Should the idea of adding a handle to Sunbeam's clipper blade really be patentable? Or put another way: Was the idea obvious to those in the field? In a 2006 federal court case, Furminator sought a preliminary injunction against three companies: Ontel Products, Inc.; Munchkin, Inc.; and the home goods retail chain Linens 'n Things. The court denied Furminator's request for an injunction because Munchkin had "designed around" the Furminator patent and did not use an "elongate" handle (as expressed in the Furminator patent). The Ontel product sold by Linens 'n Things used an elongate handle, but the handle was located at the end of the blade and parallel to it, like a knife or a comb—a design that had existed prior to the Furminator patent.

The second example is a little more complex. Document and image scanners have long included a microcontroller that controls the image sensor, the sheet-feed subsystem, and so on. Traditional scanners also have their own independent power supply. The idea of

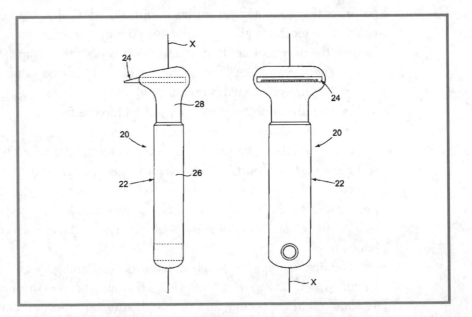

Removes unwanted pet hair: Drawings from the Furminator patent show the Sunbeam Oster Blade at 24.

Syscan's Patent No. 6,275,309 is to borrow power from a PC in order to operate the scanner so that the scanner does not have to be plugged into a wall outlet. Computing power is borrowed from the PC as well, so no microcontroller is required in the scanner. How are power and control signals from the PC coupled to the scanner? By a PCMCIA card. A related patent, No. 6,459,506, also belonging to Syscan, covers a scanner powered and controlled via a USB interface.

Syscan didn't invent the PCMCIA card, USB, or even scanners. Instead, they adopted PCMCIA and USB technology for use in scanners. The result was two patents preventing any other scanner manufacturer from using PCMCIA or USB to power or control their products—even though USB was specifically designed to allow peripheral manufacturers to power their devices from electricity supplied by the USB interface and to be controlled using software running on a connected computer. As this book went to press (October 2007), Syscan is in litigation with one original equipment manufacturer (OEM) and four other scanner companies over the two patents.

The Furminator and Syscan examples indicate that the U.S. Patent Office is willing to deem technology patentable that was developed by one company and then put to use in another company's product.

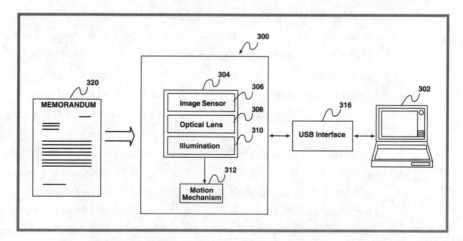

Plug and play: This flowchart from the Syscan patent demonstrates the company's innovation—a USB port can power a scanner.

In other words, these uses were new and not obvious. And that's true for many patents that cover systems made up of subsystems and components engineered by others.

There's nothing wrong with that: Thomas Edison didn't invent glass, the idea of a vacuum, or the filament, but he combined those things in a new way that was not obvious to others. By doing so he created something that has become the very icon of innovation: the light bulb.

Clearly, the line between unobvious and obvious is sometimes hard to find. To locate that line, the courts use a standard that requires proof of some prior "suggestion, teaching, or motivation" to combine the components in order to hold the combination obvious.

Which brings us to a case decided by the Supreme Court in April of 2007. Teleflex, of Limerick, Pennsylvania, owns a patent that includes the combination of two well-known components: a gas pedal that can be adjusted relative to the driver's seating position and an electronic (as opposed to a mechanical) sensor which senses and transmits to the vehicle's throttle computer the position of the pedal (Patent No. 6,237,565).

Teleflex sued its competitor, KSR International, of Canada, for supplying General Motors with adjustable gas pedals with their own sensors for use with electronic throttle controls.

The Supreme Court decided that when elements, techniques, items, or devices are combined, united, or arranged, and when, in combination, each item performs the function it was designed to perform, the resulting combination—something the court called "ordinary innovation"—is not patentable. The bottom line? Ordinary engineering that engineers perform in the course of their usual day-to-day activities may not be patentable.

Since 1952, the patent statute has forbidden patenting subject matter when the differences between the subject matter sought to be patented and the state of the art is obvious to "one skilled in the art." Understandably, this subjective standard led to unpredictable results. Especially in hindsight, many patent-worthy inventions can be easy to deem obvious. In response, the Federal Circuit established a formula to be used by the Patent Office and the lower courts in deciding whether something is obvious and thus not worthy of a patent.

A combination is not obvious, said the Federal Circuit in 1999, unless there is some prior teaching, suggestion, or motivation to make the combination. In the opinion of many people, this overly rigid test resulted in many patents for products and ideas that were, well, blatantly obvious. The patent bar had been lowered to the point you could practically step over it.

Recognizing that skilled engineers regularly piece together prior devices to meet market demand and solve known problems using obvious solutions, the Supreme Court held that even if there is no teaching, suggestion, or motivation to make the combination, the combination may still be obvious. Engineers possess common sense, said the court: "A person of ordinary skill in the art is also a person of ordinary creativity, not an automaton." Engineers, in the eyes of the Supreme Court, know that changing one component in a system often requires others to be modified as well, and that familiar items may have obvious uses beyond their primary purposes. Such may be the stuff of improvement and "ordinary innovation," but not patents.

Adjustable gas pedals designed to accommodate drivers of different sizes were well-known at the time the patent application for the "adjustable pedal assembly with electronic throttle control" was filed. So too were sensors for computer-controlled throttles and even sensors located on the pedal assembly rather than in the engine compartment. Was the combination of an *adjustable* gas pedal with a sensor on the pedal obvious? No, said the Patent Office and the Federal Circuit. Yes, said the Supreme Court: A mechanical engineer familiar with pedal control systems for vehicles would have seen the benefit of an adjustable gas pedal with its own sensor.

The patent bar has surely been raised; the real question is how high.

The Court recognized that most, if not all, patentable inventions rely on building blocks and combinations that, in some sense, are already known. So, what is still patentable, other than brand-new-never-before-seen or disruptive technologies? When the general consensus is that a known thing won't work very well in a new environment, its inclusion in a combination is patentable—especially when the result is unexpected. And, it's still the case that commercial success, addressing long-felt but unsolved needs, and finding a solution to a problem others failed to solve, points to nonobviousness.

In summary, the issue of what is and is not obvious is one of the most difficult challenges in patent law. As a manager, your opinion may be required as to what is known within your field. But, never presume that an innovation is obvious without sufficient evidence to bolster your point of view.

And don't take obviousness too far. A woman by the name of Anita Dembiczak came up with the idea of a plastic leaf bag decorated to look like a Halloween pumpkin. She filed a patent application for a flexible waterproof plastic trash bag, orange in color, with two eyes, a nose, and a mouth drawn on the bag so that when the trash or leaf bag is filled, it takes the "form and general appearance of a pumpkin with a face thereon."

The Patent Office was less than pleased with Dembiczak's application, even though the Patent Office could not find exactly the same thing in the "prior art." Instead, the Patent Office found a handbook for elementary school teachers that described how to make stuffed paper bag pumpkins. Generic plastic leaf or trash bags were not new, said the Patent Office, and neither was the idea of making *paper* bag pumpkins. Therefore, making a plastic leaf or trash bag look like a pumpkin when filled was obvious. On appeal, though, the Federal Circuit overturned the Patent Office's obviousness ruling and decided Mrs. Dembiczak was entitled to a patent for her "stuff a pumpkin."

At one level of abstraction, a plastic leaf bag tailored to look like a pumpkin is blatantly obvious: It's a combination of a known plastic leaf bag designed to hold leaves and teaching that stuffed paper bags can be decorated to look like a jack-o-lantern. The Federal Circuit previously found the combination patentable because there was no explicit teaching, suggestion, or motivation to extrapolate what was known about decorating paper bags to larger plastic leaf bags. Under

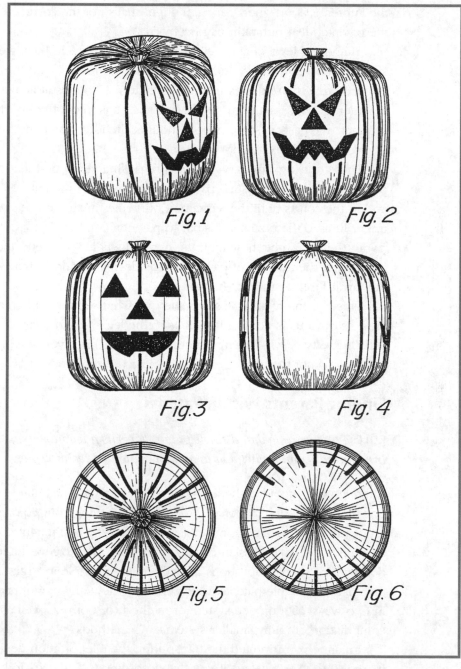

Boo! Drawings for the Dembiczak patent show plastic leaf
bags decorated to look like a Halloween pumpkin.

the Supreme Court's new ruling, though, that's not the correct test. So, the patented leaf pumpkin bag is obvious.

At another level of abstraction, however, plastic leaf bags were available for many years, and yet no one else came up with the idea of decorating them to look like jack-o-lanterns. The result achieved commercial success and turned plastic leaf bags into a dual-purpose product, and at least some people thought the idea was fairly nifty. So, the leaf pumpkin bag is not obvious.

These dueling, contrary positions regarding yet-to-be-filed, pending, and already-issued patents will play out at the Patent Office and in the courts until the Supreme Court rules again and sets an upper limit to the obviousness bar to patents.

In the meantime, how high the bar really is may be reflected in whether the number of patent awards decreases and if there is a downward trend in patent filings.

This and many other cases prove that what some people may view as obvious is not at all obvious in the legal patent sense. And it's usually pretty easy to deem something obvious once you see it. That, however, is not the test for obviousness according to patent law.

Finding Patents Within Patents

RULE: *Don't assume that a single patent governs a technology. Innovations commonly include multiple patented technologies.*

Although I've provided the legal definition of what's patentable, above, don't let that limit your perspective when reviewing your company's innovations. For example, never assume that only *one* patent covers an innovation. Like Russian nesting dolls that open to reveal another doll within, many innovations actually reveal multiple inventions that give rise to multiple patents. It's essential to view any new innovation in two ways: as a unique system or method (or both) as well as a combination of many smaller systems and methods.

Imagine you invented the transporter, the teleportation device used in *Star Trek*. (Yes, yes, we know that according to Star Trek folklore, the transporter was supposedly invented in the early 22nd century by Dr. Emory Erickson, the first human to be successfully transported.) Certainly the transporter's overall functionality—dematerializing people in one place and rematerializing them in another place— would be patentable, but along with that, the following might also be patentable:

- the user interface
- the mechanical design of the teleportation platform
- the process for illuminating the circles on the platform
- the device's individual circuits and chips
- the manner in which the circuits and chips are assembled together
- the microchip packaging
- the silicon dies inside each chip
- how the dies are electrically connected to their respective packages
- how the microprocessor chip is programmed
- how the microprocessor code was written and tested
- how the circuitry of each chip is formed in silicon
- how the silicon wafers are processed
- how the chips are cut from a wafer
- the wafer processing equipment
- the transmitter on the circuit board
- the communication protocols used by the transmitter
- the method used to fabricate the printed circuit boards
- the materials used in the printed circuit boards.

You may even be able to patent new uses for the transporter—for example, in the 24th Century, Starfleet Academy cadets apparently used the device to transport furniture instead of people. But you get the point, that a manager should not just look for a patent, but should be aware that innovations may be "multi-patented." If the transporter is too wild an idea for you, the same principles apply to any new hand-held electronic device.

> ## What's the Difference Between a System and a Method Patent?
>
> You may recall in our discussion in Chapter 2 about the Amazon dispute, that the Amazon patent covered both the computer programming that allows one-click purchases (the *system*) as well as the one-click procedure of making purchases (the *method*). Thus patents can cover products, systems, components, and things as well as methods: methods of operating a system, methods of fabricating products, methods of treating, methods of performing a procedure, and the like.

Reinventing the Wheel: Improvements and New Uses

RULE: *Don't overlook improvements and new uses of old technologies.*

When you're looking for patentable innovations, keep in mind that this includes improvements or new twists on old technologies. For example, in 2000, the Federal Circuit allowed a patent for the idea of using Bag Balm—an ointment normally used to soothe irritated cow udders—to treat human baldness.

Improvement Patents

Most patents that issue are indeed improvement patents. They attempt to protect one or a few differences between a new product and previously existing products and services of the same kind. Some people further subclassify improvement patents as either "addition" or "substitution" inventions.

An "addition invention" adds something to what came before. The Gillette Mach3 razor, for example, had three blades, where previous razors had two. Jeff Bezos, in contrast, substituted the "one-click" purchasing feature for the prior virtual shopping cart model.

Do not underestimate the value of improvement patents. In their book *Innovation: The Five Disciplines for Creating What Customers*

Want, authors Curtis R. Carlson and William W. Wilmot write that "smaller innovations can be extremely important, especially as one builds upon another. We share the passion that quality gurus W. Edwards Deming and Taiichi Ohno had about the power of accumulated small innovations."

We'll see, in later discussions, that when dealing with improvements, the real question is not, "Is this patentable?" but whether or not the patentable difference or differences provide you with a worthwhile competitive advantage.

For example, the third-blade difference in the Gillette Mach3 razor was valuable enough to Gillette to spend untold millions advertising and distributing the new razor. Compared to those costs, the patent and litigation costs incurred in going after Schick were inconsequential. And, if there is even a small chance that Gillette's patent would prohibit all of Gillette's competitors from selling razors with more than two blades, the cost was definitely worth it.

Incorporating New Technologies in Old Products

A subclass of improvement patents includes new technology in old products. For example, when microprocessors became affordable, many patents were filed and issued for devices which were previously controlled by analog circuitry. In other words, patents were granted for old products performing the same function, but now using a microprocessor instead of analog circuitry. When the next generation of microprocessors later began to include special features like their own analog-to-digital converters and internal memory, the patenting cycle started all over again and patents were awarded for products which used to include the old version of the processors but now included the new processors.

Another example, mentioned earlier in my discussion about unobviousness, involved a "new" document scanner that basically had the same configuration and architecture as old scanners but now included a universal serial bus or USB port. A USB port allows devices connected to a desktop or laptop computer to be powered directly from the computer.

Want another example? Ever hear about—aerogel? It was invented in 1931. It's is a low-density solid-state material derived from gel in which the liquid component of the gel has been replaced with gas. The result is an extremely low density solid with several remarkable properties, most notably its effectiveness as an insulator. Even though it's over seventy-five years old and no longer protectable under patent law (patents expire after approximately 17 years), some companies are now patenting uses for aerogel—for example, placing aerogel between panes of glass for insulation (aerogel transmits light), inserting it around deep sea oil well piping for insulation to prevent the oil from getting cold and clogging the piping, and placing it in fuel cells. Panes of glass, deep sea oil well piping, and fuel cells are not new, and

Crayons don't melt when shielded by aerogel, an exotic substance that is 99.8% air, yet provides 39 times more insulating than the best fiberglass insulation. © NASA

neither is aerogel, but aerogel used in these particular "new" ways is patentable because it's *different*.

New Twists on Old Ideas

Another subclass of improvements includes innovations that provide new twists on old ideas. In these cases the inventor doesn't incorporate an old invention into another device (as shown by the aerogel examples, above). Instead, an inventor finds an entirely new use for an old product.

In 2002, the Federal Circuit—the usual court of last resort for these cases (as the Supreme Court rarely hears patent matters)—reviewed these types of patents when it set out a hypothetical case that goes like this.

> **EXAMPLE:** Suppose inventor A invents a shoe polish and receives a patent for the composition of the polish. Then suppose inventor B discovers that inventor A's polish repels water when rubbed on shoes. That's not patentable, the court said, "because repelling water is inherent to the normal use of the polish to shine shoes." Next, though, suppose inventor C discovers that inventor A's polish grows hair when rubbed on the scalp. That, the court said, is patentable, because it's a new use of a known composition.

Funny example, but all too real. Don't forget that patent for the idea of using Bag Balm—an ointment normally used to soothe irritated cow udders—to treat human baldness.

Should You Patent It?

Okay, now that you have an idea of how to survey innovations for patentability, let's examine the next (and more difficult) question: Should the innovation be patented? Obviously, every innovation cannot achieve worthwhile patent protection. Companies must choose whether the cost of the patent justifies the potential benefits.

Before we analyze this question, consider a case study used by the Harvard Business School, based on real-life events, about the "X-IT" company. X-IT designed a compact, rope–like escape ladder to be used in case of a fire. The X-IT ladder was advertised as "the strongest, safest, smallest escape ladder" and was eventually patented and received several design awards.

The Walter Kidde Portable Equipment company (known as Kidde), a manufacturer of fire extinguisher products, soon became interested in X-IT and the new ladder and began selling its own version. Kidde was hardly innocent in its business dealings with X-IT, though, and, in the end, X-IT sued for various unfair business practices and won a $117 million judgment (later reduced to $12.4 million plus legal fees and interests). Kidde eventually agreed to pay X-IT $17.4 million.

Curiously, the X-IT patents weren't even a part of the lawsuit. Instead, X-IT sued for other issues such as false advertising and misappropriation of trade secrets. So in the end, X-IT incurred heavy patent costs which provided no real benefit when dealing with its primary competitor, Kidde. The reason? There were many previous versions of rope-like fire escape ladders. That meant X-IT could only patent small differences between its ladder and those that came before. Kidde, in turn, didn't include X-IT's patented design in the Kidde ladder.

I provide this cautionary tale to remind you that patents may not always offer a competitive edge in the marketplace. In some cases, for example, other types of legal protection such as trade secrets, trademark or advertising laws may provide the necessary legal ammunition to prevent unfair competition from competitors.

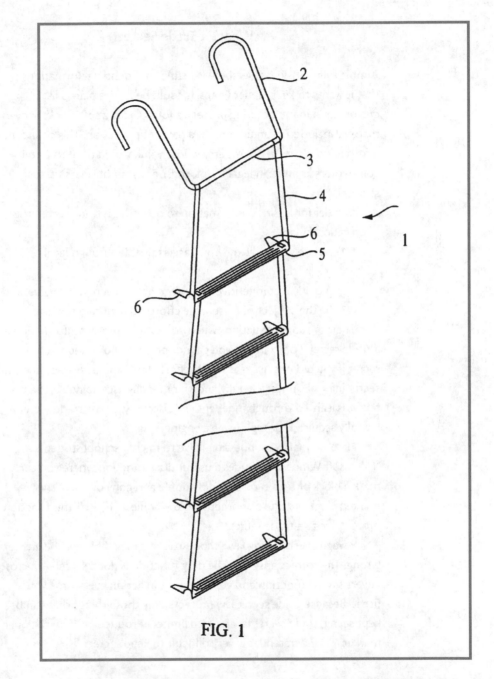

FIG. 1

We're out of here! X-IT's patented escape ladder ("Collapsible ladder having highly nesting rungs with integral stand-off projections," Pat No. 6,279,681).

What's a Trade Secret?

Almost every business has some valuable confidential information that it wants to keep under wraps. It could be a sales plan, a list of customers, a manufacturing process, a formula for a soft drink, or even material included in an unpublished patent application. This confidential information is a form of property whose value would drop to zero if competitors knew it. In legal terms, these are your business's trade secrets.

In order for business information to qualify as a trade secret, the information must:

(1) not be generally known or ascertainable through legal methods;

(2) provide a competitive advantage or have economic value, and

(3) be the subject of reasonable efforts to maintain secrecy.

There are some situations when you cannot protect information as a trade secret. For example, you cannot protect information as a trade secret if you did not use reasonable efforts to maintain secrecy, the trade secret information is generally known or readily ascertainable, the trade secret is learned through independent discovery, or the trade secret is lawfully acquired through reverse engineering.

Here's a final exam question I give to my law school students: "Microsoft Windows includes a useful 'drag' function where you can mark a block of text in one window or file and copy or move the marked block of text to another window or file. Why isn't this function protectable as a trade secret?"

Several overthinking law school students inevitably get the answer wrong. The correct answer is the drag function is not a secret—Microsoft advertises the function and you can see it in action every time you use it. Because trade secret law protects only those things that can be kept secret, trade secret law is often limited. Products sold on the open market are understandably very difficult to keep secret.

What's It Cost?

RULE: *As a ballpark figure, expect that the minimum cost for acquiring patent rights will be between $15,000 and $20,000.*

According to one survey, a company can expect to pay for the following in order to acquire a patent:

- a patent search conducted to evaluate whether a new technology is patentable in light of the state of the art, typically what is shown in prior patents ("prior art")
- filing of a patent application for the new technology, and
- dealing with the inevitable Patent Office rejections and paperwork in an attempt to win the patent (known as patent prosecution).

According to another study, the total cost of acquiring a patent is between $20,000 and $30,000. In addition, there are the costs associated with maintaining the patent for its maximum life, which can easily exceed an additional $15,000.

Filing a corresponding patent application in any single foreign country can easily equal or exceed the fees for a U.S. filing. If the patent is ever litigated—that is, you sue someone or they sue you over your rights to the innovation—expect attorney's fees to easily exceed $1 million if the case proceeds all the way through trial.

Here's a snapshot of what to expect:

Patent Costs: Average Expenses	
$20,000–30,000	Patent search, patent filing, patent prosecution
$4,000–10,000	Patent maintenance fees over life of patent
$5,000–10,000	Patent filing per foreign country
$1,000,000–3,000,000	Patent litigation

Based on the high cost and the uncertainty involved, some companies understandably say, "Why bother?" At the other end of the spectrum, other companies patent almost everything, damn the torpedoes. For example, between 1977 and 2003, IBM reportedly procured 35,341 patents. In September of 2005, Gillette introduced the Fusion five-bladed razor, allegedly protected by more than 70 patents. That's one product—70 patents!

Cost-conscious, well managed companies, however, know that sometimes the benefits associated with a given patent outweigh the costs. As expensive as patents may be, they are often worth it, especially if owning one provides market exclusivity or convinces a competitor not to compete with you. For example, would you want to start an online movie rental system, knowing that patents on certain online movie rental systems and methods are owned by the industry leader, NetFlix?

That's why the single most important factor when assessing the cost versus benefit of patenting an innovation is the impact that the patent will have on competitors.

Will This Patent Stop Competitors?

RULE: *The strongest cost-benefit justification for patent protection is the ability to prohibit competitors from copying and selling the patented invention.*

A patent allows the owner to sue a competitor who makes, uses, sells, or offers for sale the patented invention. What does that really mean? It means that if the *scope* of your potential patent is sufficiently meaningful, you can go after others and stop them from copying your innovation. And in that case, the cost of the patent may be worth the benefits derived from the patent.

Patent worth, then, entails adding up the benefits of a competitor not being able to sell a product encompassing your invention. So, if the latest version of a product sold by your company has three differences that make the product, say, faster, more reliable, and less costly, and those three differences will be used by the marketing department to hopefully increase sales, then those differences might be worth the cost of acquiring a patent.

If prior versions of that product will sell just as well, however, then the cost of acquiring the patent might not outweigh the benefits. Or, if a "next best alternative" to your patented product will compete and not infringe your patent, then the benefit of a patent may be outweighed by its cost.

Does the "Patent Pending" Statement Stop Competitors?

Once you file a patent application (or a provisional patent application), you can label your product as "Patent Pending." The use of the term "patent pending" usually provides limited legal benefit. You can't sue a competitor for patent infringement until the government awards you the patent, which can be years after you file the patent application. It's possible that some people may not know that and might refrain from copying your "patent pending" product even though they don't have to. In addition, a competitor reviewing a product marked "patent pending" also doesn't know, at least for awhile, what the scope of the patent will be or when the patent will issue. That competitor thus proceeds with competition at some risk.

Patentability and Patent Scope

RULE: *Patents that involve a new technology usually have the broadest scope.*

The primary factor that affects your cost-benefit analysis is the scope of any patent that you may acquire.

Patents range in scope from broad to narrow. What do I mean by "broad" and "narrow"? Consider the case studies described in the previous chapter. Gillette's patent for the Mach3 three-bladed razor had a broad enough scope to threaten Schick's sales of its four-bladed Quattro razor. Toro's patents were narrow enough in scope so that

John Deere was able to compete by replacing the cam-based system specified in the Toro patents with a solenoid. Amazon's one-click patent had such a broad scope that, although the Amazon patent was found infringed by Barnes and Noble, Barnes and Noble was able to put the Amazon patent in jeopardy because the breadth of the patent meant that it might have improperly covered an old idea.

In general, a patent with a broad scope will have the strongest effect on preventing competition. A patent with a narrow scope will make it easier for competitors to design around (and therefore avoid infringing) your patent.

For Gillette, the scope of the patent for a razor with more than two blades is huge, and it's worth quite a lot even in the face of a low likelihood of successfully obtaining the patent in the first place. A patent for aerogel used as insulation in deep sea oil well piping probably has a smaller scope and may not be worth all that much, especially if other types of insulating materials perform adequately. But it could be worth something just for the patent owner to be able to advertise "The only oil well piping with aerogel!" Indeed, many companies find value in just being able to advertise "Patented!"

I've generalized that the broader the scope, the more benefit and therefore the higher the cost a company is willing to pay for patent protection. Consider major innovations such as the telephone, laser, transistor, computer, and Internet. Inventors of these new (or so-called "disruptive") technologies generally acquire the broadest patents and the strongest patent rights. Certainly, owning one of these patents is worth the cost. But that's true only up to a point.

There is also often a downside to a brilliant innovation with broad patent scope. Some technologies are not, at the time of their discovery, commercially viable or even useful. It may take years—long after the patent has expired—before commercial uses are determined.

Earlier I mentioned aerogel, the "liquid smoke" discovered by a Stanford University researcher in the 1930s. This highly porous material is in the Guinness Book of World Records as "the world's lightest substance." (Aerogel is 99.8% air.) A block of aerogel as big as a person weighs less than pound but is strong enough to support a small car. It is only now, seventy-five years later, that many companies have discovered marketable uses for this substance and engineered methods to mass-produce it.

Gone Before Their Time

Aerogel is not the only broad patent to expire before commercial exploitation. Here are some other examples.

Although Teflon was invented in 1938, it was not until 1954 that two French engineers discovered that the substance could be used in frying pans to prevent food from sticking to the surface.

Disc brakes were not widely used on cars until 50 years after they were patented.

Power steering was patented in 1927 but was not introduced in passenger cars until 1951.

Stereophonic sound was invented in 1933 but was not popularized in consumer recordings until the 1960s.

The first color television system was invented in 1929 but did not become commercially practical until the 1960s.

The microwave oven was patented in 1945, but consumer models were not available until 1967.

Though patented in 1938, the first commercial electric photocopiers were not sold until 1958.

Bar code technology was patented in 1949, but it was not used for supermarket checkouts until 1974.

The first electric photocopier was patented in 1938 but not offered for sale for twenty years

The first color television system was invented in 1929 but not made commercially practical until the 1960s.

Sometimes, then, patenting even a brand-new technology isn't worth the cost; there has to be a market need. "Build it and they will come" has proven not to be a very good innovation strategy. Similarly, "patent it because we can" is not a very good patent management strategy.

Another concern raised by broad patents is that because of their breadth they often invite litigation. Highly profitable new technologies are always prone to litigation and stories like the Lasik (see "Lasik = LOL (Lots of Litigation)," below) are common. Many owners of broad patents spend their careers bogged down in patent lawsuits—Alexander Graham Bell's telephone patent was the basis of hundreds of lawsuits. The patent battles of Edwin Armstrong—inventor of FM radio—against AT&T, RCA, and Westinghouse lasted for decades and contributed to his suicide.

So, there can be a high price to pay if you attempt to enter the market with even a disruptive technology. There will be competition, and that competition could breed patents you may have to steer clear of. Patent holding companies, patent consortiums, and patent pools seem to form around the most popular new technologies. Nanotechnology is a good example. According to one study, 3,818 patents exist for the primary building blocks of nanotechnology. The result is that anyone entering or already in this field will have to carefully navigate numerous patents owned by many different firms.

In the main, though, if you can patent a brand-new technology that is expected to generate very high revenues, the benefits of the patent will generally outweigh the costs. Sometimes the benefits grossly outweigh the costs: Witness the almost $1 billion award granted to Polaroid when Kodak was found to infringe Polaroid's patents for the instant camera. Polaroid actually won twice: the $1 billion and the increased market share because Kodak was eliminated as a competitor. In Chapter 8, I'll talk about a guy who thought business people might want to receive email wirelessly, patented that idea, and won $612.5 million from the manufacturer of the BlackBerry device.

For now, though, understand that a new idea for a brand-new product, system, or method is patentable and should always be patented if the product, system, or method is marketable.

I am also aware that for many companies, there is little likelihood of a truly disruptive technology breakthrough. Keep in mind that these examples are provided as extremes on the "scope spectrum". You may never acquire a patent that is broad enough to prevent competition. Sometimes the issue is simply: Is my patent broad enough to *reduce* competition, or at least make it a little harder for the competition? Indeed, some companies patent ideas just to prevent competition: Verizon sought to prevent competition to their core cellular telephone business by patenting certain facets of Internet telephone calls. IBM, as another example, regularly patents ideas that are not used in their business but that generate significant revenue when these patents are licensed to other companies.

Other Factors

Sometimes, other factors also need to be taken into account, as patents can have value above and beyond their literal scope. Lenders, venture capitalists and other investors, distributors, potential partners or joint venturers or buyers of the company, and other business partners sometimes favor patents without any regard to their real scope. Also, remember the unintelligible patent case study regarding the dog chew patent in the previous chapter? An uneducated competitor who doesn't understand or even bother to ascertain the scope of your patent (or doesn't know how) may refrain from competition simply because "it's patented."

Patent Value as a Defense or Deterrent

Finally, some companies patent quite a few developments but never sue anyone for patent infringement. The reason for these "defensive patents" is the company knows it will likely be sued by a competitor and then the company, by virtue of its own patents, hopefully will have some trading cards to play. For example, any company in the field of laser eye surgery that did not have such defensive patents wouldn't survive for very long due to the number of patents owned by different competitors in that field. Similarly, the value of some patents is based on the fact that they provide a deterrent. These competitive companies have drawn a "patent truce." Each company has so many patents they both know that if company A sues company B for infringing company A's patent, company B will retaliate and sue company A for infringing company B's patent. The truce is that company A never sues company B and vice versa.

A Cost-Benefit Formula

If you like doing the math, one author has proposed that a patent should be applied for if **P issuance** x **P profit** x (**W−C**)>**T**.

Where:

C = the cost of prosecuting the patent application. You can fix that at, say, $20,000.

W = an estimate of the incremental profit attributable to having the patent.

P issuance = the probability the patent will issue.

P profit = the probability of realizing the estimated profit (**W**) and equals **P capitalization** x **P technical** x **P market**, where **P capitalization** is the probability of obtaining adequate funding, **P technical** is the probability of successfully manufacturing the product, and **P market** is the probability of developing the required market.

T = a threshold value set by a specific company. It is dependent upon the profit goals that a company uses in order to decide whether or not to proceed with a given project. Alternatively, one could set **T** at $98,500.

Even if you can determine **P capitalization**, **P technical**, and **P market** (one idea is to be optimistic and fix all three of these probabilities at 1.0), determining **P issuance** and **W** can be especially problematic. **P issuance** is almost always nearly 1.0 if all you cared about is a patent—any patent. But, as we have learned, if you desire a patent with a worthwhile scope, **P issuance** can be awfully difficult to predict ahead of time. **W**, the incremental profit attributable to having the patent because competitors cannot effectively compete, is tied to the scope of the patent—its worth. That value is also difficult predict ahead of time.

So, not only do **P issuance** and **W** depend on each other and can almost never be predicted ahead of time, these values also depend on numerous other variables.

Even so, doing the math when making the decision whether or not to patent is a worthwhile endeavor, even if all the relevant factors are merely discussed in gross generalities rather than actually arriving at cold, hard numbers.

Lasik = LOL (Lots of Litigation)

Lasers were not new when the Lasik eye surgery system was invented, but the system, which mapped a patient's eye and automatically trimmed just enough corneal material at the right places, was truly an innovation.

The patents granted for Lasik led to several patent battles. In late 2002, then Waltham-based Summit Technology convinced a Boston jury that Nidek Co. of Japan willfully infringed Summit's patents on the Lasik procedure. The jury assessed damages at $17.2 million, and Summit was posed to win an injunction preventing Nidek from selling its competitive EC-5000 Lasik machine as well as perhaps a trebling of the damages and even attorney's fees. The eleven-day trial pitted several well-known Lasik doctors against each other, including my client, Dr. Roger Steinert, of the Harvard Medical School (and Ophthalmic Consultants). At issue was the technique of "differential ablation," whether or not Nidek's EC-5000 machine ablated the same depth of corneal material at each pulse of the laser, and the size of the light spot produced by the laser.

Summit won the battle, but its victory was short-lived. A court in Boston overturned the jury verdict after reviewing the evidence and found that Summit failed to prove patent infringement. In April of 2004, the Federal Circuit appellate court agreed.

Nidek was now cleared to compete in the Lasik market, where Summit and Santa Clara-based Visx dominate. Nidek's business model is different from most Lasik players in that Nidek doesn't charge the per-procedure fee collected by most other manufacturers but instead prefers to build a traditional capital equipment business.

Analysts of the refractive surgery market deem it "challenging," because although Summit was the first to win FDA approval for the Lasik procedure, besides Visx, there were now many other competitors, each touting its own set of patents. The only certainty was more litigation, because none of the Lasik players were strangers to the courtroom. Summit and Visx, for example, once sued each other and then settled by pooling their patents and jointly profiting each time a Summit or Visx laser was used to correct a patient's vision. A number of class action lawsuits were filed in response to this "patent pool" on behalf of both doctors and

Lasik = LOL (Lots of Litigation) (continued)

patients. The U.S. Federal Trade Commission ruled in 1998 that the patent pooling partnership was anticompetitive, and the partnership was ultimately dissolved. Visx and Summit then cross-licensed their respective patents.

Visx also sued and ultimately settled with LaserSight, Inc.; Bausch & Lomb; and even Nidek, resulting in a $9 million payment to Nidek. Summit and Visx both sued individual surgeons who were using custom-made or gray market laser systems. Nidek, for its part, sued both Summit and Visx. You might think, given this history of competing devices and patents, no one would be crazy enough to enter the fray.

The next technological improvement in the Lasik procedure, however, was the use of a laser instead of a blade or microkeratome to create the flap that is folded back to provide access to the corneal tissue during the laser surgery. The company that holds the patents on that technique is Interlase Corp. of Irvine, California. Interlase's management team consists largely of ex-Summit executives who left Summit after or shortly after it was sold for almost $1 billion to Alcon, a Nestle SA subsidiary. Interlase has secured FDA approval and now has 120 machines in use.

Interlase has not yet sued or been sued for patent infringement, but Vice President of Business Development Bernard Haffey, a resident of Dover, MA, told me there is a competitor in Germany attempting to establish its own patent position for the new flap-creation technique. Given his previous experience at Summit, he wants to "avoid litigation at all costs." But still, he relies on patents.

What Are Copyrights and Trademarks?

Copyrights and trademarks are often confused with patents, but they are really quite different.

Copyright law protects music, architecture, writing, computer programs, plays, movies, dance, or visual arts such as graphic arts, sculptures, photographs, or paintings. The creator of a copyrightable work (known as an author) automatically acquires copyright protection for the life of the author plus 70 years (for works created by a single author). Other works are protected for 120 years from date of creation or 95 years from first publication, whichever is longer. Additional benefits are acquired if the copyright is registered with the U.S. Copyright Office. But, generally only patents can protect ideas, new functionality, improvements, and innovations.

A trademark is any word, symbol, design, device, logo, or slogan that identifies and distinguishes one product or service from another. Trademarks inform consumers that a product comes from a particular source. For example, the Apple trademark informs consumers that an iPod has a certain quality or reliability. This consumer connection, known as "goodwill," strengthens the value of all Apple products.

A trademark does not have to be a word. It can be anything that identifies and distinguishes a product or service, for example, the yellow McDonald's arches, the color pink for Corning fiberglass, or the shape of the Absolut vodka bottle.

The owner of a trademark can exclude others from using a similar trademark on similar or related goods or services. In some cases, use of a similar trademark may be stopped if a court determines that the use of the similar mark dilutes or tarnishes the trademark. For example, the unauthorized use of the Adidas trademark made to look like a marijuana leaf would dilute or tarnish the shoe maker's image. Trademark protection lasts for as long as a business continuously uses the trademark in connection with goods or services. Many valuable marks such as Jell-O have been in existence for over a century. Additional trademark rights can be acquired if a business registers the trademark with the U.S. Patent and Trademark Office. Trademarks protect the name of a product or service but not the product or service itself.

Design and Plant Patents

This book is devoted to utility patents, the most common patent issued by the Patent Office. There are two other, less common forms of patents:

- Plant patents, which cover plants that can be reproduced through the use of grafts and cuttings (asexually reproducible), such as flowers.

- Design patents, which cover the unique, ornamental, or visible shape or design of a nonnatural object. Design patents can be used to protect a wide range of designs including toys, jewelry and crafts, and computer icons. The difference between a utility patent and a design patent is that a utility patent protects the way a product functions, while a design patent protects the way a product looks. You can acquire both design and utility patents for an innovation that is useful and has an ornamental appearance. A design patent lasts for 14 years. A utility patent lasts for 20 years from the date of filing (typically 17 to 18 years from the date the patent issues).

The Claim Game: How to Read a Patent

Anatomy of a Patent 85

    The Title Page...86

    Patent Filing and Issue Dates 90

    The Body of the Patent 91

    Field of Invention...94

The Claim Game...105

    Claiming the Ladder 109

    Claiming a Fiber Optic Switch Generically 116

    Reading Claims for Infringement 119

    Independent and Dependent Claims...119

    The Importance of Words 121

    Means Plus Function 123

What a Patent Doesn't Tell You 125

    Stuff Happens After the Patent Issues 125

    Patents Have Relatives...127

    Patents May Not Reflect All Prior Art...127

There are two types of patent documents available for the public to read: patents issued or granted by the Patent Office, and patent applications that have been published by the Patent Office (typically 18 months after filing). The biggest difference between these two documents is that only owners of issued patents can go after infringers. Another distinction is that a published patent application may never become a patent (approximately fifty percent of applications become patents). Finally, a patent application may change in scope before it issues.

> *"'When I use a word,' Humpty Dumpty said in rather a scornful tone, 'it means just what I choose it to mean— neither more nor less.'"*
>
> —LEWIS CARROLL

Since an application may not become a patent and is not enforceable against infringers, why bother reading applications? One reason is to get an idea what your competitors are developing. And, as I'll explain in Chapter 6, if an application is published and your company infringes the invention after publication but before issuance, the owner can still sue your company for these infringements once the patent issues.

CAVEAT: *Know what you're reading. Patents and published applications look similar. The difference? A published application has the letter A at the end of its patent number.*

Patents and patent applications are nearly identical in appearance, but you can tell them apart by examining the upper right-hand portion of the title page. On a patent application, the publication number will contain the letter "A," a designation that means a patent has not yet been granted.

You can search applications published since March 15, 2001 at the Patent Office website. We explain searching in detail in Chapter 6, but if you'd like to get started now, go to the Patent Office website (www.uspto.gov), click Patents, click Search, and then choose the option search Published Applications on the right side of the screen. Design patents, plant patents, and provisional patent applications are not published and therefore won't show up in your search.

Anatomy of a Patent

As you will see, each patent application, like each invention, is different. There is no "standard application" used for preparing patents. (I wish I had a nickel for every time someone asked me for a "blank" patent application form they could fill out and submit themselves. If only it were that easy.)

A patent is a document with a split personality. The technical side of it—part functional specification and part design specification—is intended to explain your great idea and what makes it new and patentable. The legal side of the patent, particularly the claims, explains what others cannot copy, use, or sell. So, in effect, the patent says look (the technical side) but don't touch (the legal side).

For example, if the legendary Dr. Frankenstein were to patent his process for reanimation, the patent would describe the biological engineering—the methods and processes—by which the body is brought back to life. But the patent, with its built-in legal limitations, would also function to effectively prevent anyone from reanimating their own creatures under threat of lawsuit.

Okay, let's look at some patents. You've never seen a patent? Don't worry. At the beginning of each semester, many of my patent law school students haven't, either. Once you read through a few, you'll quickly get the hang of deciphering them.

BOTTOM LINE: *You can and should learn how to read patents.*

Where to Find Patents ...

In Chapter 6, I discuss how to search and find patents online. If you'd like to get started immediately, you can find and read U.S. patents for free by using the databases at www.uspto.gov. If you know the patent number, click Patents, click Search, and then choose Patent Number Search. If you don't know the number, follow the searching instructions provided in Chapter 6. You can also have access to free patents by using Google's new patent search engine (Go to www.google.com, click more and choose Patents.) Chapter 6 also explains other online sources for patents as well as how to obtain paper and PDF copies of patents. You can also get a general idea of all the newly published patent applications, organized by industry, inventor, and category, at FreshPatents.com. Herein I'll discuss the official patent format as a patent issues. Some on-line search engines do not allow a printout of the patent in this format.

All patents share a basic format, adhered to, at least in part, in the patents of most foreign countries. This format includes proscribed sections, some archaic language, and various bureaucratic idiosyncrasies. In the following sections we analyze each of these sections.

The Title Page

All U.S. patents include a title page, the first page of the patent, which includes a summary of important information. An example is provided below of the title page for Amazon's "one-click" patent.

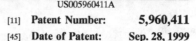

US005960411A

United States Patent [19]

Hartman et al.

[11] Patent Number: **5,960,411**

[45] Date of Patent: **Sep. 28, 1999**

[54] **METHOD AND SYSTEM FOR PLACING A PURCHASE ORDER VIA A COMMUNICATIONS NETWORK**

[75] Inventors: **Peri Hartman; Jeffrey P. Bezos; Shel Kaphan; Joel Spiegel**, all of Seattle, Wash.

[73] Assignee: **Amazon.com, Inc.**, Seattle, Wash.

[21] Appl. No.: **08/928,951**

[22] Filed: **Sep. 12, 1997**

[51] Int. Cl.[6] **G06F 17/60**

[52] U.S. Cl. **705/26**; 705/27; 345/962

[58] Field of Search 705/26, 27; 380/24, 380/25; 235/2, 375, 378, 381; 395/188.01; 345/962

[56] **References Cited**

U.S. PATENT DOCUMENTS

4,937,863	6/1990	Robert et al.	380/4
5,204,897	4/1993	Wyman	380/4
5,260,999	11/1993	Wyman	384/4
5,627,940	5/1997	Rohra et al.	395/12
5,640,501	6/1997	Turpin	395/768
5,640,577	6/1997	Scharmer	395/768
5,664,111	9/1997	Nahan et al.	705/27
5,715,314	2/1998	Payne et al.	380/24
5,715,399	2/1998	Bezos	705/27
5,727,163	3/1998	Bezos	705/27
5,745,681	4/1998	Levine et al.	395/200.3
5,758,126	5/1998	Daniels et al.	395/500

FOREIGN PATENT DOCUMENTS

0855659 A1	1/1998	European Pat. Off.	G06F 17/30
0855687 A2	1/1998	European Pat. Off.	G07F 19/00
0845747A2	6/1998	European Pat. Off.	G06F 17/60
0883076A2	12/1998	European Pat. Off.	G06F 17/60
WO 95/30961	11/1995	WIPO	G06F 17/60
WO 96/38799	12/1996	WIPO	G06F 17/60
WO 98/21679	5/1998	WIPO	G06F 17/60

OTHER PUBLICATIONS

Jones, Chris. "Java Shopping Cart and Java Wallet; Oracles plans to join e–commerce initiative." Mar. 31, 1997, Info-World Media Group.

"Pacific Coast Software Software creates virtual shopping cart." Sep. 6, 1996. M2 Communications Ltd 1996.

"Software Creates Virtual Shopping Cart." Sep. 5, 1996. Business Wire, Inc.

Terdoslavich, William. "Java Electronic Commerce Framework." Computer Reseller News, Sep. 23, 1996, CMP Media, Inc., 1996, pp. 126, http://www.elibrary.com/id/101/101/getdoc . . . rydocid=902269@library_d&dtype=0–0&dinst=. [Accessed Nov. 19, 1998].

"Internet Access: Disc Distributing Announces Interactive World Wide." Cambridge Work–Group Computing Report, Cambridge Publishing, Inc., 1995, http://www.elibrary.com/id/101/101/getdoc . . . docid=1007497@library_a&dtype=0–0&dinst=0. [Accessed Nov. 19, 1998].

(List continued on next page.)

Primary Examiner—James P. Trammell
Assistant Examiner—Demetra R. Smith
Attorney, Agent, or Firm—Perkins Coie LLP

[57] **ABSTRACT**

A method and system for placing an order to purchase an item via the Internet. The order is placed by a purchaser at a client system and received by a server system. The server system receives purchaser information including identification of the purchaser, payment information, and shipment information from the client system. The server system then assigns a client identifier to the client system and associates the assigned client identifier with the received purchaser information. The server system sends to the client system the assigned client identifier and an HTML document identifying the item and including an order button. The client system receives and stores the assigned client identifier and receives and displays the HTML document. In response to the selection of the order button, the client system sends to the server system a request to purchase the identified item. The server system receives the request and combines the purchaser information associated with the client identifier of the client system to generate an order to purchase the item in accordance with the billing and shipment information whereby the purchaser effects the ordering of the product by selection of the order button.

26 Claims, 11 Drawing Sheets

[54] **Patent Title**. Usually, the title of the patent is a short, simple summary of the invention ... although in some cases, titles get a bit long-winded and/or do not really accurately reflect the legal protection afforded by the patent.

[75] **Inventors**. The inventors block lists the names of the actual inventors, who usually assign their rights in the patent to the assignee.

[21] **Application Number.** Once an application is filed, it is given a serial number for tracking purposes.

[22] **Filed ("Filing Date")** The filing date determines the patent's age—patents are now valid for 20 years from the date they are filed. The filing date is also key when companies attempt to void a patent.

[58] **Field of Search**. This is where, among the many classes, the Patent Office Examiner searched for prior patents in the process of determining if the patent application described something new and unobvious.

[56] **References Cited**. These are the prior patents, published patent applications, and other literature cited by the applicant and/or the Patent Office Examiner.

United States Patent [19]

Hartman et al.

[54] **METHOD AND SYSTEM FOR PLACING A PURCHASE ORDER VIA A COMMUNICATIONS NETWORK**

[75] Inventors: **Peri Hartman; Jeffrey P. Bezos; Shel Kaphan; Joel Spiegel**, all of Seattle, Wash.

[73] Assignee: **Amazon.com, Inc.**, Seattle, Wash.

[21] Appl. No.: **08/928,951**

[22] Filed: **Sep. 12, 1997**

[51] Int. Cl.^{6} G06F 17/60
[52] U.S. Cl. **705/26**; 705/27; 345/962
[58] Field of Search 705/26, 27; 380/24, 380/25; 235/2, 375, 378, 381; 395/188.01; 345/962

[56]   **References Cited**
                   U.S. PATENT DOCUMENTS

4,937,863	6/1990	Robert et al.	380/4
5,204,897	4/1993	Wyman	380/4
5,260,999	11/1993	Wyman	384/4
5,627,940	5/1997	Rohra et al.	395/12
5,640,501	6/1997	Turpin	395/768
5,640,577	6/1997	Scharmer	395/768
5,664,111	9/1997	Nahan et al.	705/27
5,715,314	2/1998	Payne et al.	380/24
5,715,399	2/1998	Bezos	705/27
5,727,163	3/1998	Bezos	705/27
5,745,681	4/1998	Levine et al.	395/200.3
5,758,126	5/1998	Daniels et al.	395/500

FOREIGN PATENT DOCUMENTS

0855659 A1	1/1998	European Pat. Off.	G06F 17/30
0855687 A2	1/1998	European Pat. Off.	G07F 19/00
0845747A2	6/1998	European Pat. Off.	G06F 17/60
0883076A2	12/1998	European Pat. Off.	G06F 17/60
WO 95/30961	11/1995	WIPO	G06F 17/60
WO 96/38799	12/1996	WIPO	G06F 17/60
WO 98/21679	5/1998	WIPO	G06F 17/60

OTHER PUBLICATIONS

Jones, Chris. "Java Shopping Cart and Java Wallet; Oracles plans to join e–commerce initiative." Mar. 31, 1997, Info-World Media Group.

[73] **The Assignee.** The assignee is the individual or company who acquired the patent rights from the inventor—typically an employee of the company. The patent reflects the assignee's name as of the date of issuance. Subsequent assignments are usually but not always recorded with the Patent Office and can be researched at the Patent Office and online. Sometimes, even patent licenses are recorded.

[51] **Intl. Class** and [52] **U.S. Cl.** The Patent Office classifies inventions according to classes and subclasses. Amazon's one-click patent is classified in the data processing class (class 75) and in the electronic shopping subclass (class 26), among other classes and subclasses.

Amazon's "One Click" Patent—Title Page (left-hand side)

[45] Date of Patent. The date the Patent Office granted the patent.

[11] **Patent Number:** 5,960,411

[45] **Date of Patent:** Sep. 28, 1999

[11] Patent Number. The upper right-hand portion of every title page includes the patent number, a series of numerals that reflect the sequential order in which patents are issued by the Patent Office. Underneath the patent number is the date the patent issued. If the publication number includes the letter A at the end, then the document is an application, not a patent. Sometimes, people will refer only to the last three numbers (e.g., the "411 patent").

"Pacific Coast Software Software creates virtual shopping cart." Sep. 6, 1996. M2 Communications Ltd 1996.
"Software Creates Virtual Shopping Cart." Sep. 5, 1996. Business Wire, Inc.
Terdoslavich, William. "Java Electronic Commerce Framework." Computer Reseller News, Sep. 23, 1996, CMP Media, Inc., 1996, pp. 126, http://www.elibrary.com/id/101/101/getdoc . . . rydocid=902269@library_d&dtype=0–0&dinst=. [Accessed Nov. 19, 1998].
"Internet Access: Disc Distributing Announces Interactive World Wide." Cambridge Work–Group Computing Report, Cambridge Publishing, Inc., 1995, http://www.elibrary.com/id/101/101/getdoc . . . docid=1007497@library_a&dtype=0–0&dinst=0. [Accessed Nov. 19, 1998].

(List continued on next page.)

Examiner. This is the name of the Patent Office Examiner(s) who processed the patent application.

Primary Examiner—James P. Trammell
Assistant Examiner—Demetra R. Smith
Attorney, Agent, or Firm—Perkins Coie LLP

[57] **ABSTRACT**

[57] Abstract. The abstract is a synopsis of the invention, similar to the abstract of a technical or scientific paper.

A method and system for placing an order to purchase an item via the Internet. The order is placed by a purchaser at a client system and received by a server system. The server system receives purchaser information including identification of the purchaser, payment information, and shipment information from the client system. The server system then assigns a client identifier to the client system and associates the assigned client identifier with the received purchaser information. The server system sends to the client system assigned client identifier and an HTML document identifying the item and including an order button. The client system receives and stores the assigned client identifier and receives and displays the HTML document. In response to the selection of the order button, the client system sends to the server system a request to purchase the identified item. The server system receives the request and combines the purchaser information associated with the client identifier of the client system to generate an order to purchase the item in accordance with the billing and shipment information whereby the purchaser effects the ordering of the product by selection of the order button.

26 Claims, 11 Drawing Sheets

Enable Single-Action Ordering

301 Retrieve client ID

302 Set client ID/customer mapping

303 Set single-action ordering for client ID/customer

304 Return confirming web page

Done

Drawing. The bottom of the title page includes a reproduction of one of the patent drawings or figures. The drawing on the title page of the "one-click" patent is a flow chart depicting how "one-click" works. More drawings are usually included with the patent, and we discuss them in more detail below.

Amazon's "One Click" Patent—Title Page (right-hand side and bottom)

Patent Filing and Issue Dates

CAVEAT: *The filing date listed on the left-hand side of the title page may not always be the earliest filing date.*

RULE: *In patent prosecution or patent litigation, the parties and attorneys sometimes use a shorthand to refer to patents, using the last three numbers of the patent number—for example, Amazon's "411 patent." Other times, the name of the first-listed inventor is used—for example, the Hartman patent.*

There are two important dates in a patent: the filing date and the issue date. Patents are now valid for 20 years from the date they are filed (the filing date). Since it takes an average of two to three years for the Patent Office to examine and finally approve an application, patents last, or are valid, on average, for about 17 years from the day they issue.

Prior to 1995, patents lasted 17 years from the date of *issue.* So, if you are reading a patent whose filing or issue date is prior to June 8, 1995, then the patent will expire 17 years after the issue date or 20 years from the filing date, whichever is greater. This change in the law was to thwart "Submarine Patents": patent applications that were purposefully kept pending until an industry built up around the invention. Then, the "submariner" would allow the patent to issue and sue numerous infringers. Today, a patent that is pending too long means a patent with less of a useful life.

If the patent dates indicate that the patent is expired, your company is free to use, copy, or sell the invention, provided you don't begin competition until *after* the patent expires. Generic drug manufacturers understand this principle all too well and typically offer for sale generic versions of popular drugs the very day after they "come off patent."

The filing date is also important if your company is engaged in a dispute over a patent. It's possible to invalidate an existing patent if you can show that a highly relevant patent or product or technical paper (prior art) was in existence more than one year before the filing date of the patent to be invalidated. For example, the filing date for the

Amazon patent is September 12, 1997. Therefore, if Barnes & Noble wanted to invalidate this patent, they had to locate prior art dated before September 12, 1996. Also keep in mind that the filing date may not always be the earliest filing date. Some patents are related to older patents with earlier filing dates. That information can be ascertained in "Related Applications," below.

Because the filing date listed on the patent may not always be the earliest filing date, you cannot always rely on it to determine when the clock begins running. A fair number of patents, for example, have their genesis in a foreign patent office or arrive at the U.S. Patent Office via a multinational treaty.

A last thing to keep in mind about filing dates: If a long period of time elapsed between the filing date and the issue date, that fact could indicate that the patent applicant faced difficulty in convincing the Patent Office that the invention was patentable. Sometimes, the patent owner's difficulty can be your salvation, especially when the patentee sought broad protection but ended up only with a patent of a very narrow scope.

The Body of the Patent

Following the title page, the patent is divided into several distinct sections. In the best-written patents, those sections are cohesively tied together by a thesis, one that describes the realization of the inventors that led to the invention. Below, I've highlighted the sections you can expect to find following the title page.

Drawings

Patent drawings (also known as "drawing sheets") are visual representations of the invention and must be included with the application, if necessary, to understand the patent. Sometimes, chemical and biological patents do not have drawings, but most others do. The drawings must show every feature recited in the claims (I'll discuss claims below). In other words, a patent will include a visual reference for everything that's novel about the invention.

There are strict standards for patent drawings as to materials, size, form, symbols, and shading. For example, writing is not permitted in the margins and there can be no holes punched in the drawing sheet. Some examples of patent drawings are shown below.

Innovations, inventions, and improvements are commonly depicted in different views or figures—for example, top views, side views, perspective views, or disassembled (exploded) views. Inventors seek to present as many views as necessary to demonstrate an invention, including all of its embodiments. Each view provides another way of "seeing" the invention. Each view is given a discrete figure number (abbreviated as "Fig." in patent law).

Sometimes, the patent drawings provide an exploded view in which the parts of the invention are separated but shown in relation to each other. Other views, such as schematics or flowcharts, are not drawings in the traditional sense. Some patents include perspective views (in which you can see several angles and sides of an invention).

When you see broken (dashed) lines instead of straight lines, that indicates hidden lines (lines that you could not see from that perspective).

There are three types of numbers used in patent drawings. First, each drawing sheet is numbered on the top using a fraction in which the numerator is the number of the particular drawing sheet and the denominator is the total number of drawing sheets (for example 1/4, 2/4, 3/4, and so on).

Second, there are "figure numbers" consecutively numbered in Arabic numerals—for example Fig. 1, Fig. 2, Fig. 3—and arranged in numerical order in the patent. Sometimes if several related views are grouped together, letters are used as suffixes after the numbers—for example, Fig. 1A, Fig. 1B, Fig. 2A, Fig. 2B, and so on.

Third, and perhaps of greatest importance in deciphering a patent, each drawing includes reference numbers. These reference numbers (and letters) identify the parts or elements of the invention. The general rule is that every component mentioned in the application is numbered. The reference number helps the reader understand what component or element is being discussed and is included in the written description of the invention, commonly with the part name

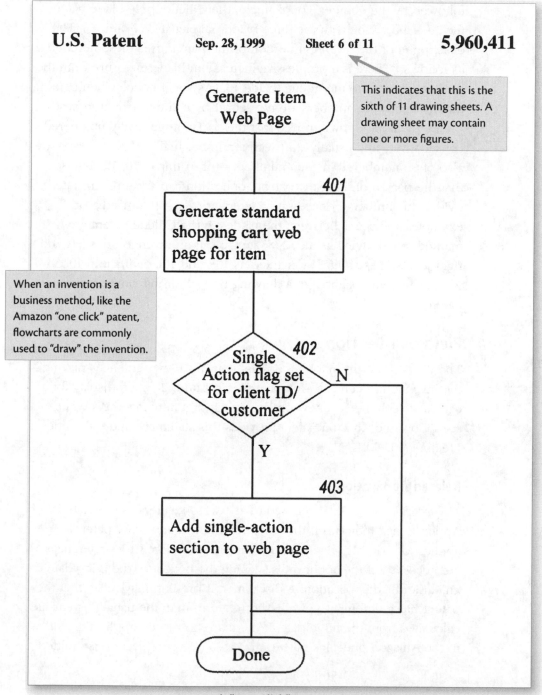

U.S. Patent   Sep. 28, 1999   Sheet 6 of 11   **5,960,411**

Generate Item Web Page

This indicates that this is the sixth of 11 drawing sheets. A drawing sheet may contain one or more figures.

401
Generate standard shopping cart web page for item

When an invention is a business method, like the Amazon "one click" patent, flowcharts are commonly used to "draw" the invention.

402
Single Action flag set for client ID/ customer

N

Y

403
Add single-action section to web page

Done

Amazon's "One Click" Patent—Drawing

followed by the number. For example, the Gillette three-blade patent includes a drawing with the three blades labeled 11, 12, and 13. The description of the invention portion of the patent uses these numbers as follows: "There is a progressive increase in blade exposure from the leading blade 11 to the trailing blade 13." As you'll notice when reading these patents, the numbers are not set off by commas or parentheses.

In addition, you will notice that the parts are generally numbered consecutively and usually start with a number higher than 10. Parts are also often numbered in even numbers—for example, 10, 12, 14—so that the person drafting the patent application can add in items later (with odd numbers) if necessary. Letters are also often used. For examples, the spans between the blades in the Gillette patent are marked in a drawing as S1, S2, S3, and S4. If an invention has left and right levers, these might be marked as 10R and 10L or 10a and 10b.

Above is an example of a drawing from the Amazon one-click patent.

Field of Invention

The Field of the Invention section is typically a few sentences placing the invention in context—for example, is it an LCD microdisplay for a cellular telephone or a new optical switch or a new razor? As you can see below, the Amazon patent provides this statement under the title "Technical Field."

Related Applications

This section, sometimes referred to as "Cross References to Related Applications," indicates if the patent owner has any other patent applications on file relating to the current invention. Cross-references are necessary if the applicant is seeking the benefit of the filing date of an earlier filed application. A disclaimer, if present, may recite that the patent has a different, typically shorter, term than the usual 20-year life calculated from the filing date. If there are no related applications, as in the Amazon one-click patent, the cross reference section is omitted.

5,960,411

1

METHOD AND SYSTEM FOR PLACING A PURCHASE ORDER VIA A COMMUNICATIONS NETWORK

TECHNICAL FIELD

The present invention relates to a computer method and system for placing an order and, more particularly, to a method and system for ordering items over the Internet.

BACKGROUND OF THE INVENTION

The Internet comprises a vast number of computers and computer networks that are interconnected through communication links. The interconnected computers exchange information using various services, such as electronic mail, Gopher, and the World Wide Web ("WWW"). The WWW service allows a server computer system (i.e., Web server or Web site) to send graphical Web pages of information to a remote client computer system. The remote client computer system can then display the Web pages. Each resource (e.g., computer or Web page) of the WWW is uniquely identifiable by a Uniform Resource Locator ("URL"). To view a specific Web page, a client computer system specifies the URL for that Web page in a request (e.g., a HyperText Transfer Protocol ("HTTP") request). The request is forwarded to the Web server that supports that Web page. When that Web server receives the request, it sends that Web page to the client computer system. When the client computer system receives that Web page, it typically displays the Web page using a browser. A browser is a special-purpose application program that effects the requesting of Web pages and the displaying of Web pages.

Currently, Web pages are typically defined using Hyper-Text Markup Language ("HTML"). HTML provides a standard set of tags that define how a Web page is to be displayed. When a user indicates to the browser to display a Web page, the browser sends a request to the server computer system to transfer to the client computer system an HTML document that defines the Web page. When the requested HTML document is received by the client computer system, the browser displays the Web page as defined by the HTML document. The HTML document contains various tags that control the displaying of text, graphics, controls, and other features. The HTML document may contain URLs of other Web pages available on that server computer system or other server computer systems.

The World Wide Web is especially conducive to conducting electronic commerce. Many Web servers have been developed through which vendors can advertise and sell product. The products can include items (e.g., music) that are delivered electronically to the purchaser over the Internet and items (e.g., books) that are delivered through conventional distribution channels (e.g., a common carrier). A server computer system may provide an electronic version of a catalog that lists the items that are available. A user, who is a potential purchaser, may browse through the catalog using a browser and select various items that are to be purchased. When the user has completed selecting the items to be purchased, the server computer system then prompts the user for information to complete the ordering of the items. This purchaser-specific order information may include the purchaser's name, the purchaser's credit card number, and a shipping address for the order. The server computer system then typically confirms the order by sending a confirming Web page to the client computer system and schedules shipment of the items.

Since the purchaser-specific order information contains sensitive information (e.g., a credit card number), both

2

vendors and purchasers want to ensure the security of such information. Security is a concern because information transmitted over the Internet may pass through various intermediate computer systems on its way to its final destination. The information could be intercepted by an unscrupulous person at an intermediate system. To help ensure the security of the sensitive information, various encryption techniques are used when transmitting such information between a client computer system and a server computer system. Even though such encrypted information can be

TECHNICAL FIELD

The present invention relates to a computer method and system for placing an order, and, more particularly, to a method and system for ordering items over the Internet.

catalog, the server computer system metaphorically adds that item to a shopping cart. When the purchaser is done selecting items, then all the items in the shopping cart are "checked out" (i.e. ordered) when the purchaser provides billing and shipment information. In some models, when a purchaser selects any one item, then that item is "checked out" by automatically prompting the user for the billing and shipment information. Although the shopping cart model is very flexible and intuitive, it has a downside in that it requires many interactions by the purchaser. For example, the purchaser selects the various items from the electronic catalog, and then indicates that the selection is complete. The purchaser is then presented with an order Web page that prompts the purchaser for the purchaser-specific order information to complete the order. That Web page may be prefilled with information that was provided by the purchaser when placing another order. The information is then validated by the server computer system, and the order is completed. Such an ordering model can be problematic for a couple of reasons. If a purchaser is ordering only one item, then the overhead of confirming the various steps of the ordering process and waiting for, viewing, and updating the purchaser-specific order information can be much more than the overhead of selecting the item itself. This overhead makes the purchase of a single item cumbersome. Also, with such an ordering model, each time an order is placed sensitive information is transmitted over the Internet. Each time the sensitive information is transmitted over the Internet, it is susceptible to being intercepted and decrypted.

SUMMARY OF THE INVENTION

An embodiment of the present invention provides a method and system for ordering an item from a client system. The client system is provided with an identifier that identifies a customer. The client system displays information that identifies the item and displays an indication of an action (e.g., a single action such as clicking a mouse button) that a purchaser is to perform to order the identified item. In response to the indicated action being performed, the client system sends to a server system the provided identifier and a request to order the identified item. The server system uses the identifier to identify additional information needed to generate an order for the item and then generates the order.

The server system receives and stores the additional information for customers using various computer systems so that the server system can generate such orders. The server system stores the received additional information in association with an identifier of the customer and provides

Amazon's "One Click" Patent—Field of Invention

Background

As you wade into most patents, you will see that the first important written section, known as the Background, typically discusses the "prior art," technology that pre-dates the alleged invention. This is often quite interesting stuff, because it explores the state of the art for that particular field of invention and emphasizes the shortcomings associated with the state of the art. This is done to bolster the applicant's argument that the innovation is really new and a nonobvious solution to a problem.

For example, if the invention is a new kind of optical switch, the primary make-up and functions of a typical optical switch might be explained first in the patent to educate the reader. This makes sense, because a portion of the patent audience (judges, members of the jury, investors, venture capitalists, and even some Patent Office examiners) might not be familiar with optical switches. The patent might also point out certain limitations associated with prior optical switches: too slow, too large, too expensive to manufacture, and the like.

For example, the Background section of the Amazon one-click patent describes the Internet generally, then shopping on the Internet, and finally the "cumbersome" online shopping process (the shopping cart model) that was in place before the one-click invention.

Sometimes the background section will refer to prior patents or technical or scientific papers and explain, in summary fashion, what those prior documents represent. One patent for X-it's collapsible fire escape ladder (reviewed in Chapter 3), for example, discusses seven prior patents for collapsible fire escape ladders. In reading just one page of X-it's patent, then, you can then deduce two things: First, X-it did not invent the very idea of a collapsible fire escape ladder, and second, X-it's patent cannot protect X-it against competitors who make fire escape ladders the "old way" as represented in those seven prior patents. That can be valuable information if you are seeking to enter the collapsible fire escape ladder market. A patent which fully explains, in the background, the state of the art for a technology can be an excellent source of information for engineers and project managers.

For example, the purchaser selects the various items from the electronic catalog, and then indicates that the selection is complete. The purchaser is then presented with an order Web page that prompts the purchaser for the purchaser-specific order information to complete the order. That Web page may be prefilled with information that was provided by the purchaser when placing another order. The information is then validated by the server computer system, and the order is completed. Such an ordering model can be problematic for a couple of reasons. If a purchaser is ordering only one item, then the overhead of confirming the various steps of the ordering process and waiting for, viewing, and updating the purchaser-specific order information can be much more than the overhead of selecting the item itself. This overhead makes the purchase of a single item cumbersome. Also, with such an ordering model, each time an order is placed sensitive information is transmitted over the Internet. Each time the sensitive information is transmitted over the Internet, it is susceptible to being intercepted and decrypted.

METHOD AND SYST[...]
PURCHASE O[...]
COMMUNICATI[...]

TECHNIC[...]

The present invention relate[...] system for placing an order [...] method and system for orderi[...]

BACKGROUND OF [...]

The Internet comprises a v[...] computer networks that are ini[...] nication links. The intercon[...] information using various serv[...] Gopher, and the World Wide [...] service allows a server compu[...] Web site) to send graphical W[...] remote client computer system[...] system can then display the W[...] computer or Web page) of the [...] by a Uniform Resource Locato[...] Web page, a client computer s[...] that Web page in a request [...] Protocol ("HTTP") request). T[...] Web server that supports that[...] server receives the request, it[...] client computer system. Whe[...] receives that Web page, it typically displays the Web page using a browser. A browser is a special-purpose application program that effects the requesting of Web pages and the displaying of Web pages.

Currently, Web pages are typically defined using Hyper-Text Markup Language ("HTML"). HTML provides a standard set of tags that define how a Web page is to be displayed. When a user indicates to the browser to display a Web page, the browser sends a request to the server computer system to transfer to the client computer system an HTML document that defines the Web page. When the requested HTML document is received by the client computer system, the browser displays the Web page as defined by the HTML document. The HTML document contains various tags that control the displaying of text, graphics, controls, and other features. The HTML document may contain URLs of other Web pages available on that server computer system or other server computer systems.

The World Wide Web is especially conducive to conducting electronic commerce. Many Web servers have been developed through which vendors can advertise and sell product. The products can include items (e.g., music) that are delivered electronically to the purchaser over the Internet and items (e.g., books) that are delivered through conventional distribution channels (e.g., a common carrier). A server computer system may provide an electronic version of a catalog that lists the items that are available. A user, who is a potential purchaser, may browse through the catalog using a browser and select various items that are to be purchased. When the user has completed selecting the items to be purchased, the server computer system then prompts the user for information to complete the ordering of the items. This purchaser-specific order information may include the purchaser's name, the purchaser's credit card number, and a shipping address for the order. The server computer system then typically confirms the order by sending a confirming Web page to the client computer system and schedules shipment of the items.

Since the purchaser-specific order information contains sensitive information (e.g., a credit card number), both

very flexible and intuitive, it has a downside in that it requires many interactions by the purchaser. For example, the purchaser selects the various items from the electronic catalog, and then indicates that the selection is complete. The purchaser is then presented with an order Web page that prompts the purchaser for the purchaser-specific order information to complete the order. That Web page may be prefilled with information that was provided by the purchaser when placing another order. The information is then validated by the server computer system, and the order is completed. Such an ordering model can be problematic for a couple of reasons. If a purchaser is ordering only one item, then the overhead of confirming the various steps of the ordering process and waiting for, viewing, and updating the purchaser-specific order information can be much more than the overhead of selecting the item itself. This overhead makes the purchase of a single item cumbersome. Also, with such an ordering model, each time an order is placed sensitive information is transmitted over the Internet. Each time the sensitive information is transmitted over the Internet, it is susceptible to being intercepted and decrypted.

SUMMARY OF THE INVENTION

An embodiment of the present invention provides a method and system for ordering an item from a client system. The client system is provided with an identifier that identifies a customer. The client system displays information that identifies the item and displays an indication of an action (e.g., a single action such as clicking a mouse button) that a purchaser is to perform to order the identified item. In response to the indicated action being performed, the client system sends to a server system the provided identifier and a request to order the identified item. The server system uses the identifier to identify additional information needed to generate an order for the item and then generates the order.

The server system receives and stores the additional information for customers using various computer systems so that the server system can generate such orders. The server system stores the received additional information in association with an identifier of the customer and provides

Amazon's "One Click" Patent—Background

Summary of the Invention

The Summary section of a patent sometimes lists the objectives to be carried out by the invention—for example, the new invention may be faster, more accurate, and less costly to manufacture than the prior art.

You will notice that the language of the Summary section often repeats elements already stated in the Field of Invention and Background. For example, whatever may be lacking in the prior art is now present in the new patent. This repetition is common in patents. Like musical compositions, patents repeat common themes throughout the document. In the Summary above, Amazon's one-click patent provides a succinct explanation of the one-click process.

Web server that supports that Web page. When that Web server receives the request, it client computer system. When receives that Web page, it typic using a browser. A browser is a program that effects the reque displaying of Web pages.

Currently, Web pages are typ Text Markup Language ("HTM dard set of tags that define displayed. When a user indicate Web page, the browser sends puter system to transfer to the HTML document that defines requested HTML document is puter system, the browser displ by the HTML document. The various tags that control the controls, and other features. contain URLs of other Web pa computer system or other server computer systems.

The World Wide Web is especially conducive to conducting electronic commerce. Many Web servers have been developed through which vendors can advertise and sell product. The products can include items (e.g., music) that are delivered electronically to the purchaser over the Internet and items (e.g., books) that are delivered through conventional distribution channels (e.g., a common carrier). A server computer system may provide an electronic version of a catalog that lists the items that are available. A user, who is a potential purchaser, may browse through the catalog using a browser and select various items that are to be purchased. When the user has completed selecting the items to be purchased, the server computer system then prompts the user for information to complete the ordering of the items. This purchaser-specific order information may include the purchaser's name, the purchaser's credit card number, and a shipping address for the order. The server computer system then typically confirms the order by sending a confirming Web page to the client computer system and schedules shipment of the items.

Since the purchaser-specific order information contains sensitive information (e.g., a credit card number), both

billing and shipment information. In some models, when a

SUMMARY OF THE INVENTION

An embodiment of the present invention provides a method and system for ordering an item from a client system. The client system is provided with an identifier that identifies a customer. The client system displays information that identifies the item and displays an indication of an action (e.g., a single action such as clicking a mouse button) that a purchaser is to perform to order the identified item. In response to the indicated action being performed, the client system sends to a server system the provided identifier and a request to order the identified item. The server system uses the identifier to identify additional information needed to generate an order for the item and then generates the order.

such an ordering model, each time an order is placed sensitive information is transmitted over the Internet. Each time the sensitive information is transmitted over the Internet, it is susceptible to being intercepted and decrypted.

SUMMARY OF THE INVENTION

An embodiment of the present invention provides a method and system for ordering an item from a client system. The client system is provided with an identifier that identifies a customer. The client system displays information that identifies the item and displays an indication of an action (e.g., a single action such as clicking a mouse button) that a purchaser is to perform to order the identified item. In response to the indicated action being performed, the client system sends to a server system the provided identifier and a request to order the identified item. The server system uses the identifier to identify additional information needed to generate an order for the item and then generates the order.

The server system receives and stores the additional information for customers using various computer systems so that the server system can generate such orders. The server system stores the received additional information in association with an identifier of the customer and provides

5,960,411

3

the identifier to the client system. When requested by the client system, the server system provides information describing the item to the requesting client system. When the server system receives a request from a client system, the server system combines the additional information stored in association with the identifier included in the request to effect the ordering of the item.

BRIEF DESCRIPTION OF THE DRAWINGS

FIGS. 1A–1C illustrate single-action ordering in one embodiment of the present invention.

FIG. 2 is a block diagram illustrating an embodiment of the present invention.

4

mation already stored at the server system, there is no need for such sensitive information to be transmitted via the Internet or other communications medium.

FIGS. 1A–1C illustrate single-action ordering in one embodiment of the present invention. FIG. 1A illustrates the display of a Web page describing an item that may be ordered. This example Web page was sent from the server system to the client system when the purchaser requested to review detailed information about the item. This example Web page contains a summary description section 101, a shopping cart section 102, a single-action ordering section 103, and a detailed description section 104. One skilled in the art would appreciate that these various sections can be

Amazon's "One Click" Patent—Summary

What's an Embodiment

"Embodiment" refers to the physical manner in which an invention is implemented—that is, how the invention achieves its objective. An invention can have several embodiments. For example, one embodiment of a ladder can be made with wood; another embodiment can be with aluminum. By listing various embodiments, the owner of an invention can expand the scope of the patent. The preferred embodiment, also known as "the best mode," must be included in the patent.

Description of the Drawings

The Description of the Drawings section is just that: When the reader is later referred to a particular drawing in the patent, what that drawing represents is explained in the Description section. As I mentioned in my discussion of drawings, above, each figure presents a unique view of some embodiment (or portion of the embodiment). For example, in Amazon's one-click patent, Figure 3 is described as a flowchart depicting how the one-click system works.

Sometimes there will be one or more drawings depicting the way the task was accomplished in the prior art. This is done as a way of comparing and contrasting what is old with that alleged to be new. Comparing these drawings can allow you to quickly ascertain the differences between the alleged invention and what came before—something the patent does not cover or protect.

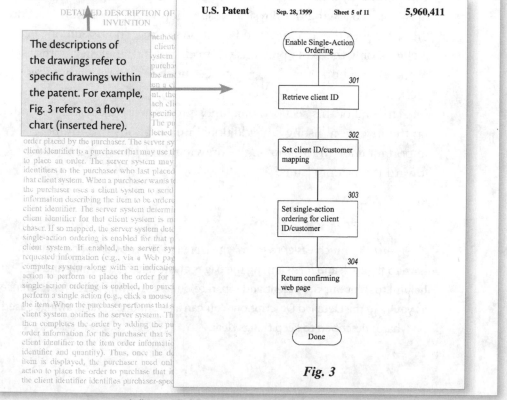

5,960,411

3

the identifier to the client system. When requested by the client system, the server system provides information describing the item to the requesting client system. When the server system receives a request from a client system, the server system combines the additional information stored in association with the identifier included in the request to effect the ordering of the item.

BRIEF DESCRIPTION OF THE DRAWINGS

FIGS. 1A–1C illustrate single-action ordering in one embodiment of the present invention.

FIG. 2 is a block diagram illustrating an embodiment of the present invention.

FIG. 3 is a flow diagram of a routine that enables single-action ordering for a customer.

FIG. 4 is a flow diagram of a routine to generate a Web page in which single-action ordering is enabled.

FIG. 5 is a flow diagram of a routine which processes a single-action order.

FIG. 6 is a flow diagram of a routine for generating a single-action order summary Web page.

FIG. 7 is a flow diagram of a routine that implements an expedited order selection algorithm.

FIGS. 8A–8C illustrate a hierarchical data entry mechanism in one embodiment.

DETAILED DESCRIPTION OF INVENTION

The descriptions of the drawings refer to specific drawings within the patent. For example, Fig. 3 refers to a flow chart (inserted here).

4

mation already stored at the server system, there is no need for such sensitive information to be transmitted via the Internet or other communications medium.

FIGS. 1A–1C illustrate single-action ordering in one embodiment of the present invention. FIG. 1A illustrates the display of a Web page describing an item that may be ordered. This example Web page was sent from the server system to the client system when the purchaser requested to review detailed information about the item. This example Web page contains a summary description section 101, a shopping cart section 102, a single-action ordering section 103, and a detailed description section 104. One skilled in the art would appreciate that these various sections can be omitted or rearranged or adapted in various ways. In general, the purchaser need only be aware of the item or items to be ordered by the single action and of the single action needed to place the order. The summary description and the detailed description sections provide information that identifies and describes the item(s) that may be ordered. The shopping cart section provides the conventional capability to add the described item to a shopping cart. The server system adds the summary description, the detailed description, and the shopping cart sections to each Web page for an item that may be ordered. The server system, however, only adds the single-action ordering section when single-action ordering is enabled for that purchaser at that client system. (One skilled

U.S. Patent   Sep. 28, 1999   Sheet 5 of 11   5,960,411

Enable Single-Action Ordering

Retrieve client ID   301

Set client ID/customer mapping   302

Set single-action ordering for client ID/customer   303

Return confirming web page   304

Done

Fig. 3

Amazon's "One Click" Patent—Brief Description of Drawings

Detailed Description of the Preferred Embodiment(s)

Did you ever assemble a model airplane? You may remember the instructions that came with it, a detailed explanation of how to make the model referencing the different parts with drawings and part numbers. The Detailed Description in a patent is similar. It describes the invention's structure and explains its performance, usually in two separate subparts: a physical description and an explanation of how the invention operates. Both of these explanations reference the numbered parts in the drawings. The Detailed Description is thus a hybrid design/performance specification.

When the patent describes an invention's physical structure or arrangement, it usually starts with the base, frame, bottom, or input, or some other logical starting place of the invention, and then works up, out, or forward in a logical manner. Each part is named and numbered and is usually related to the numbering in the patent drawings. Following the physical description is an "operation" section that describes the action of the invention's parts. The operation section includes only the parts previously introduced in the earlier portion of the description. Again, you may see much repetition within this section.

The end of this section sometimes provides a conclusion, summing up the invention, listing any additional ramifications that are not important enough to show in the drawing, and pointing the reader toward the patent claims.

TIP

It's much easier to follow the Detailed Description when you don't have to flip back and forth among the pages of the patent. You may find it helpful to print out the patent and separate out the drawing pages for reference as you read the Detailed Description. You can also annotate the drawings based on what is described to keep things clear.

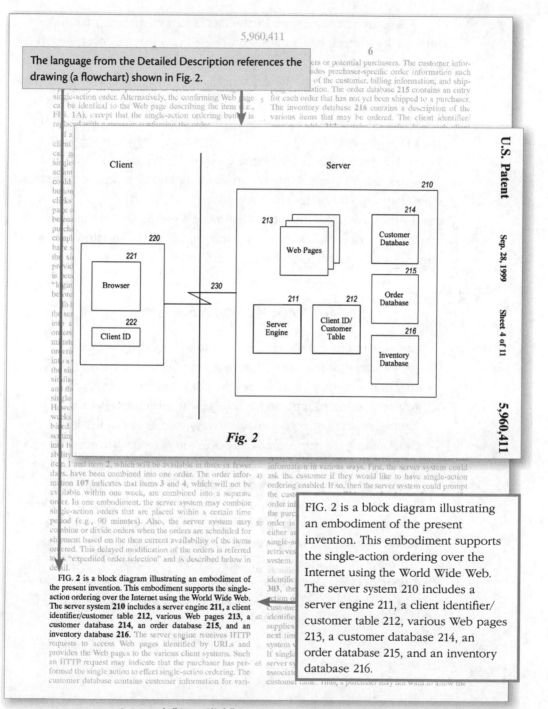

The language from the Detailed Description references the drawing (a flowchart) shown in Fig. 2.

5,960,411

U.S. Patent   Sep. 28, 1999   Sheet 4 of 11   5,960,411

Fig. 2

FIG. 2 is a block diagram illustrating an embodiment of the present invention. This embodiment supports the single-action ordering over the Internet using the World Wide Web. The server system 210 includes a server engine 211, a client identifier/customer table 212, various Web pages 213, a customer database 214, an order database 215, and an inventory database 216.

FIG. 2 is a block diagram illustrating an embodiment of the present invention. This embodiment supports the single-action ordering over the Internet using the World Wide Web. The server system 210 includes a server engine 211, a client identifier/customer table 212, various Web pages 213, a customer database 214, an order database 215, and an inventory database 216. The server engine receives HTTP requests to access Web pages identified by URLs and provides the Web pages to the various client systems. Such an HTTP request may indicate that the purchaser has performed the single action to effect single-action ordering. The customer database contains customer information for vari-

Amazon's "One Click" Patent—Detailed Description

There are a few features of the Detailed Description that make it a little tricky to decipher. I discussed one element that affects readability previously, and that is use of the reference numbers for each part of the invention (shown in the drawing figures). The Detailed Description may state (or "recite," as patent professionals say), "LCD microdisplay 10, Fig. 1 for cellular telephone 12 ...." In this case, the reader of the patent is being referred to Fig. 1, which would show a microdisplay labeled 10 on a cellular telephone labeled 12. (That's one reason it pays to unstaple the patent you are reading and remove the drawings. That way you can better track the parts.)

In the case of an invention that has no physical structure, such as the Amazon one-click patent, the steps or blocks of the flowcharts and drawings are identified and referenced.

What Is the Specification?

Patent attorneys and courts often refer to the Detailed Description section as the "Specification." However, the official definition of the specification states that it includes the title of the invention, a cross-reference to related applications (unless included in the application data sheet), a statement regarding federally sponsored research or development, the names of any parties to a joint research agreement, reference to a "Sequence Listing" (a table, or a computer program listing appendix submitted on a compact disc), the Background, the Summary of the Invention, the Description of the Drawings, the Detailed Description, the Claims, and the Abstract. In other words, from the Patent Office's point of view, the specification includes everything that's written in the patent except for the title page. For purposes of reading a patent, it doesn't matter how we define the specification, although you may find it helpful to know that the term has different meanings.

The Claim Game

BOTTOM LINE: *The claims are an attempt to describe what's new about the invention and, at the same time, to alert competitors as to what they may not do.*

BOTTOM LINE: *If it's not claimed, it's generally not protected.*

Remarkably, the claims—the key part of any patent—come last in the patent. That's odd considering that everything else being equal, the three most important things about any patent are the claims, the claims, and the claims. The level of misunderstanding about this truism is astonishing, especially among people unfamiliar with patents. One reason for the misconception is people sometimes measure the strength or value of a patent by the wrong part of the patent. For example, I've had clients who mistakenly fretted over the title of a patent because the title described a mechanism the client wanted to manufacture. There are over 1,800 patents with the word "ladder" in the title. Obviously, not all of these patents cover the basics of a traditional ladder. Also, there are probably numerous patents for ladders that do not include the word "ladder" in the title. A ladder, for example, could also be called a "climbing apparatus." It may even be possible that a figure of a given patent shows exactly your latest and greatest design. Still, there may be no infringement of the patent, unless the claims are infringed.

Everything that matters in the patents—whether someone is infringing, whether a patent is valid—hinges on the claims. In fact, if you think about it, the Patent Office doesn't really grant patents—it grants patent claims. And it is the claims that are subject to the most rigorous examination during patent prosecution (the process of applying for a patent).

What Are Patent Claims?

Patent claims are statements included in a patent application that describe (or "recite") the structure of an invention in precise and exact terms, using a long-established formal style and precise terminology. Claims serve as a way:

- for the Patent Office to determine whether an invention is patentable, and
- for a court to determine whether a patent has been infringed (someone has made, used, or sold an invention or a device without the patent owner's permission).

In a sense, claims are the boundaries for the invention, much like a fence can delimit the boundaries of real property. Most patent applications contain more than one claim, each of which describes the invention from a slightly different viewpoint. Claims may be "independent" (standing on their own) or "dependent" (referring to other claims on which they depend for some or all of their elements).

Written in a somewhat archaic form, patent claims can, at least initially, be difficult to read and comprehend. The claims section begins with words like "what is claimed is" or "we claim" followed by the patent claims themselves, which are sequentially numbered paragraphs at the very end of the patent. The last claim is followed by five asterisks denoting the end of the patent and the claims. The claims are stated in "units" (sentence fragments that can and almost always do have numerous clauses and subclauses). Grammatically, they're often quite strange—always starting with a capital letter and only containing one period. They rarely have parentheses or quotation marks (except for chemical or mathematical formulas). No doubt about it: Patent claims can be difficult. They are so important, though, that you as a manager need to understand claim basics. I'll try to simplify them, so stick with me for awhile.

We claim:

1. A method of placing an order for an item comprising:

under control of a client system,

displaying information identifying the item; and

in response to only a single action being performed, sending a request to order the item along with an identifier of a purchaser of the item to a server system;

under control of a single-action ordering component of the server system,

receiving the request;

retrieving additional information previously stored for the purchaser identified by the identifier in the received request; and

generating an order to purchase the requested item for the purchaser identified by the identifier in the received request using the retrieved additional information; and

fulfilling the generated order to complete purchase of the item

whereby the item is ordered without using a shopping cart ordering model

---

6. A client system for ordering an item comprising:

an identifier that identifies a customer;

a display component for displaying information identifying the item;

a single-action ordering component that in response to performance of only a single action, sends a request to a server system to order the identified item, the request including the identifier so that the server system can locate additional information needed to complete the order and so that the server system can fulfill the generated order to complete purchase of the item; and

a shopping cart ordering component that in response to performance of an add-to-shopping-cart action, sends a request to the server system to add the item to a shopping cart.

Independent Claims

960,411

10

selection using any pointing device may be effected by the purchaser. Although a single action may be preceded by multiple physical movements of the purchaser (e.g., moving a mouse so that a mouse pointer is over a button), the single action generally refers to a single event received by a client system that indicates to place the order. Finally, the purchaser can be alternately identified by a unique customer identifier that is provided by the customer when the customer initiates access to the server system and sent to the server system with each message. This customer identifier could be also stored persistently on the client system so that the purchaser does not need to re-enter their customer identifier each time access is initiated. The scope of the present invention is defined by the claims that follow.

We claim:

1. A method of placing an order for an item comprising:

under control of a client system,

displaying information identifying the item; and

in response to only a single action being performed, sending a request to order the item along with an identifier of a purchaser of the item to a server system;

under control of a single-action ordering component of the server system,

receiving the request;

retrieving additional information previously stored for the purchaser identified by the identifier in the received request; and

generating an order to purchase the requested item for the purchaser identified by the identifier in the received request using the retrieved additional information; and

fulfilling the generated order to complete purchase of the item

whereby the item is ordered without using a shopping cart ordering model.

2. The method of claim 1 wherein the displaying of information includes displaying information indicating the single action.

3. The method of claim 1 wherein the single action is clicking a button.

4. The method of claim 1 wherein the single action is speaking of a sound.

5. The method of claim 1 wherein a user of the client system does not need to explicitly identify themselves when placing an order.

6. A client system for ordering an item comprising:

an identifier that identifies a customer;

a display component for displaying information identifying the item;

a single-action ordering component that in response to performance of only a single action, sends a request to a server system to order the identified item, the request including the identifier so that the server system can locate additional information needed to complete the order and so that the server system can fulfill the generated order to complete purchase of the item; and

a shopping cart ordering component that in response to performance of an add-to-shopping-cart action, sends a request to the server system to add the item to a shopping cart.

7. The client system of claim 6 wherein the display component is a browser.

8. The client system of claim 6 wherein the predefined action is the clicking of a mouse button.

9. A server system for generating an order comprising:

a shopping cart ordering component; and

Amazon "One Click" Patent—Claims

Patent claims of the type we know today were not required in patents back in 1880 when Thomas Edison received his patent for the light bulb (actually a patent more specifically directed to the filament of the light bulb). Nevertheless, as a teaching tool, many journeymen patent attorneys have "claimed" the basic light bulb something like this:

What is claimed is:

1. A light source comprising:
   an airtight chamber with a light-transmitting wall,
      the chamber being evacuated or containing an
      inert gas;
   a resistance element in the chamber; and
   a connection between the resistance element and
      an electrical power supply to cause the resistance
      element to glow.

Most patent applications contain more than one claim, each of which describes the invention from a slightly different viewpoint. Claims may be "independent" (standing on their own) or "dependent" (referring to other claims on which they depend for some or all of their elements).

Patents always consist of at least one independent claim. Claim 1 of any patent is always an independent claim, but other claims may also be in independent form. Amazon's patent has four independent claims: claims 1, 6, 9, and 11. Amazon had to prove only that Barnes & Noble's Express Lane feature infringed *one* of these independent claims in order to win.

Patent attorneys also draft "dependent" claims. These are claims that depend upon a primary independent claim and add one or more additional elements (to establish other embodiments of the invention).

How Are Claims Infringed?

In an infringement case, a court examines the claims of the patented invention and then compares them to the "accused" device or process. (The device or process accused of infringing the patent claims). The court determines if the claims cover (or "read on," as patent professionals say) the allegedly infringing device or process. To infringe a patent, a competitor's device must physically have or perform all of the elements contained in one of the claims. For example, if a patent claim recites two elements, (1) a luggage tag with an LCD screen, and (2) a snap that makes the tag detachable, a device that contains only a luggage tag with an LCD screen won't infringe. A dependent claim cannot be infringed unless the allegedly infringing product also infringes the related independent claim. In other words, if an independent claim is not infringed, then the dependent claims cannot be infringed.

Claiming the Ladder

Let's drive home the importance of patent claims with a simple example. Go back in time and imagine you invented the first ladder. Suppose your patent application claim states:

> 1. A climbing apparatus comprising:
>   a pair of spaced parallel lengthy wooden side rails; and
>   a plurality of spaced short wooden rungs extending between the side rails.

Don't worry about the legalese here: "comprising" means "including" and "plurality" means more than one. (See "Common Claims Terms," below.)

Let's map these claim elements or requirements onto a picture of our ladder:

First Ladder

Looks pretty good. This claim will provide protection at least against anyone who sells a ladder as shown in the picture. Will the Patent Office allow this claim and grant us a patent? Yes, unless elements A (the two side rails) and B (the rungs) are proven to be shown in a prior patent or patents.

Suppose, for example, a prior patent shows a "climbing apparatus" with a single post or bar to which rungs are affixed, as shown below.

If this single-post ladder existed, we should still be able to get our patent—that is what we claimed above. The prior art single-post ladder does not include everything we've claimed—what's missing is a pair of side rails and, in the prior art, the rungs don't extend between two spaced parallel side rails. It's possible that the Patent Office examiner might conclude our invention is obvious in light of this prior ladder, but I'll bet we would ultimately win a patent.

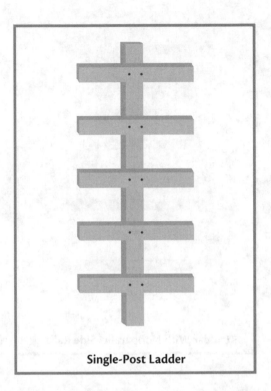

Single-Post Ladder

However, keep in mind that if this single-post ladder existed before we created our ladder, then our patent will not protect us against competitors who sell this old ladder. Still, our ladder is better, and the marketing department reports that it's expected to sell well. So, we proceed with the patent.

Is there any way for a competitor to devise a ladder that is more like ours than the prior single-post ladder? Perhaps the competitor's ladder wouldn't be exactly like ours nor quite as good but still marketable.

Think again about claim elements as being requirements, and try to design around your own claim. What word or words could I underline in the patent claim that might not be required in a competitive ladder? What structure could I remove from the claim?

How about a competitor's ladder that didn't have parallel side rails, as shown below?

Ladder With Nonparallel Side Rails

Does our patent claim protect us from a competitor who creates a ladder whose side rails are not parallel? Probably not: We *specified* parallel side rails in the claim.

What about a ladder that looks just like ours (it's got parallel side rails and the rungs) but is made out of aluminum or fiberglass instead of wood like we specified?

In both cases, the competitor has designed around our patent, and its value has diminished. So, knowing this, we play the claim game before we file our patent application and instead file claims that include an independent claim and two dependent claims, like this:

1. A climbing apparatus comprising:
   a pair of spaced lengthy side rails; and
   a plurality of spaced short rungs extending between the side rails.
2. The climbing apparatus of claim 1 in which the spaced side rails are parallel to each other.
3. The climbing apparatus of claim 1 in which the side rails and the rungs are made of wood.

Now our competitor can't legally make our ladder out of aluminum or fiberglass, because independent claim 1 doesn't require any specific material for the side rails or the rungs. In other words, our claim 1 will cover a ladder irrespective of what it's made of: wood, aluminum, fiberglass, or aerogel. Moreover, there is now no requirement in claim 1 that the side rails be parallel. Indeed, our dependent claims 2 and 3 make it clear that parallel side rails and a wooden construction are *not* requirements of claim 1.

So far, so good. We get our patent and its value is high.

Suppose now our competitor sees a market for ladders that stand on their own. The competitor designs a device consisting of two sections joined by center brackets, as shown below.

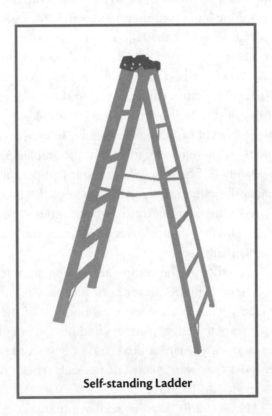

Self-standing Ladder

Suppose the competitor who comes up with this design gets a patent with the following independent claim:

> 1. A climbing apparatus comprising:
>   a pair of spaced side rails;
>   a plurality of spaced rungs extending between the side rails; and
>   a leg hingedly connected at or near the top of each side rail for supporting them in a free standing configuration.

Okay, now the competitor enters the market with the stepladder. Is there anything we can do?

Yes—the competitor's stepladder product infringes our patent, because the stepladder includes two side rails and the rungs. It's true that it has something in addition to what we've claimed—the supporting legs—but their ladder still infringes our patent because it meets at least all our claim requirements.

Their standalone ladder exceeds our claim requirements, but that's okay as we learned in the Gillette case (where a razor with four blades infringed Gillette's patent covering three blades). Note, too, that the addition—the legs—was how the competitor was able to get his own patent in light of our earlier patent. In other words, even though the Patent Office may recognize that the stepladder infringes our patent, the Patent Office will still issue our competitor's patent because it claims something new. The attitude of the Patent Office is that patent owners must sort out infringement issues. The job of the Patent Office is only to judge inventions for novelty and nonobviousness, not infringement.

So, although the competitor has a patent for a stepladder product, he cannot sell it because of our patent. We, in turn, cannot sell a stepladder like our competitors' because of the competitor's patent. If we want to sell stepladders and our competitor also wants to sell stepladders, perhaps a deal could be worked out where both sides get what they want via licensing each other's patents. Licensing is discussed in Chapter 10.

This scenario helps us rectify a huge misconception: Patents don't give you the right to do anything except sue someone for patent infringement. Patents don't somehow allow you to sell patented products, they don't guarantee market success, and they can never stop competitors from doing things the old way.

In summary, the claims of a patent describe the metes and bounds of the invention somewhat like a property description in a deed. The claims thus describe where others may not trespass.

BOTTOM LINE: *Management should attempt to design around their own company's patent claims before the patent application is filed.*

Why Bother With the Specification?

If the claims are so important, why not just read them and forget about reading the rest of the patent? One reason is that claims don't exist in a vacuum. If something is claimed, it must be both disclosed in the specification and also typically shown in a drawing. Also, if a particular claim term is ambiguous or has multiple meanings, the specification may be used in court to interpret the claim language. So, the specification is built on the claims, and usually there are no absolutes. Also, patent attorneys try not to include extraneous matter in the specification that is not claimed.

In one notable case, a patent specification for a printed circuit board stated one layer of the board could be made out of aluminum or steel. The claims of the patent, however, specified aluminum. A competitor of the patent owner then entered the market with a printed circuit board including a layer of steel. When the patent owner sued the competitor, it was agreed that the use of steel or aluminum was specified in the patent and that these materials were functionally equivalent. The jury assessed damages in the amount of $1,138,764 against the competitor. On appeal, however, the Federal Circuit overturned the verdict. The higher court determined that since the patent claims required aluminum, the use of steel was not an infringement of the patent. In other words, even though steel was referenced in the specification, anyone was free to use a steel embodiment of the invention, because it was not mentioned in the claims.

BOTTOM LINE: *Ideas disclosed in a patent specification but not properly claimed might be free to use by everyone.*

Claiming a Fiber Optic Switch Generically

Let's take a second pass through patent claims, this time using a fiber optic switch as our example. Most patent claims include "elements" denoted by some type of separating indentation and/or punctuation. The teaching tool light bulb claim includes three elements: A—the airtight chamber, B—the resistance element or filament, and C—the connection. The ladder claim includes two elements: A—the side rails and B—the rungs.

In our example, the generic form of a claim for a new faster, smaller, and less costly switch used in fiber optics might include structural elements A, B, C, and D, thus:

> 1. An optical switch comprising:
>   element A;
>   element B;
>   element C; and
>   element D.

Claims are required to put competitors on notice as to which structural combinations do and which do not constitute patent infringement. In our optical switch example, the structural elements A, B, C, and D will generally be those parts of the switch that make it faster, smaller, and less costly.

Besides the rule that a claim must recite structural elements, another important rule is this: At least one of those structural elements must be something new (at least, in our example, with respect to optical switches).

So, if a prior optical switch—one that existed over a year before the date of invention—included elements A, B, C, and D, then claim 1 above is not patentable, because it is not new. Or, if one prior optical switch (optical switch 1) included elements A and B and another prior optical switch (optical switch 2) included elements C and D, the combination of prior optical switches 1 and 2 might render our claim example obvious and therefore not patentable.

But, new combinations of old elements are definitely patentable—most patent claims are just that. As we already know, most patented inventions are improvements and thus, in our example, if a typical prior optical switch included parts A, B, and C and we added D, that's patentable. In a substitution invention, a prior optical switch may have had parts A, B, C, and E. We substituted D for E and that, too, may be patentable. Whether or not claimed subject matter is obvious is a fairly subjective determination. For patentability, think "addition" (add an element) or "substitution" (substitute one element for another).

Let's now suppose that our claim 1 above is both novel and nonobvious, and it issues in a patent. Once the patent issues, a competitor cannot legally make, use, sell, or offer to sell an optical switch including elements A, B, C, and D. If the competitor makes an optical switch including elements A, B, C, and D and also a new element X, that optical switch still infringes the patent: In patent attorney parlance, the claim "reads on" the optical switch. That was the situation in the Gillette case: Schick added a fourth blade in a case where Gillette's patent claim recited three blades. That was also the situation in the stepladder example, where two supporting legs were added to the ladder to make it a stepladder.

If, however, element X in the optical switch example is novel and unobvious, the competitor may be able to patent the combination A, B, C, D, and X for itself as an improvement, but your patent is still said to be the "dominant patent," because practicing the patent covering A, B, C, D, and X would infringe the dominant patent with only claim elements A, B, C, and D. Typically, that is exactly how technology and patents evolve: Imagine that the first patented optical switch was claimed fairly broadly. All later improvements to the optical switch are then required to be claimed more narrowly. With improvements on improvements, the number or at least the preciseness of the claimed structural elements usually grows.

So far, so good, but is there any problem with our original claim combination (reproduced below)?

1. An optical switch comprising:
   element A;
   element B;
   element C; and
   element D.

Yes, if a competitor can enter the market with a competitive switch including only elements A, B, and D. That switch wouldn't infringe the claim—it doesn't include all of the claimed elements—because, in this particular example, element C is missing. To escape infringement, the competitor's device must not include at least one of the claimed elements: Omission of a claimed element equals a design around and no infringement. For noninfringement, think "subtraction."

Thus, the three combinations A, B, and C; A, C, and D; and B, C, and D also do not infringe the patent claim, and the competitor has successfully designed around the patent. If you are the competitor, that's good; if you are the patent owner, it's bad. Also recall the Toro lawn aerator: How a claim element is described can severely impact the value of a patent claim.

To prevent such design-arounds, patent attorneys attempt to include in claims only the bare number of elements required to make a patent distinguishable over the prior art. And they attempt to describe those elements as generically as possible. Additional unnecessary elements and/or specificity only provides competitors with possible design-arounds. And you can never prevent the competitor from selling a device that exists in the prior art, as in the X-It case.

In summary, all the claimed requirements must generally be met in order to successfully sue someone for infringement. As a general rule, the fewer the requirements, the higher the value. Conversely, a requirement in a patent claim that need not be met in a competitor's product lowers the value of the patent. And that's exactly how you should think about patent claims: They include requirements that must be met in order to sue someone for patent infringement.

For example, in the Gillette case, the penultimate question was whether Gillette's patent claim required only three and therefore not four blades or, conversely, at least three blades but perhaps four, too. In the Toro case, the question was whether Toro's patent claim required a mechanical cam-based system.

Reading Claims for Infringement

As you review a given patent, you can easily make a record of infringement or noninfringement or at least narrow the issues as follows: Suppose first you want to document whether your new optical switch infringes a claim of a competitor's optical switch patent. Underline (or highlight) the words in the claim that require something not present in your optical switch. The more underlining the better, but usually all that is needed to escape infringement is underlining of one requirement. Sometimes, underlining of a single word is enough. If questions arise, put a question mark in the margin of the claim next to the unclear claim language. A patent attorney can then more easily confirm whether or not you have a good case of noninfringement.

When it's your patent application, you play this game in reverse: Underline that which is required in your claim that might not be found in a hypothetical competitor's product. We hope, of course, there is no underlining. If there is, however, or if there are questions, again a patent attorney will have to perform the final analysis. Once your patent issues and a competitive product arrives on the scene, match each requirement of your claim with proof that requirement is met by the competitor's product. Patent attorneys call this a "claim chart": On the left is each requirement of a claim and on the right is evidence showing how each requirement is met in the infringing product. This evidence is sometimes the words used by the competitor in marketing or engineering literature; sometimes it's pictures of or drawings representing the competitor's product, sometimes it's both.

Independent and Dependent Claims

Most of my discussion has been about independent claims: claims that stand by themselves. Amazon had to prove only that Barnes & Noble's "Express Lane" feature infringed one of these independent claims in order to win. Patent attorneys also draft "dependent" claims, that is, claims that depend on a primary independent claim and add one or more additional elements. For example, we could add the following to the claims for the fiber optic switch:

> 2. The optical switch of claim 1 further including element E.

Why make this addition? Usually dependent claims are drafted to fully describe the actual product expected to be marketed by the company.

So, element E might actually be required in order to make a functioning optical switch work well, and we draft a dependent claim directed to it.

Why, if element E is required, don't we include element E in broader independent claim 1? First of all, there is no rule that a claim must describe a complete device. That is, if you claim a new feature of an automobile engine, you don't have to claim the tires or the dashboard. Second, technology advances. In the future, element E may not be required or element E could be supplanted with something else.

Why then draft a dependent claim at all including element E?

First, by including element E in dependent claim 2, it is usually clear that element E is *not* required in order to infringe independent claim 1, and therefore E cannot be implied as a requirement of claim 1.

Second, claims don't have to describe a complete device, but the patent specification does. The specification must describe how to make and use the claimed invention. Since the specification is written from the claims, patent attorneys claim the preferred example or version ("embodiment") of a complete device at least in dependent claims.

Sometimes there are two or more embodiments or versions of the inventive design. We claim the invention broadly in an independent claim and cover each of the inventive embodiments more specifically in separate dependent claims. Suppose, for example, a laser-based device could be embodied using a YAG laser (a laser commonly used in ophthalmology and dentistry), a CO2 laser (one of the earliest gas lasers and commonly used in construction), or a diode laser (the most common laser, built around a semiconductor, and used for various applications including telecommunications and barcode readers). The general recitation for the laser in the independent claim might be "a source of electromagnetic radiation." A more specific dependent claim might then recite that the source of electromagnetic radiation is a laser and further dependent claims may recite that the laser is a YAG laser, a CO2 laser, or a diode laser.

Third, dependent claims provide us with a fallback position. The Patent Office Examiner may not be willing to ever allow the broadest claim 1 but might agree to allow the narrower claim 2.

If, in our example, the combination of both claims 1 and 2 (requirements A-E) still has value—that is, it is unlikely a competitor could design around that combination easily—the business decision might be made to accept claim 2 rather than incur the expense of further arguments with the Patent Office or an expensive appeal in order to secure broader patent protection.

And, as you now know, issued patents are subject to challenge. Suppose a competitor, in court, is able to knock out independent claim 1 but not dependent claim 2, and the competitor still infringes claim 2. That's enough: You've got him even though claim 1 is held to be invalid. That's one reason we typically draft a lot of claims and, for important products, even more than one patent. Claims are arrows in a quiver, and even if the first two arrows miss the target, perhaps the third will be a bull's eye.

The Importance of Words

It's not just claim elements (generically represented with the letters A-E above) that are important—so too are the words used to describe each element and/or its relationship to other claimed elements. Does the word "on," as in "one component being on another component," mean that the two components must actually touch each other? Does "including," as in "one component includes another," mean the two components must be a part of each other or only just somehow associated? These were the questions in real patent cases, where quite often someone, either the patent owner or the company accused of patent infringement, was left unhappy (and perhaps broke) with the meaning ascribed certain patent claim terms by a court. Million-dollar court cases can literally hinge on the meaning of just one or a few words of a patent claim. In the Gillette case, the word was "three." In the Toro case, the words were "control means."

That's why you should always keep in mind that when reading patents, words are sometimes inexact and subject to challenge. Consider the following. Two things communicate with each other in a variety of ways: electrically, optically, magnetically, or even mechanically, as for, example, a membrane deforms and touches some kind of sensor responsive to touch. Electrical signals can be in analog or digital form, and wireless communication can take numerous forms.

If two remotely located electronic subsystems "talk" to each other, it could be via optical signals sent from a transmitter to a receiver. But a communication channel could also, in this day and age, be via a speech synthesizer that forms words heard by a speaker hooked up to a processor equipped with speech recognition software.

Similarly, two parts can be connected to each other in a myriad of ways. Fasteners such as screws and bolts can be used, there are thousands of different kinds of adhesives, and there is welding and laminating and a pressure fit. The two parts could also be integral— molded from the same material, for example.

To give you an idea of the swirling confusion that words can trigger, here are just a few of the many ways to describe joining: anchored; attached; bolt; dowel; pin; conduit; clamp; fastener; clip; coupled; joined; mated connection; joint; engage; fix; fastener; rivet; screw; gluing; joining; hinge; pivot; hook; clasp; interconnect; interlock; interface; seam; coupling; juncture; union keeper; key; latchkey; securing means; latch; lock; secure link; linkage; closure; latch; mate; coupled mount; nail; pin; nut; paste; adhesive; glue peg; post; peg fulcrum; seal; fasten; secure; secure stitch; tape; bind; bond.

This is one reason patent applications cost a lot: Patent attorneys must carefully choose each word of the patent claims and brainstorm with the inventor(s) how recitations that are too specific might lower the value of the resulting patent.

Below, I provide some common terms and their popular meanings. This may prove helpful in deciphering the arcane language of patent claims. But as with all things patent, there are no guarantees regarding word usage. Consider the term "about." It could be used as "about 10 inches" (does that include *exactly* 10 inches?), or a sleeve could be "about" a rod (does that mean all the way around the rod, just over the top of the rod, fixed to the rod, sliding on the rod?). So these terms are provided only as a basic guide to patentspeak.

about: a nonspecific quantity

contiguous: elements are touching

disposed: a part is positioned in a particular place

further including: additional parts

heretofore: something previously recited

means for: claiming something in terms of its function, rather than specific hardware (see "Means Plus Function," below)

member: a mechanical part, when no other word is available

multitude: a large, indefinite number

pivotably: a part that's rotatably mounted

plurality: more than one of an element

predetermined: a part that has a specific parameter

respectively: relating several parts to several other parts in an individual manner

said: a previously recited part

thereby: specifying a result or connection between an element and what it does

whereby: introducing a function or result at the end of a claim

wherein: reciting an element (part) more specifically in a claim

Means Plus Function

Because in patents invention must be reduced to words, and because words may not exist to properly describe a given invention, one technique allowed under the patent laws to ease the burden of claim drafting is the use of so-called "means plus function claim language." Basically, the idea is the use of special claim language approved by Congress as a shorthand reference to specific structure disclosed in the patent.

Suppose an invention includes a light source, but the light source could be an incandescent bulb, an LED, or even a laser. It might be tempting to draft a claim wherein the light source is simply referred to as "means for producing light." The thought used to be that such a shorthand reference to the light source protected all possible light sources—those referred to in the patent and those not.

Older patent claims for many different types of technologies regularly used the special "means" language. Sometimes, a patent claim would recite first means, second means, third means ... and so on. Toro's patents included the claim language "control means" as a way to describe the mechanical cam-based system for opening and closing a valve and, hopefully for Toro, other mechanisms (such as, say, a solenoid) that did the same thing.

As Toro discovered, however, there is a price to pay for the convenience of employing this special means language in patent claims. If drafting claims is challenging (like Newtonian physics), interpreting patent claims to determine whether they are infringed is extraordinarily difficult (like quantum physics). Paradoxes abound, such as, the fact that the specification of the patent can be used to interpret the claims but limitations from the specification are not to be imported into the claims. Claim interpretation, say the courts, is not an exact science.

Building upon a series of cases where patent claims including "means" clauses were found to be rather restrictive, the court in the Toro case gave patent attorneys another good reason not to ever use the means short hand technique in claims drafting.

There is also a growing (and disconcerting) body of law which transforms some commonly used electronic patent language into the more limiting and restrictive means short hand even though the word "means" is not even used. Some trial courts, for example, have opined that words like "input processing section," "processing circuit," "rectifier circuit," and just plain old "circuit" are actually highly restrictive, while other courts have decided that patent language like "programming circuit," "electronic circuit," "control circuit," and even "circuit means" are not. In fact, two judges, in the same courthouse, in different cases, disagreed with each other over the meaning of "inverter circuit" and "inductor means" in the same patent.

In the only case tested on appeal, "circuit" used by itself in a claim could, in some cases, be highly restrictive, but "interface circuit" and "logic circuit" may not. The reason for the "could" and the "may" is because that portion of the high patent court's opinion is something lawyers call dicta, which is Latin for "this is not necessarily the law." In the Toro case itself, Toro's patents also recited a "control mechanism" as opposed to "control means," but the result was the same: "Control mechanism" is a means type restriction even though the word "means" is not used. The "control mechanism" was thus interpreted to include the cam, and Deere's solenoid was sufficiently different enough from a cam for Deere to escape infringement. In summary, be wary of means type claim language in your patents.

What a Patent Doesn't Tell You

Now that you've been exposed to the elements of a patent and you're ready to start reading them, here are some things you won't find in the patent.

Stuff Happens After the Patent Issues

CAVEAT: *Things can change after a patent is issued. In other words, it's always possible that the patent you are reading may no longer be correct.*

Patents Die

When you read a patent, it reflects the invention as it was issued. But a lot of stuff happens to patents that does not show up in the reading. For example, more than half of all patents expire before their full term is run because the patent owner fails to pay periodic maintenance fees, fees that commonly run several thousand dollars every few years. In other words, the government terminates the patent owner's monopoly because someone failed to make the payments. Keep in mind, though, that under some conditions expired patents can be revived.

Patents can also be invalidated or restricted by a court, for example, as discussed in Chapter 2, when a court narrowed Toro's patents, determining they did not cover the use of a solenoid in a soil aerator. You would not know that by reading Toro's patents.

CAVEAT: *"Expired" patents can be revived under certain conditions.*

Patents Get Reexamined and Reissued

Sometimes, patents are reexamined and reissued by the Patent Office (we'll learn more about this in Chapter 9 when we discuss the BlackBerry litigation). Patents can also be corrected and disclaimed.

Unfortunately the Patent Office does not republish the patent when many of these critical events occur. So how do you find this stuff out? Attorneys often review the patent owner's communications with the Patent Office—called the prosecution history or "file wrapper"—or they use others means of reviewing Patent Office records.

It is possible for anyone to obtain a patent's file wrapper (see "What Is a File Wrapper?," below) but generally, post-issuance research, considering the patent bureaucracy, is traditionally best left in the hands of a patent attorney or other qualified person.

What Is a File Wrapper?

A file wrapper is the collection of documents (including correspondence and other paperwork) that the Patent Office maintains for each issued patent. Each file wrapper contains all of the paperwork that flows between the patent applicant (and the applicant's lawyer) and the Patent Office.

Once the patent issues, the file wrapper is made available to the public so that others can see exactly how the Patent Office processed the application. The file wrapper is useful for two main inquires: 1) Did the patentee actually receive the scope of protection desired? and 2) Are there any special meanings of the words used in the claims?

You can get a file wrapper for any issued patent or published application at the USPTO website at www.uspto.gov. Click Patents, then, under eBusiness, click Buy Copies.) The USPTO charges approximately $200 to $400 for most patent file wrappers, depending on the size. You can also download the contents of the file wrapper of fairly new patents for free.

Patents Have Relatives

Another fact that does not necessarily show up when reading a patent is whether this patent has bred others, an issue of increasing importance when valuable technology is at stake. For example, it would be unfortunate if a competitor's patent for an LCD micro display is determined not to be violated, and then you later learned the competitor has four additional LCD micro display patents that *are* infringed.

Worse, a given patent lists its parents and grandparents (related patents that precede it), but it does not list its children (related patents that follow it). A competitor could even have patents pending for additional innovations concerning LCD micro displays.

Remember, too, that some patents have parents and grandparents and/or originated in a foreign patent office. Thus, in some cases, the date to beat is not the filing date but the date of the patents or applications listed in the "prior publication," "related application," and/or "priority" data fields on the title page.

Patents May Not Reflect All Prior Art

A patent will include a listing of "references cited" on the title page including, as applicable, other U.S. Patents, foreign patents, and other publications. Some of those references may be from a listing provided by the company seeking a patent when the patent application was filed. Other references may have been uncovered and cited by the Patent Office Examiner.

CAVEAT: *Prior art references that have been uncovered by the USPTO examiner (and not the applicant) are typically marked with an asterisk.*

Attempting to prove a patent invalid is difficult enough; attempting to prove a patent invalid because of one of these listed references can be an uphill battle—those items listed on the patent were presumably reviewed by the examiner who granted the patent. It can be hard to convince a court or jury that the Patent Office made a mistake (but it can and has been done). Therefore, the best way to knock out a patent is to uncover other patents or references having the correct date but not cited on the title page of the patent to be invalidated. In other words, the patent may not reflect valuable prior art that could result in a finding of patent invalidity.

What to Do When Your Candy Bar Melts: Capturing Patents

Patent Policies and Ownership 132

    Written Agreements 133

    Employed to Invent... 135

Trade Secret Considerations 136

    Employee Confidentiality 138

    Nonemployee Confidentiality... 138

Documentation 139

    Inventor's Notebooks.. 140

    Invention Disclosure Forms 143

    When Employees Fail to Document 146

Patent Committees.. 148

    The Committee Process 149

    Who Is on the Committee?.. 149

BOTTOM LINE: *Every company with innovative products should institute a patent management system to document and review company discoveries.*

I n 1945, Dr. Percy Spencer, a scientist at Raytheon, was surprised to find that the candy bar in his pocket had melted as he stood in front of a magnetron (a device that generates microwaves). After testing other foods in front of the device—popcorn, and then eggs— he realized that microwaves can cook food.

> *"An innovated success is as good as a successful innovation."*
>
> —ARCHIBALD PUTT, PUTT'S LAW AND THE SUCCESSFUL TECHNOCRAT, 1981

Spencer reported his claims to Raytheon executives, and after further testing, documentation, and review, Raytheon pursued a patent application for a "Method of Treating Foodstuffs" (later issuing as Pat No. 2,495,429; see below).

Raytheon introduced its Radar Range in 1947. The device did not sell well initially—probably because it was six feet tall, weighed 750 pounds, required a plumbing hookup (the magnetron tube had to be water cooled), and was priced at $5000. But within six years, a smaller, more commercial consumer model was introduced and an industry was born.

Percy Spencer and Raytheon were no strangers to patents. (Spencer was named as an inventor in over 300 Raytheon patents.) Most important, Raytheon had a process in place for documenting and reviewing company discoveries made by Spencer and his fellow scientists and engineers.

As you read this book, someone somewhere could be making a key discovery. But that discovery may dry up and blow away unless the company employing that brilliant innovator has a system in place to claim, document, and review the discovery.

That concern keeps many CEOs awake. For example, Mark Tauscher, the CEO of Massachusetts-based PLC, Inc., which develops high tech medical devices, told me that his greatest fear is that his employees may be generating great ideas that they are not reporting or recording. (I'll talk more about Mark's company in Chapter 8.)

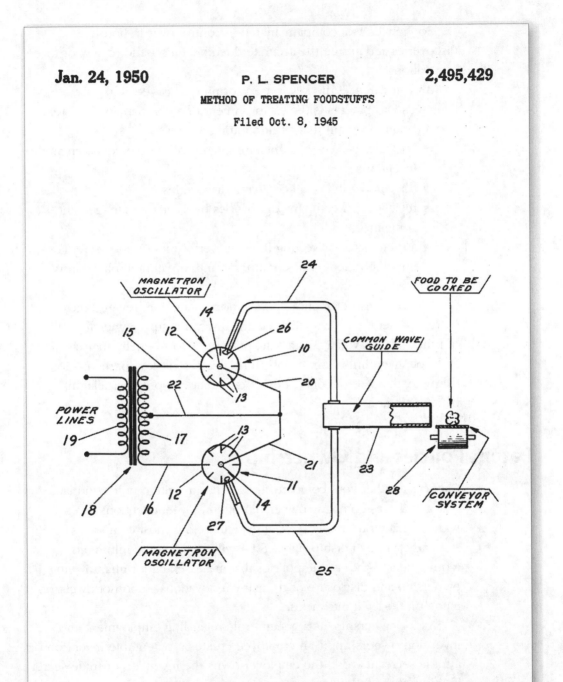

Raytheon Microwave Patent

So, how does a company maintain control over in-house discoveries and assure the accurate documentation and review of these innovations?

As you will see, the key to transforming discoveries like Dr. Spencer's into patents is the establishment of a company-wide patent management program that, at minimum requires:

- company polices guaranteeing ownership of employee-created inventions
- documentation of all company discoveries
- review of all company discoveries by a patent management committee, and
- a process for protecting the discovery (under trade secret laws) until the patent issues or at least until a patent application is filed.

Without these elements—policy, documentation, review, and secrecy—there is no way that a company can assure ownership of innovations, evaluate its assets, perform a cost-benefit analysis, and document important events in the history of development—for example, the date of conception (a date that can prove crucial in patent litigation).

Patent Policies and Ownership

Chances are that your company already has a written policy in place that guarantees company ownership of employee inventions. Even without that written policy, as I'll explain below, most companies still can claim ownership rights. So, I will focus on the minimum requirements—that is, the policies that are essential for guaranteeing ownership and disclosure of company innovations—and not dwell too much on the legal intricacies.

As for ownership, as a general rule regarding employment and invention ownership, if an employee creates a patentable invention or a trade secret at work, the employer owns the invention or trade secret if either of the following is true:

- The employee signed a written agreement (usually an employment agreement) assigning invention rights to the company
- The employee was specifically hired (even without a written agreement) for the purpose of innovating or creating a specific invention (known as "hired to invent").

Even if the employer does not acquire ownership under one of these two methods, the employer may still acquire a limited right to use an employee's patent or trade secret (called a shop right) without paying the employee. Under a shop right, the employee retains ownership of the patent or trade secret, but his company has a right to use the invention without paying the employee. A shop right can occur only if the employee uses the employer's resources (materials, supplies, time) to create an invention. Other circumstances may be relevant, but use of employer resources is the most important criterion.

Written Agreements

Most companies have something in writing—either an employment agreement or a company employment manual—that establishes that the employee assign any inventions to the employer. Because these employment agreements are often signed before the employee creates an invention, this paperwork is sometimes called a preinvention assignment. Most preinvention assignments have three parts:

- an assignment provision that guarantees the employer's ownership of any inventions
- a power of attorney provision that allows the employer to register and administer the ownership rights, and
- a disclosure provision that requires the employee to report any discoveries to the employer.

Sample provisions from a preemployment agreement appear below. As with any provision or restriction, the language may vary from agreement to agreement and may even be set out under a separate title or heading.

Employer Ownership Innovations

Assignment of Innovations. Employee agrees that any invention, process, system, or patentable creation (Innovations) conceived, originated, discovered, or developed in whole or in part by Employee: (1) as a result of any work performed by Employee with Company's equipment, supplies, facilities, trade secret information, or other Company resources; or (2) on Company's time, shall be the sole and exclusive property of Company. Employee agrees to sign and deliver to Company (either during or subsequent to his employment) such documents as Company considers desirable to evidence: (1) the assignment to Company of all rights of Employee, if any, in any such Innovation, and (2) Company's ownership of such Innovations.

Power of Attorney. In the event Company is unable to secure Employee's signature on any document necessary to apply for, prosecute, obtain, or enforce any legal right or protection relating to any Innovation or copyrightable work referred to above, Employee irrevocably designates and appoints Company (and each of its duly authorized officers and agents) as his agent and attorney-in-fact, to act for and in his behalf and to execute and file any such document and to do all other lawfully permitted acts to further the prosecution, issuance, and enforcement of patents, copyrights, or other rights.

Disclosure. Employee agrees to promptly disclose in writing to Company all discoveries, developments, designs, programs, code, ideas, innovations, improvements, inventions, formulas, processes, techniques, know-how, and data (whether or not patentable or registrable under copyright or similar statutes) made, written, conceived, reduced to practice, or learned by Employee (either alone or jointly with others) during the period of his employment, that are related to or useful in Company's business, or that result from tasks assigned to Employee by Company, or from the use of facilities owned, leased, or otherwise acquired by Company.

Sample Provisions: Employer Ownership of Innovations

What the Employer Can't Own

Eight states—California, Delaware, Illinois, Kansas, Minnesota, North Carolina, Utah, and Washington—impose restrictions on what inventions *cannot* be claimed by an employer. These restrictions apply only to "inventions" an employee creates—that is, items for which a patent may be sought. Typically, these provisions provide that the only inventions an employer can't claim are true independent inventions—those that are developed completely without company resources and that don't relate to the employee's work or the employer's current business or anticipated future business.

If your company is in California, Illinois, Kansas, Minnesota, or Washington, state law requires that your company give written notice of your state's restrictions to employees. If this is not done, the assignment could be unenforceable. What if you live in one of the 42 states that do not have laws restricting invention assignments? Even in most of these states, preinvention assignments can't be grossly unfair. Employers in these states sometimes track the rules used in the eight states because they want their preinvention assignment agreements to be legally enforceable.

Employed to Invent

The Supreme Court once ruled that, "One employed to make an invention, who succeeds, during his term of service, in accomplishing that task, is bound to assign to his employer any patent obtained." In other words, even without a written employment agreement, an employer will own rights to an employee's patent or trade secret if that employee was hired for inventing or designing skills. Most companies prefer to use a written agreement, which is more reliable and easier to enforce than this implied agreement. However, this is always a suitable fallback position for a company with some doubts about ownership of an innovation.

Here's an example of how this works: An engineer had no written employment agreement with his employer. He was assigned as the chief engineer on a project to devise a method of welding a "leading edge" for turbine engines. The engineer spent at least 70% of his time on the project. He developed a hot forming process (HFP) for welding a leading edge and built the invention on his employer's time and using his employer's employees, tools, and materials. The engineer claimed that he was the sole owner of patent rights. A court held that the company owned the patent rights because the engineer was hired for the express purpose of creating the HFP process. That fact, combined with the use of the employer's supplies, payment for the work, and payment by the employer for the patent registration, demonstrated that there was an implied contract to assign the patent rights to the employer. Therefore, even without a written employment agreement, the employer acquired ownership.

What About Independent Contractors?

The rules above for employees generally won't apply to independent contractors. If your company uses contractors or consultants to develop products, you'll need to make sure that written agreements are in place guaranteeing your company's ownership of their work—especially software.

Trade Secret Considerations

Regardless of whether your company plans to patent an innovation, it should treat the discovery as a trade secret to the maximum extent possible. That means no publication or dissemination of the innovation unless your are authorized to do so by your company (or your patent attorney).

That also means that employees keep the innovation a secret whether talking to family, friends, or contractors. Any disclosure (unless to other employees or persons who have signed nondisclosure agreements or NDAs) will result in the loss of trade secrecy rights. That won't necessarily kill your company's patent chances (unless a public disclosure is made more than year before filing your patent application), but it can seriously impact your ability to outmarket the competition.

The Patent Office treats patent applications as confidential, making it possible to apply for a patent and still maintain the underlying information as a trade secret, at least for the first 18 months of the application period. Unless the applicant files a Nonpublication Request at the time of filing and doesn't file for a patent outside the U.S., the Patent Office will publish the application within 18 months of the filing date. At that point, trade secrecy rights (as to what is disclosed in the application) are lost.

Publication after 18 months does provide one advantage for a patent applicant: If a patent later issues, the patent owner can later recover damages from infringers from the date of publication, provided that the infringer had notice of the publication and the patent claims do not significantly change.

Developing and testing an invention should not compromise the trade secret status of the invention. For example, lab notebooks should be shown only to those persons willing to maintain confidentiality. There is an implied understanding that witnesses must maintain confidentiality when signing the lab notebook. Some inventors prefer that witnesses also sign a confidentiality agreement (or NDA).

Although a confidentiality agreement will assure the inventor's right to sue someone who discloses confidential information, it will not guarantee success in court. As noted above, the company must also be able to prove that reasonable steps were taken to protect the confidential information and that the information has not become known to the public.

What's a Trade Secret?

A trade secret is any information that has commercial value, that has been maintained in confidence by a business, and that is not known by competitors. A business that owns trade secrets is entitled to court relief against those who have stolen the secrets or divulged them in violation of a legal duty—for example, after signing an agreement not to disclose (a nondisclosure agreement or NDA).

Employee Confidentiality

Each state has laws that prohibit employees from making unauthorized disclosures of company trade secrets. In some cases, an employer may obtain financial damages from the employee for such disclosures. Although it is always advisable to use a nondisclosure agreement with employees (at least those with access to innovations), these state laws provide a second line of defense in the event trade secrets are stolen. In addition to state laws prohibiting disclosure, certain management and high-level employees—for example, an engineer, scientist, or corporate executive—who come in contact with trade secrets during the course of their work have a special obligation (referred to as a "fiduciary duty" or "duty of trust") to treat secrets as confidential. The higher the level of expertise or responsibility possessed by the employee, the more likely this special fiduciary relationship exists. This offers an employer another method of preserving trade secrecy.

Nonemployee Confidentiality

Again, your company is probably already aware of this requirement, but if you are disclosing trade secret information regarding an innovation, an NDA should be used with vendors of supplies, prototype makers, manufacturers, and companies that want to license the invention. But, as noted in Chapter 3, if a product is sold on the open market, it can be freely reverse-engineered and copied without violating any trade secret laws. Only a patent can protect the product in such cases.

Documentation

Inventor documentation may be the single most important element in a company's patent management program. I recommend two types of inventor documentation:

- an inventor's notebook, and/or
- an invention disclosure form.

Why Documentation Matters

Documentation is used to prove two foundations of patent rights: conception and reduction to practice. Conception is the mental part of inventing, the discovery or formulation of an invention, or the moment a problem is solved—for example, Dr. Spencer's realization that microwaves could heat food. Conception is documented by the use of inventor notebooks or other witnessed records of the discovery.

Reduction to practice occurs in two ways: actual reduction to practice (by building and testing the invention) or constructive reduction to practice (by preparing a patent application or provisional patent application). Inventor notebooks and invention disclosure forms are used to document both conception and reduction to practice.

In the event of a dispute or a challenge at the Patent Office, this documentation helps to prove the "how and when" of conception and reduction to practice, and it is useful in defeating prior art references and patent applications by competitors covering the same idea as yours. The goal is to demonstrate with your notebooks that your invention was conceived and reduced to practice before another invention.

Documentation has a related noninventor purpose. It may assist in demonstrating to the IRS that your company is entitled to deduct certain expenses related to the invention process.

Inventor's Notebooks

CAVEAT: *Have all notebook entries reviewed and signed by two witnesses.*

CAVEAT: *Don't enter anything in an inventor's notebook that you wouldn't eventually want printed on the front page of the* New York Times.

Most likely some engineers, scientists, and developers working for your company are already using some form of an inventor's notebook (sometimes known as "lab notebook"). These permanently bound notebooks are the most reliable and efficient ways to document an invention. The pages in an inventor's notebook should be numbered consecutively and contain lines at the bottom of each page for signatures and signature dates of the inventor and the witnesses. Any bound notebook is suitable, as long as each discrete description is dated, signed, and witnessed.

Here's what you should expect to find in an inventor's notebook:

- detailed descriptions of the innovations, particularly any novel features
- an explanation of the procedures used in the building and testing of the invention
- any visual representations of the work accomplished, whether it is a drawing or sketch entered directly in the notebook or a photograph taped on the page
- testing procedures, results, and conclusions, if any, and
- third-party documentation if relevant, for example correspondence regarding the innovation or purchase receipts.

Here are four rules to follow regarding inventor's notebooks:

- **Sign and witness everything.** Notebooks entries should be witnessed because an inventor's own testimony, even if supported by a properly completed notebook, may be inadequate if your company is involved in a dispute at the Patent Office or with another company. If information is included that has not been directly entered into the notebook—for example, photos, receipts, computer printouts, or correspondence—those elements should be separately signed and witnessed using the procedures described below. Some inventors and engineers prefer to draw a line across the pages and continue the line through across the additional material. That way, it's clear if a photo has been removed or substituted.

- **Use two witnesses.** Witnesses do more than verify the inventor's signature; they actually read or view and understand the technical subject material in the notebook. For this reason, the witnesses should have some background or knowledge in the field of the invention. While one witness may be sufficient, two are preferred, because this enhances the likelihood of at least one of them being available to testify at a later date. If both are available, the inventor's case will be very strong. Also, the company should have a policy guaranteeing that any witness who signs the notebook entries is not a relative.

- **Don't enter anything in a notebook that you wouldn't want printed on the front page of the *New York Times*.** If a dispute ever develops, the contents of your notebook may become part of a public record available for all to read.

- **Regularly collect notebooks.** It's a good company practice to collect and secure all inventor notebooks on a regular basis to prevent the temptation to rewrite history.

The Case of the Forged Notebook

Here's a wild case involving inventor notebooks. Dr. Amr Mohsen of Aptix Corp. maintained inventor's notebooks as he developed programmable circuit boards (which he later patented). When Aptix sued its competitor Quickturn Design Systems, Inc. (now known as Cadence Design Systems, Inc.), Dr. Mohsen was required to deliver his inventor notebooks to Quickturn and to the court in order to prove Aptix's case.

Everything might have gone well were it not for the fact that the copy of Dr. Mohsen's 1989 notebook supplied to the Judge had extensive text and diagrams not present in a copy of the "same" 1989 notebook provided by his attorneys.

It gets worse. Mohsen reported he found a copy of a 1988 notebook, and he later submitted still another copy of the 1989 notebook he had furnished to the court.

Where were the original notebooks? Mohsen reported that they were stolen from his car. Mohsen then produced additional evidence to corroborate his asserted invention conception date, including his 1989 "Daytimer," which included various entries referring to the engineering notebooks.

Forensic evidence, however, showed that these entries were written with an ink that was not manufactured until 1994—five years after the supposed entries. Ooops!

Then, some of the original notebook pages mysteriously showed up in a priority mail package, which the judge determined was actually prepared by Dr. Mohsen or his accomplices.

As you might expect, the lawsuit was dismissed based on the fraudulent efforts of Dr. Mohsen. Quickturn, the defendant in the patent lawsuit, was awarded its attorney fees, and Aptix's patent was held unenforceable.

It gets stranger. Mohsen appealed, and although the Federal Circuit upheld the attorney fees award and the dismissal of the lawsuit, the court of appeals—in an unusual quirk—found the Aptix patent was still enforceable.

Dr. Mohsen didn't accept his fate willingly. While in jail for criminal charges for lying to the court, he solicited a cellmate to murder the judge, torch the house and car of a government witness, and threaten other witnesses. What Mohsen did not know was that the cellmate was wearing

The Case of the Forged Notebook (continued)

a wire. Mohsen's brother was also indicted for forging his signature as a witness to the fake inventor notebooks. Three days before his trial Mohsen was arrested with an Egyptian passport and $20,000 in cash.

In January 2007, Dr. Mohsen was sentenced to 17 years in prison for perjury, attempted intimidation of witnesses, and solicitation of arson. As part of his sentence, Mohsen was ordered to pay restitution to Cadence. Although this case is extreme to be sure, the lessons are clear: Use inventor notebooks, but don't let anyone change them at a later date. Some people get lost in this world, and engineers and scientists are no exception.

Invention Disclosure Forms

TIP: *Your company should institute a process to number invention disclosure forms so that they are indexed for future reference and tracking.*

Okay, let's say an engineer has diligently recorded the events (in a lab notebook) that lead to a discovery. The engineer thinks there may be something patentable. What happens now? At this point, I recommend that the employee prepare and file an "invention disclosure" form (sometimes called an "invention capture" form).

I've seen a wide range of invention capture forms, but I recommend—given the hectic work schedules of engineers and scientists—that companies use a concise form that can be filled out quickly without any assistance or explanation. Lengthy and complicated disclosure forms will discourage usage and could add an unwieldy aspect to the patent review process. Keep in mind that the point of this form is to capture a potentially patentable idea on a document that can be circulated for review. Below is an example of a one-page form.

AB Corp.   Date _____

Invention Capture   No. _____

Title of the Invention: _____

Your Name: _____

Group/Division: _____

Brief Description of the Invention (what does it do?): _____
_____

What problems does it solve? _____
_____

Applicability to what products or services? _____
_____

☐ Fully engineered?

☐ Sold?   If so, when _____

Disclosed in any manner to anyone outside the company?   ☐ Yes   ☐ No

Attach any previously written descriptions of the invention and any known prior patents or competitive product descriptions.

Patent Committee Decision: ☐ Proceed with patent

                              ☐ Do not patent

                              ☐ Revisit at a later date

Date: _____

Reasons(s): _____
_____
_____
_____

Blank Invention Disclosure Form

AB Corp.   Date ___6/5/06___

Invention Capture   No. ___No. 06-14___

Title of the Invention: ___Optical switch___

Your Name: ___Lora Carter___

Group/Division: ___Optics___

Brief Description of the Invention (what does it do?): ___Switches among___
___optical fibers___

What problems does it solve? ___Faster, smaller, less costly___

Applicability to what products or services? ___IBX series of switches___

☑ Fully engineered?

☑ Sold?   If so, when ___3rd quarter 2007___

Disclosed in any manner to anyone outside the company?   ☐ Yes   ☑ No

Attach any previously written descriptions of the invention and any known
prior patents or competitive product descriptions.

Patent Committee Decision: ☑ Proceed with patent

                                          ☐ Do not patent

                                          ☐ Revisit at a later date

Date: ___6/12/06___

Reasons(s): ___Easily reverse engineered. Provides competitive___
___advantage. Broad protection possible.___

Completed Invention Disclosure Form (For Wholly Fictional, Optical Switch)

Your company should institute a process to number these forms so that they are indexed for future reference and tracking. Copies of the inventor's notebook pages or other write-ups concerning the invention can be attached to the form, as can other patents and the like. Then, the patent attorney will have enough information to begin the patenting process.

When Employees Fail to Document

CAVEAT: *Financial incentives to encourage employee disclosures may limit broad patent protection.*

What should a manager to do when an engineer or scientist fails to keep an inventor's notebook or fails to turn in an invention disclosure forms? Many companies avoid this problem by implementing financial incentives—for example, a reward of $1,000 or so per inventor for each patent application filed and granted by the Patent Office.

There's a downside to this incentive, though. To secure the patent and thus the financial reward quickly, the inventors may sacrifice the goal of broad, encompassing, valuable patent claims and simply take whatever narrow, low-value claims the Patent Office is willing to allow.

A different, nonmonetary incentive used by some companies is recognition. Patentees' names and pictures are published in the company newsletter, and the individuals are recognized at company meetings. Alternatively, patent plaques, each with the title page of the patent and listing the inventors' names, line the halls of many corporate offices. A less expensive method of providing recognition is simply to frame the title page of a patent.

Sometimes these monetary and nonmonetary incentives work, sometimes they don't. Alternatively, these incentives may ultimately discourage disclosures. Why? People may start trying to patent everything and now management, due to budget constraints, has to deny their employees their efforts. This can lead to patent ambivalence, wherein the employees again stop turning in invention disclosures.

Some companies prefer the stick to the carrot. Because employees are required to disclose all new innovations (under the terms of company policy, discussed above), any failures in this area can be the subject of discipline or negative performance reviews.

Another problem regarding disclosure is that employees sometimes fight over claims of inventorship. For example, two engineers conceive of a new idea for a product, and soon several other engineers and managers assert they are inventors, too. In these cases, the patent attorney much decide who actually contributed to the conception and/or reduction to practice of the claims. These are the inventors for patent purposes and are listed in the application.

One way to minimize these sorts of issues is to develop a pro-patent company culture at your company—that is, to make the document-and-disclosure process as simple as possible. This can be done by providing seminars for employees on how to spot patentable innovations and how to best document them—that is, basically simplifying how employees capture and report their ideas. In that regard, here are a few other tips:

- Periodically include a patent attorney at project design review meetings and let the attorney capture ideas, thereby assuring full disclosure.
- Conduct "walkabouts," again with a patent attorney, where a visit is made to engineers working on a specific project to get them talking about their innovations.
- Hold a luncheon and invite the engineers in to get them excited about patents and talk about new ideas.
- At corporate retreats, include a lecture by a patent attorney about patent basics, patent law, or perhaps a case that's in the news.

Personally, I gain valuable information about each of my clients at these types of meetings and lectures, and I think the client benefits from my suggestions, as well. If cost is an issue, see if the patent attorney will reduce rates for an informal group lunch near the attorney's office.

Patent Committees

The patent committee is the group that reviews all potentially valuable ideas, improvements, innovations, and inventions to determine whether a patent application should be filed. Why do you need a patent committee? Because somebody needs to do the appropriate cost-benefit analysis. This is where a patent committee enters the picture. The committee engages in the cost-benefit analysis necessary to determine whether the innovation merits patent protection.

One survey revealed that large companies such as IBM, Intel, and Hewlett-Packard regularly file thousands of U.S. patent applications each year. To do this, their domestic intellectual property (IP) budget alone must be in the millions. Sometimes, these costs are borne by the company as overhead. For other companies, though, these expenses are treated as direct costs attributable to business units, manufacturing lines, or product divisions.

When the patent costs are allocated to general overhead, there may not be any real incentive for the business units to manage costs, and some companies may put a periodic "hold" on patents as a way to increase profitability projections in a given fiscal quarter. When patent costs are borne solely by the business units, they may decide to lower costs by not pursuing patent protection as often as needed.

Because of the sheer cost, no company would file a patent for every invention disclosure submitted by its employees. Instead, a patent committee is formed and meets on a periodic basis to decide which inventions—as disclosed by the company's scientists and engineers—merit protection via a patent.

In start-up companies, the "committee" can be just one or two employees; larger companies may form a committee for each division and/or site. Keep in mind that an invention might be conceived by one person, but it takes a team effort to bring that invention to the market as an innovation. Inventions that are interesting from a scientific or engineering standpoint but for which there is no potential profitable market can be weeded out of the costly patenting process.

The Committee Process

The basic notion is that would-be patentees—or at least their inventions—are brought before the multidisciplinary committee to discuss the merits of invention. The committee then decides either by vote or by consensus whether to spend any of the currently budgeted intellectual property budget on a particular technology. Collectively, of course, the committee knows that patents can help keep the competition at bay, but it also understands that patents can serve other purposes. Patents are assets looked upon favorably by investors and would-be acquiring companies; patents can be used as trading cards in licensing deals, litigation, and settlement negotiations; and patents can prevent others from patenting what the company already knows.

If approved, an invention disclosure with the patent committee's seal of approval is sent off to the patent attorney. And so begins the patent pending process, discussed in more detail in the next chapter.

Who Is on the Committee?

Ideally, a company's patent committee should comprise members from many different areas of the company and from a variety of job functions. It should always include people with a reasonable cross-section of technical knowledge representative of a company's main technologies. This makes sense, because at least one member of the committee must understand the invention being evaluated and be able to provide a reasonable explanation of its significance to the other patent committee members. Remember, the value of a patent lies in its scope. Internal research and development managers have an awareness of a company's strategic technology investments critical to appreciating where the company should be investing its patent dollars. An R&D manager can bring to a patent committee both insight into a company's most promising or critical R&D efforts and also receive from the committee an understanding of the intellectual property position being developed around different technology areas.

Here are some suggestions for members of your committee:

- **Corporate Counsel.** Your in-house counsel, if you have one, can contribute by explaining the costs associated with a patent application in the United States and/or in various foreign countries and the time limitations for patenting in the U.S. and abroad. Even if in-house counsel is not a patent attorney, her position on the patent committee is essential because she typically knows the various reasons patents are sought and the pros and cons of patents versus trade secrets and other forms of intellectual property protection. In-house counsel is also familiar with the personalities, skills, and traits of the patent attorneys used by the company and may be able to match the given scientist or engineer with the most appropriate patent attorney. In-house counsel understands the company's policies, procedures, and strategies regarding patenting and can keep the committee's efforts in line with the same.

- **Engineering Manager** or **Chief Technology Officer.** It's important to have a committee member who can offer opinions on the technical merits of the invention as well as some insight into the particular market. This committee member may also be able to provide input regarding competitors of the company and how to tailor a given patent to protect present and future markets.

- **Inventor or Patent Holder.** It sometimes helps to have a seasoned inventor or patent holder who knows the ins and outs of the patent system and can contribute to the committee by advising on which inventions are likely to be held patentable and which have little chance of success. Based on previous experiences working with patent attorneys, this committee member can also provide insight to new, would-be patentees on how to most efficiently prepare for the stage where the patent application ultimately is filed.

- **Marketing Representative.** This member provides input regarding the relevant market, the expected market share, and the potential return on investment via the patent. A marketing expert may also be able to provide a prediction as to how the company will tout the new technology—advantages of the technology that can be set forth in the patent application itself (the only deep sea oil piping with aerogel!). Understanding where a company is marketing and the demands of its customers is an important component of formulating and implementing a patent strategy. Sales, marketing, and business development personnel have the requisite customer-facing experience to be able to recognize when a particular invention can add value to a company's product line. You can be sure Gillette took a marketing approach when it decided to develop and patent the Mach3 razor.

- **Chief Financial Officer.** Your CFO or other finance personnel can assist with the cost-benefit analysis and can also advocate for a patent committee's budget. In addition, financial and accounting personnel often review innovations as strategic investments or assets rather than as simple expenses.

- **Champion.** This might be the inventor, or it may not. A champion is someone who is willing and able to tout the technology and explain its relevance in the marketplace. If there is no champion, that could indicate perhaps the technology is really not worth the cost of a patent.

At the end of the day, there are basically two types of companies. Company A runs in cycles—first patenting nothing, then patenting everything, then nothing, and so on. Perhaps a new product is developed and no one thought about patents. The product is a hit, and so it breeds competition. Now management wants patents, but the product has been on the market for two years so no patents are possible.

The next revision of the product is now being engineered. In panic mode, every single difference between the new and old versions of the product is patented, no matter how trivial. Patent costs are out of control and the patent budget is exceeded.

As a result, a hold is put on patents. That causes the engineers and scientists to become ambivalent to patents. No invention disclosures are turned in to management. No patent applications are in the pipeline. Later in time, the panic mode begins once again.

Company B, in contrast, establishes a patent budget each year. Its engineers and scientists continually turn in invention disclosures.

A patent committee meets regularly and decides to patent ideas, improvements, and innovations which will really add value. Patent panic rarely occurs. Mistakes are sometimes made but the decision to pursue and win patents is an informed management decision.

Company B is patent savvy; Company A is not.

The Long and Winding Road to "Patent Pending"

Playing the Claim Game: Part Two 155

    How Does a Company Analyze Claims in Relation
        to Existing Patents? 155

    Can a Nonattorney Properly Review the Claims? 156

    Should the Claims be Global or Local? 157

    How Do You Win the Claim Game? 157

To Search or Not to Search? 158

Things to Keep in Mind About Patent Searching 160

    The Trouble With Computer Searching 160

    Searching Does Not Always Recover All Relevant Patents 163

    Don't Ask, Don't Tell? 164

    Be Wary of Clearance Searches 165

The Patentability Study 165

The Patent Application 167

    Preparing for the Meeting 169

    The Meeting 172

    After the Application Is Prepared 174

    How Managers Help in the Patent Review Process 174

    Tracking Patent Costs ... So Far 176

The Provisional Patent Application 177

By now you're aware that the value of the patent lies in its claims. So, how does your company properly bring those claims to the attention of the Patent Office? And, equally important, how does your company decide whether it's worth spending the $10,000-plus price tag—the costs commonly associated with obtaining a patent—to pursue the rights to those patent claims?

> "Life is either a daring adventure or nothing. Security is mostly a superstition. It does not exist in nature."
>
> —HELEN KELLER

In Chapter 4, I discussed the claim game in some detail, explaining how claims fall within a continuum that ranges from very broad to very narrow. In this chapter, I'll explain a different perspective on the claim game—specifically how to review your patent claims in relation to existing patents.

What's Patent Pending?

Strictly speaking, patents are never pending; patent *applications* are pending. A patent is "pending" during either:

- the period between the filing of a regular patent application and when the patent issues (is granted) by the Patent Office, or
- the period between the filing of a provisional patent application (discussed later in this chapter) and when a patent issues, provided that a regular patent application is filed within one year of the provisional's filing date.

During these periods, you can advertise a product as "patent pending," and let others know about your invention's status. However, because you don't yet have a patent, you cannot sue infringers during this period. Why then do companies regularly brag about patent pending when the law is clear no action can be taken against a competitor who copies the innovation? Well, some people may not know the law and may be of the opinion that "patent pending" means protection. Also, a competitor does not know when the patent will issue, at least for awhile, or what it will cover. So, the competitor competes during the patent pending period at some risk—the risk that product sales will have to stop once the patent issues.

Playing the Claim Game: Part Two

I provided an explanation of how claims are drafted in the section entitled "The Claim Game" in Chapter 4. In this chapter, I'll take a more practical view by comparing our potential claims with existing technology:

How Does a Company Analyze Claims in Relation to Existing Patents?

Let's consider this example: We've decided to patent a new liquid crystal display with elements A, B, C, and D. Suppose (as discussed in previous chapters), that elements A, B, and C are standard in all LCDs but our new component, element D, makes LCDs consume less power.

We should file a patent … If our patentability study reveals a group of patents that disclose elements A, B, and C but not D, then the decision is simple; we can prepare and file a patent application, relatively secure that our patent will not be opposed on the basis of a prior art patent.

We should not file a patent … If we find a single prior patent which somewhere, anywhere discusses the idea of combining elements A, B, C, and *also* our power-reducing component D. Then, we know that it's best *not* to file a patent application unless we add something else to our patent application claim, say, element E. Of course, that patent would have a lesser value than the one we'd hoped for, because all of our competitors (if the prior patent is expired or doesn't properly claim elements A, B, C, and D), can make an LCD including our no-longer-novel idea (component D—the power-reducing component).

Often, however, the claim game is more confusing. For example, you might find a prior patent disclosing elements A, B, our power-reducing component D, but not component C. Or perhaps component C has been replaced by component C'. Or, you might find a patent discussing in detail power-reducing component D and a reference to its potential use in many different products and systems but not identifying LCD displays by name. In any of these scenarios, the Patent Office might conclude that your invention is obvious. Ouch!

At the very least, the cost of securing a patent of value probably just went up and—even more important—the value of our potential patent may have dipped below its expected cost.

That, of course, is the challenge of the claim game. It requires that you reevaluate the cost versus benefit of the patenting effort based on the results of your patent research. Remember: The more restrictions present in your claims, the easier it will be to win a patent, but the more restrictions, the lower the value of the patent.

Can a Nonattorney Properly Review the Claims?

To some extent, inventors, engineers, managers, and other nonattorneys are often excellent sounding boards for the claims.

After all, the claims of the application must serve a definite purpose, and these people can help to determine if that purpose has been fulfilled. For example, is the goal to thwart competition? Then the claims must clearly protect the product to be sold and also predictable variations of it engineered by competitors. Is one possible goal to license this patent? Consider adding claims covering different uses of the product, and/or consider adding claims covering the product in different environments.

Let's suppose the idea is a new fuel filter. Can claims be drafted not only for the construction of the fuel filter but also for a fuel filter so constructed as a component of an automotive fuel system? How about as a component in the fuel system of an aircraft or riding lawnmower? The reason for such claims is the chance of a heftier license fee based on the price of the fuel system as a whole instead of just the price of the fuel filter component of the fuel system. Also, the patent can be separately licensed to automotive fuel system suppliers, aircraft fuel system suppliers, and riding lawnmower fuel system suppliers.

Right now, perhaps one component of the product to be patented is limited to an existing technology. Is it possible that in the future, other technologies can serve as that component? Quite often, things that exist only on paper or are too expensive today soon become real things at affordable prices.

Should the Claims Be Global or Local?

The claims must also cover a product or service someone will buy in the country where the patent is filed. If a service involves, for example, an electronic unit, relay stations, and a central processing station, note that one competitor might sell competing electronic units and a different competitor could provide relay stations and the central processing station. One set of claims, then, should cover just the electronic unit and another set of claims, either in the same or a different patent, should cover the relay stations and the central processing station. We'll learn later how some U.S. patent claims for the notion of a wireless email system failed because the market leader implemented a part of the system in Canada instead of in the U.S. I discuss foreign patent filing in Chapter 8.

In the end, the claims should address a customer need that so far, nobody else is meeting, and the claims should explain your approach to addressing that need, and perhaps even the benefits of your approach. The other portions of the patent application discuss competitive products or services and how the innovation is superior to the competition. For all these reasons, it's wise to have nonattorneys review the claims as well as the complete patent application to verify that it delineates the company's value proposition for the innovation.

How Do You Win the Claim Game?

Since I refer to it as "the claim game," you may wonder how a company wins.

That's easy. You win it simply by playing it properly. And to play it properly you must understand patent searching, patent applications, and provisional patents, all of which I'll discuss in this chapter. You will also need to understand patent prosecution (a process I'll describe in more detail in the next chapter).

To Search or Not to Search?

BOTTOM LINE: *Deciding whether to search involves a cost-benefit analysis.*

In order for you to make your claims decision, you must have knowledge of existing patents and their claims. The best way to obtain that information is with a search of existing patents. Many people believe that such a search is a prerequisite for filing a patent application.

Surprise! It's not.

There is no law or Patent Office regulation that requires that you perform a patent search before (or after) filing a patent application. In fact, the Patent Office will always conduct a patent search relating to your invention once you file a patent application.

So why pay for a professional patent search which might cost, say, $2,000 or more?

It's a cost-benefit decision, and it's part of the claim game strategy. If the searcher uncovers evidence that demonstrates you won't get a patent, you'll save the money you would have spent to prepare and prosecute a patent application. So the decision comes down to whether you want to spend $2,000 to see if it's worth saving $10,000 or more?

The answer to the question of whether or not to search can often be "No." The engineer or scientist who devised the innovation may already know quite a lot about the current state of technology in this particular field of endeavor—for example, she reviews the latest scientific literature and attends all the relevant conferences. The particular inventor may also hold previous patents in the field and may regularly keep abreast of later patents filed by others.

Such a person may actually know *more* than the Patent Office because the patents and even the published patent applications that can be searched are behind the times. Once filed, a patent application can take one-and-a-half years to publish and three to five years to issue. Patent filings for the latest and greatest technology, then, are simply not searchable. So in these cases, a company that is already aware of what's out there doesn't need to spend money on research that may already be outdated.

In other cases, a patent search can be worthwhile—for example, when moving into a new technology field or where company engineers are not aware of the state of that particular technology.

Patent Searches: One Size Does Not Fit All

Patent searches come in all sizes and shapes. Here are some of the common types.

Basic Knock-Out Search. This type of search is a "quick and dirty" search, usually performed on the Internet for free. The purpose is to get a rough idea of whether an existing patent or product will prevent (or "knock out") your patent from issuing. If this search does not knock out your patent, the company may then wish to proceed with a full-blown patentability study.

Patentability Search or Study. The purpose of a more formal patentability study is to compare your invention with prior and pending patents (to the extent they are published), as well as with existing literature and products. The goal is to determine if any "prior art" will prevent your patent from issuing. The study is often accompanied by an oral or written opinion.

Clearance Search. This type of search is used to determine whether a planned product infringes any of the claims of someone else's existing or pending patents. The study is often accompanied by an oral or written opinion that includes an analysis as to whether existing or pending patents are enforceable.

As you can imagine, the focus of the search may change midstream as more details about a particular patent are revealed—for example, a patentability study (can we patent this?) can evolve into a clearance search (do we infringe their patent?).

Things to Keep in Mind About Patent Searching

Companies often feel that patent searching provides extra security, shielding them from potential liability. After all, why pay thousands of dollars for inconclusive results? Patent searching is generally very helpful and often essential, but it has degrees of reliability.

The Trouble With Computer Searching

CAVEAT: *Keyword searching of databases may not uncover relevant patents.*

There are a number of computerized patent databases available. These patent databases are great resources and should always be included within your patent searching arsenal. You're probably familiar with the basic searching methods used for these databases: Boolean logic, a searching method based on the use of keywords—words, terms, and phrases that appear within the text of the patent. Keywords are used in conjunction with field searching and connectors. The "fields" of the patent are the various discrete sections we learned about in Chapter 4. For example, you can search a keyword within patent abstracts (patent summaries), titles, inventors' names, assignee, or other sections of the patent specification. "Connectors" are terms such as "and" or "or" that allow alternative searching choices.

The trouble with keyword searching is that highly relevant patents may not be uncovered. For example, suppose an engineer is looking for patents in the field of liquid crystal displays. Entering the key words "liquid," "crystal," and "display" in the abstract field of the patent title page will uncover over a thousand patents that were issued in just the last three years. The searcher will then likely narrow the search to only those patent abstracts discussing a particular environment for LCD displays—cellular telephones, for example. But a patent can cover liquid crystal displays for use in cellular telephones without the abstract ever mentioning cellular telephones.

In addition, the choice of language by the patent's drafter can throw off the search results. Perhaps the abstract of the patent mentions "handheld communication devices" or "wireless communication devices" instead of cellular telephones. Relevant patents in the field of LCDs for cellular telephones could exist that don't even mention "liquid crystal" in the abstract or, for that matter, in any part of the patent. Instead, "pixel electrodes" or other equivalent terms could be used throughout the patent instead of "LCD." Similarly, patent attorneys (who sometimes seem to loath plain English) can, for example, call the common screw a "mechanism for converting rotational motion into linear motion." You say "fan," I say "wind generator," she says "motorized air movement apparatus."

There are computer searching workarounds for overcoming the keyword issue. For example, you can search inventions by classification. Every inventions falls within a relevant search classification organized by classes and subclasses. Remember that the Amazon "one-click" patent was classified, on the title page, as belonging to the data processing class (class 75) and the electronic shopping subclass (class 26). As another example, if you invented something that had to do with sewing, you would search in Class 112. If the invention had to do with sewing gloves, it would be in Class 112, Subclass 16. You can find the appropriate classifications in either the Index to the U.S. Patent Classification, which lists all possible subject areas of invention alphabetically, from "abacus" to "zwieback," or the Manual of Classification, which lists all classes and subclasses, numerically. Both of these resources are available at the PTO website. Again, though, be careful: There is no guarantee that an examiner always correctly classifies a given patent.

Computer Search Resources

Free databases include:

- The U.S. Patent & Trademark Office (www.uspto.gov). The PTO website has a full-text searchable database of patents and drawings that cover the period from January 1976 to the most recent weekly issue date (usually each Tuesday).
- Google Patent Search (www.google.com/patents). Google has entered the free patent searching business by converting the entire image database of U.S. Patents (from 1790 to the present) in a format that's easy to search. At the time this book went to press, it did not include patent applications, international patents, or U.S. patents issued over the last few months, but the company plans to expand coverage in the future.
- European Patent Office (http://ep.espacenet.com). The EPO site permits searches of patents worldwide back to the 1920s.

Fee-based databases include:

- Delphion (www.delphion.com). The Delphion website has evolved from the former IBM patent website. The site offers U.S. patents searchable from 1971 to the present (it is expected to add pre-1971 patents) as well as full-text patents from the European Patent Office, the World Intellectual Property Organization PCT collection, and abstracts from Derwent World Patent Index (which includes 40 international patent-issuing authorities).
- Micropatent (www.micropatent.com). Micropatent offers U.S. and Japanese patents searchable from 1976 to the present, International PCT patents from 1983, European patents from 1988, and the *Official Gazette* for patents.
- LexPat (www.lexis-nexis.com). This site provides U.S. patents searchable from 1971 to the present. In addition, the LEXPAT library offers extensive prior art searching capability of technical journals and magazines.
- PatentMax (www.patentmax.com). At PatentMax, you can search U.S. and foreign patent databases and perform batch loading, a process that automates patent downloads.
- ICO Suite (www.patentcafe.com). The ICO Suite offers various levels of patent research and reports.
- PatBase (www.patbase.com). PatBase is a relatively new database that can search back to the 1800s through many nations' patents and permits batch downloading.

Searching Does Not Always Recover All Relevant Patents

CAVEAT: *There's no publicly available information as to patent applications that have not been published.*

Keep in mind that there is never a guarantee that all relevant patents will be uncovered during a patent search. As we have learned, patents can take two years or longer to issue from the date they are filed. And the Patent Office is behind in publishing patent applications. So, there may be relevant patents pending that you (or an experienced patent searcher) simply cannot find. Say you want to offer a product similar to a new product on the market advertised as "patent pending." You cannot find a patent application, because it has yet to be published. You're in the dark and uncertain. What does their patent cover? Will it issue? This is the "FUD" (fear, uncertainty, and doubt) principle behind "patent pending."

Wouldn't-It-Be-Nice Products

When it comes to low tech consumer products, a patent search is almost always recommended. Here, I'm talking about the "wouldn't it be nice"-type products that many inventors hope will turn into the next hula hoop, Aero-Garden, or The Club. Prior patents or previous products may already exist for these products. A patent search can save the inventor a great deal of time and money. A basic knock-out patent search is always advisable even if the inventor decides not to patent the product (many wouldn't-it-be-nice products sell well without being patented). That search may help to avoid a patent infringement lawsuit from an inventor who's already "been there, done that."

Don't Ask, Don't Tell?

CAVEAT: *In some cases, it's better not to perform an extensive patent search*

You're probably familiar with the concept, "Don't ask, don't tell." In a sense, a company that's considering filing a patent application is faced with a similar situation. Should they ask for a search report that discloses relevant information about potentially competing (or infringed) patents? Or is it better not to know?

If a competitor can prove that you knew of a patent, that you disregarded the knowledge, and then you infringed the patent, your company may be liable for three times the amount of financial damages as a willful infringer. And, you may have to pay the other side's attorneys' fees! For example, suppose that, during the discovery portion of a patent lawsuit, documents were furnished showing that a search had been performed and among the hundreds of patents uncovered was the patent at the center of the lawsuit. Even though you may have never focused on or discussed that particular patent, your company might be in an uncomfortable position.

So, the question of whether you know about a certain patent and when you first knew about it can affect the amount of money recoverable against your company in a patent infringement action. It's an unfortunate fact of life that a diligent, regularly conducted review of patents can adversely impact your company's liability.

At the same time, when your company files a patent, there is an affirmative duty to cite all relevant patents you know about to the Patent Office. As I mentioned, you don't have to do a patent search, but, if you do, the search results *must* be disclosed to the Patent Office.

Different companies have different policies and procedures in this area, which attempt to work a viable trade-off between unintentionally being put on notice of a patent and the need to learn more about existing patents.

The best route to take is to search periodically but not to print or electronically store every result. (Note: Computers keep a record of all searches forever unless some affirmative action is taken.) Retain records only of patents that are relevant to your company or to the invention at hand. And when doing so, follow your company's procedures regarding record keeping. The goal here is to avoid storing irrelevant patent information that may come back to haunt your company in the event a competitor litigates and goes on a fishing expedition during the lawsuit's discovery phase.

Be Wary of Clearance Searches

BOTTOM LINE: *It's not always feasible to perform a clearance search for every new product.*

A "clearance search" is usually a specially commissioned search, the purpose of which is to see if any patents have claims that would be infringed were your company to sell Product X. As you can imagine, searching for all the possible patents for a specific type of product and then reviewing all the claims of all those patents is exorbitantly expensive. For example, you can quickly watch an attorney's billing meter spin out of control reviewing the claims of thousands of LCD patents!

My advice: If you are aware of a particular patent or two, study those patents. If you know your prime competitors in this market space, study their patents. No company I know of, though, performs a clearance search for each new product the company introduces into the marketplace. It's just too expensive and unreliable. Some investors require clearance searches, and that's fine—just try to keep the search focused.

The Patentability Study

Okay, we've explained some of the caveats regarding patent searches. Now, let's examine the procedures for one of the most common types of searches: the patentability study. The main goal of a patentability study is to predict, by researching historical technology, whether the

Patent Office will award you your patent claims and if so, whether the projected scope of the patent claims merit incurring the patent costs.

As you know by now, an invention is *not* patentable unless it is new and not merely an obvious variant of what is already known. So initially you need to determine if any existing patents preclude a Patent Office examiner from issuing your patent.

Although patents are understandably the primary types of references used by Patent Office examiners, they aren't the only thing used to measure the patentability of your invention. They sometimes use other sources as well, including technical articles, scientific databases, and Internet research.

For this reason, companies must conduct their own patentability studies using similar resources to avoid any surprises in the patent prosecution process. A patentability study often produces a mountain of paperwork, and companies must sort through the results.

If your company has been keeping abreast of the patents in a particular engineering field, the patentability study will complement that research, with one additional twist: When it comes down to patentability, extraneous information—for example, who owns the patent, whether the patented device was commercialized, or whether the patent is expired—doesn't matter. A prior patent that discloses your idea—even if that disclosure is not in the claims—is enough to preclude obtaining your own patent. That's why when I hear about "title" or "abstract only" searches, I cringe. Sometimes, a single paragraph deep within the specification of a prior patent is enough to knock out your patent.

A professional patentability search is carried out by a patent agent, a specialist patent searcher, or an attorney. The steps are as follows:

1. The searcher is sent a search request.
2. The searcher reviews the request to gain an understanding of the scope of the search.
3. The searcher conducts the search, usually online at first and then at the Patent Office.
4. The searcher reports the search results.

The search request should be focused and to the point. You should begin with a statement that clearly sets out your goals. For example:

Dear Searcher—

We are seeking all relevant prior art in which aerogel is used as insulation in deep sea oil well piping.

The request letter should bring the searcher up to speed quickly. For example, if we've decided to attempt patenting the combination of claim elements A, B, C, and D for a new liquid crystal display, tell the searcher what liquid crystal displays do, where they are used, and that you already know prior LCD displays include components A, B, and C. Tell the searcher *not* to search for patents explaining that liquid crystal displays include components A, B, and C. Instead, focus on the invention in the request and tell the searcher you want to review only patents featuring liquid crystal displays with components A, B, C, *and D*. Outline a claim you hope to obtain. You are basically telling the searcher to try and knock out this claim via prior patents.

The format of a typical search request letter is shown below.

The best search requests are less than a couple of pages in length and include a schematic drawing or two so the searcher sees as well as reads about the invention to be patented. Remember those inventor notebooks and invention capture forms? *Do not* send those to the searcher because rarely do those items appropriately focus the searcher on the task at hand.

Once the search has been completed, the results become part of the claim game, as I discussed at the beginning of this chapter—that is, we compare the claims in the existing patents and determine whether the patent scope obtainable is worth the cost of the patent.

The Patent Application

The next step in the patenting process is the preparation and filing of a patent application. As you're already aware, a patent application is one of the most difficult legal instruments to draw with accuracy

Dear _____:

Please perform a patentability search for the subject invention that relates to [*here describe the subject matter—is the invention a new use for aerogel, a new LCD, or a new climbing apparatus?*].

The components of a typical [*subject matter*] are shown in Fig. 1. [*Here, and in Figure 1, describe the "prior art" and educate the searcher regarding the same. Many searchers have engineering degrees, but you should write at the lowest level possible*].

The problems with prior [*subject matter*] include: [*here describe the problems and limitations associated with the state of the art shown in Figure 1*].

The invention is shown in Fig. 2. [*Here describe the difference(s) between the invention as shown in Figure 2 and the prior technology as shown in Figure 1*].

The subject invention thus is a [*subject matter*] including:

[*here list the elements of a broad claim for the invention*].

Please provide us with a copy of each reference found in your search, and do not hesitate to telephone the undersigned if you have any comments, questions, or suggestions.

Sample Search Request Letter

(remember the Gillette and Toro cases from Chapter 2?). Your goal here is to avoid "term paper syndrome"—where an attorney hopes the correct ideas in the patent application will somehow reveal themselves in the third or fourth rewrite.

Lack of quality control in the management of a given patent project can end up costing you money. This is especially true in patent drafting, where the attorney's meter is always running. The more efficient and the more prepared you are, the lower your bill. Let's discuss a few ways to ensure the attorney's time is well spent.

Preparing for the Meeting

BOTTOM LINE: *Start the application process with a meeting between patent attorney and inventor.*

Make no mistake about it: The inventor has to *meet* with the patent attorney face to face. Engineers and scientists are always busy—that's a given—but a patent attorneys who begins working on a patent application based solely on an invention disclosure or lab notebook entries often produces work that ends up wasting more of the inventor's time than had the inventor and the attorney sat down to discuss the invention in the first place.

I recently reviewed a fifty-page PowerPoint presentation a company sent me in order to prepare for a meeting with several engineers. Proud that I was up to speed, I told the inventors that I had studied the presentation. The project manager told me, pointing to the presentation, "Well, that's what *didn't* work."

So I'll say it again: The patent attorney must meet with the inventors, first.

Before the meeting, the inventor need not and probably should not attempt to pen a draft of a complete patent application. But the inventor should understand the basic format of a patent and the topics likely to be covered at the meeting with the patent attorney. Remember the invention disclosure or capture form in Chapter 5? Working from that, the inventor should write down, in two or three pages or less, a background explanation of the prior art (known ideas and technology) and the problems with the prior way of doing things that gave rise to the need for the invention. Remember, the patent attorney will examine these elements in order:

1. the state of the art
2. the limitations of the state of the art
3. the deltas between the invention and the state of the art, and
4. how those deltas overcome the limitations associated with the state of the art.

Here's a simple example:

1. prior razors had two blades
2. a closer shave was not possible
3. more blades might induce undesirable drag forces
4. we've got three blades in a special geometry
5. drag forces are reduced and a closer shave is now possible.

Gather Background Information

These notes will ultimately form the background section of the patent application. I call this the "slow, inaccurate, and unreliable" part of the patent application, because many patent applications do indeed describe prior techniques as slow, inaccurate, and unreliable and then go on to tout that the innovation renders the new product faster, more accurate, and more reliable. This patent application section usually starts out with a general description of the field to which the invention relates—for example, is the invention a new razor, an LCD, a new use for aerogel, or an optical switch?—and gradually provides more specifics until all the problems confronting the inventor and solved by the invention are spelled out.

Create the Advantages

A list should be compiled of all the advantages of the invention. These advantages are the solutions to the problems raised in the background and should be in functional terms—for example, the invention is faster, less expensive, more compact, uses fewer toxic chemicals, has more and faster memory, provides a closer shave without skin irritation, and the like.

There should be a one-to-one relationship between the problems noted with the prior art in the background section and the advantages or objects of the invention, stated in the summary portion of the patent application. Why, for example, would you note that prior art optical switches are expensive to manufacture if your new optical switch is not, indeed, less expensive to manufacture? Conversely, if your optical switch is less expensive to manufacture, why would you fail to state that manufacturing costs associated with prior optical switches are high?

Prepare the Drawings

Third, a set of drawings should be prepared, which may range from detailed computerized CAD/CAM drawings to simple hand sketches. The drawings should start with a broad (10,000 foot) view of the environment of the invention and gradually get more and more detailed until the necessary details of the invention itself are revealed. These items, provided to the attorney, become the tools he or she then uses to draft the patent application.

Summarize the Concepts

Finally, the inventor should attempt to express, in one sentence, the basic inventive concept. The reason? Such an expression can serve to form the thesis of the patent application—remember, it's a legal document as well as a technical one—a document to be read and hopefully appreciated by a judge, a jury, and others typically without any technical background.

For example, the Gillette Mach3 patent recites the following thesis:

> It has been found that with a blade unit comprising three blades, the frictional drag forces can be kept at an acceptable level while allowing an improved shaving efficiency, by setting the blades relative to each other and to guard and cap surfaces positioned in front of and behind the blade edge, according to a particular geometrical disposition.

And, in the Amazon "one-click" patent, this is the thesis presented:

The present invention provides a method and system for single-action ordering of items in a client/server environment. The single-action ordering system of the present invention reduces the number of purchaser interactions needed to place an order and reduces the amount of sensitive information that is transmitted between a client system and a server system.

Good patent attorneys know that people tend to appreciate that which they can understand and discount or ignore that which they cannot. There is an art to explaining the complex at a 10th-grade reading level, and even patents need to be understandable at least on some level.

Summary

The manager's role here is to capture and confirm a value proposition, including a crisp description of the problem the innovation addresses, the distinguishing features of the innovation, and its benefits, including the reasons it's better than the competition. Some people are of the opinion that the patent attorney need not be told this value proposition. The patent attorney just needs to be told the engineering details and to handle the legal stuff. Wrong. The patent attorney's primary job is to protect your value proposition, which he cannot do unless you relate it to him.

The Meeting

The meeting between inventor and patent attorney should result in a meeting of the minds as to the following:

- the true invention and its scope and the value proposition discussed above
- proposed wording of the broadest claim(s)
- the scope of the prior art and its disadvantages, and the benefits made possible by the invention
- how the actual device to be patented works, is used, and is made
- all possible variations of the device (examples or embodiments)

- an understanding of why patent protection is sought in this particular instance
- the basic layout of this particular patent application including which figures will be presented to the reader, why, and in what order, and
- a thesis which cogently ties everything together.

If these goals are accomplished, the back-and-forth proofing of the draft application will be much more efficient. Because these goals must be accomplished in a short time at the meeting, the inventor may feel he is being subjected to a type of cross-examination, and he may have to be patient with the attorney. That's the nature of the beast: Presumably the invention is new and therefore the patent attorney will not have seen it before.

Schedules permitting, it can be a good idea to include, at the drafting meeting, certain members of the patent committee—they can not only contribute to the patent attorney gaining an understanding of the invention but also ensure the attorney is aware of the reason(s) the company is seeking patent protection and the value expected in the resulting patent.

I like it when I first meet with one or two inventors to gain and understanding of the technology behind the invention and then close the meeting with representatives from management and even marketing to make sure our goals are aligned for the patent application I'm about the draft.

In this way, the "term paper syndrome" and frustration often associated with preparing the patent application is minimized and the true invention is captured in a clear, cogent, and readable patent application.

Here are some other possible questions for the inventors and/or management:

- Has a patent search been conducted, and what are the results?
- Is there a deadline for filing this patent application? Remember, it's best to file before the invention is made public in any way and before it's included in a product offered for sale.
- What's the product that will be sold, and within that product, where is the invention?

- Why is the invention important to the marketing of the product?
- Will foreign patents be sought and, if so, in what countries?
- Has a provisional patent application been filed? Are there any other pending patent applications associated with this invention, this product, or this project?

After the Application Is Prepared

Once the patent application has been prepared by the patent attorney and reviewed by the inventor, management and personnel from the patent committee, and perhaps even noncommittee personnel, should review the application. What are these people looking for? They should be asking questions such as:

- Is it understandable?
- Does it present a cogent thesis?
- Has the claim game been played?
- Has your company analyzed and addressed existing products and patents?
- Does this patent have a scope that will likely give your company a return on investment?

You may find that writing out the value proposition of a patent application can be a good idea—for example:

> This patent will prevent our competitors from selling any climbing apparatus with side rails and rungs made of any material.

or

> This patent will prevent our competitors from using aerogel in deep sea oil well piping, but they can still use other insulating materials.

How Managers Help in the Patent Review Process

Here are some other tips for managers in the patent review process:

- **Keep good configuration control.** Is this the first or third draft or the patent application? Keep track of who has already reviewed the application by having all the reviewers review a single hard copy draft.

- **Have everyone review the same application.** Your patent committee should make any necessary additions, modifications, or comments, writing their remarks in red on the draft or on additional sheets as necessary. It is more efficient if all the reviewers review the same document; that way, each reviewer can view comments made by the other reviewers. Disagreements sometimes ensue, but those fights can provide valuable insight into the "true" invention. In cases with multiple inventors, I've sometimes received some comments by email, some comments by fax, and some comments by phone. In one case, I received five different versions of an edited patent application by email. You can bet the cost of that particular patent application fell on the right of the bell curve.

- **Do not let anyone retype any portion of the application.** This effort will make it more difficult for the attorney to see exactly what was changed, and he will have to spend additional time and effort assessing the changes.

- **Don't fret over informal, messy-looking drawings in the first draft.** Costly patent draftsman's time should not be spent until everyone agrees the drawings are correct. At the final version stage of the application, formal drawings can be prepared. You can even file an application with informal drawings and then file the formal drawings later.

- **Are there numerous comments throughout the specification portion of the draft patent application but not a single change to any claim?** That could reflect a reviewing inventor who doesn't understand patent claims or their importance. Play the claim game with the inventor. Moreover, since the specification is properly drafted from and therefore *after* the claims, it would be a rare case that a change to the specification wouldn't reflect a change needed in the claims.

Once finalized, the patent application is filed. Filing a patent means that it has been transmitted the U.S. Patent Office. And it can take a year or more for the Patent Office examiner to first review the application. When he does, we enter the "prosecution" phase of the patent project.

Tracking Patent Costs ... So Far

BOTTOM LINE: *Expect to pay between $10,000 to $12,000 to prepare and file a patent application.*

At the point of filing, the patent attorney's job is completed for now, and you should soon be receiving a bill for these services. In addition, the Patent Office also levies its fees—fees that go up annually. The fee for a U.S. patent application filed by a small business company is currently $500 and is broken into three parts—a basic filing fee ($150), a search fee ($250), and an examination fee ($100). All the fees are mandatory, so don't ask me why the U.S. Government divvies them up.

There are other fees, as well. One fee penalizes an applicant for long utility patent applications—you must pay $125 for each set of 50 pages exceeding 100 pages. You also must pay for numerous claims. Each excess independent claim above three is $100.

The cost structure of any given U.S. patent project looks roughly like this:

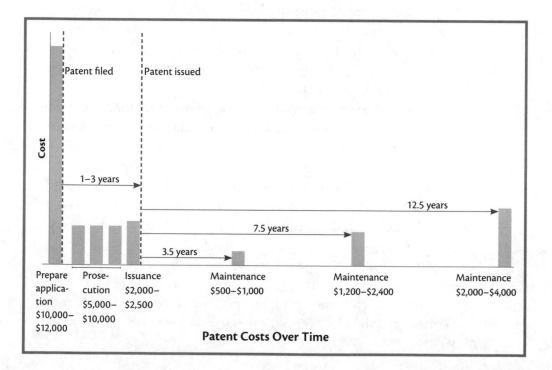

Patent Costs Over Time

Real patent filing figures vary based on the complexity of the invention, the scope of the prior art, the number of claims, and the law firm used. Ballpark costs are $10,000-12,000 to prepare and file a patent application prepared over the course of a month or two (add $2,000-3,000 more in cost and a month more in time if a search is performed). The costs are then usually fairly low for a year or two after filing (the patent attorney will report on the filing and may check to ensure the application is properly pending from time to time), then expect to pay $3,000-5,000 for prosecution over the course of a year or more; $1,000-2,000 to issue the patent; and then maintenance fees: $500-1,000 at 3.5 years after issuance; $1,200-2,400 at 7.5 years; and $2,000-4,000 at 12.5 years (depending on the size of the patent owner). In the next chapter, we'll break out the costs a little further and also take into account foreign patent applications and their costs.

The Provisional Patent Application

CAVEAT: *Provisional patent applications can preserve your place in line at the Patent Office but if done improperly can result in a patent of no or little value.*

Management and engineers, pushed by product release dates, may not always have the time to fully pursue a "real" (aka "utility") patent application. Budget constraints may also prevent patent filings. As we'll see in the next chapter, there are strict time limits on when a patent application can be filed. In the United States, for example, you can commercialize a product and then up to one year later still file a patent application. In most foreign countries, however, the patent application must be filed before the invention is made public. One way for management to meet these deadlines without incurring heavy costs is to file a provisional patent application.

First allowed in the United States in 1995, provisionals have been touted as quick, easy, and inexpensive vehicles for achieving patent pending status for new products. In 2002, for example, over 80,000 provisional patent applications were filed with the Patent Office. Unlike full utility patent applications, a provisional requires no claims. Nor is a provisional required to be in any specific format. In fact, provisionals are not even reviewed by the Patent Office. Once filed, however, the invention can be labeled as "patent pending." After one year, that status will end unless a regular patent application is filed for the invention.

Provisionals can come in many shapes and sizes. There are no rules. They can be the design specification for a product; a scientific paper; a short invention disclosure; a white paper; or even, in some cases, a short memorandum describing the invention. In the dotcom era, these "idea" provisionals were often so minimal they were deemed "napkin provisionals."

By filing a provisional, the invention can be disclosed or sold without fear of losing patent rights, provided a full utility patent application is filed within a year of the provisional. In fact, if patent protection is desired only in the U.S., one can sell a product to be patented, up to a year later file a provisional, and then up to a year after that file the full patent application.

Because of their simplicity and low cost, provisionals are often filed when there isn't enough time or money to prepare and file a full application—for example, because of an impending trade show, product release, or presentation, or when the budget won't support a full application. They are also suitable when the feasibility or marketability of the technology is presently questionable.

So far, so good—but all this assumes the provisional does at least one thing right. The law requires that even the lowly provisional patent application contain a written description of the invention detailing how the invention is made and used sufficient to enable others to practice the invention *claimed* in the later filed utility application.

This is the *quid pro quo* of our patent system: In return for government-approved exclusivity regarding the patent protected discovery, the patent must teach others how to make and use the invention so they can practice it after the patent expires, thus furthering the constitutional goal of promoting progress in science and the useful arts.

So, if the provisional lacks sufficient content, the provisional fails and so too may the later issuing patent based on the provisional. In other words, an improperly drafted provisional can be worthless. Here's one worst-case scenario: A product is sold, a provisional is filed within a year of the sale, and a full patent application is filed within another year—but the provisional fails to adequately describe the invention actually *claimed* in the full patent application. The result? The patent is invalid, because the provisional failed to provide the mandated *quid pro quo* disclosure.

In 2002 that very scenario came occurred in the case of *New Railhead Mfg. Co. v. Vermeer Mfg. Co. & Earth Tool Co.* New Railhead patented a drill bit for horizontal drilling in rock useful for installing utilities under a roadway. When New Railhead's competitors began using similar drill bits, New Railhead sued. Unfortunately, New Railhead's provisional did not adequately describe one fairly minor feature of the drill bit claimed in the utility application. The provisional application was deficient, and without the important provisional filing date within a year of the sale of the drill bit by New Railhead, the full utility patent application—filed more than a year after the sale—was in violation of law. New Railhead's later issuing patent was invalid and thus worthless.

There are other challenges with provisionals. For example, although no legal claims are required, the provisional application must support the all important claims in the later-filed utility application. Therein lies the rub: Without the claims, how can a provisional be drafted to support the claims?

As you probably realize after reading about the ladder claims example in Chapter 3, regular patents are normally written by drafting the claims first to fully capture the invention and all its possible variations. The drafting is done in a way that makes it difficult for a competitor to escape infringement by making unimportant and insubstantial changes to the claimed discovery.

The specification is then drafted *from* the claims to support them, because of a simple rule of patent law: What is claimed must be supported in the specification section of the patent application. The patent specification can contain more than what is claimed, but it can't contain less.

Provisionals turn that time-honored practice on its head-resulting in later-drafted patent claims possibly not supported by the provisional specification (and an invalid patent). And since the Patent Office does not endeavor to check the provisional to ascertain whether it supports the claims of the later-filed utility application, a deficient patent will still issue only to be knocked down in court when a competitor's attorney carefully reviews the provisional to evaluate whether it fully supports the claims. You can bet your competitor's attorney will be happy to see a napkin provisional.

This problem, however, can be solved by at least considering the invention that will be claimed or, better yet, by drafting actual claims and then ensuring that the provisional specification fully supports the claims, real or imagined. This solution may require the services of a patent attorney. That adds to the cost of the provisional but the benefit—a viable provisional versus a voidable patent—generally outweighs the cost.

Another tactic is to throw the kitchen sink into the provisional— that is, add in all the design documentation, computer code, white papers, whatever—in the hopes that somewhere there will be adequate support for the later-drafted claims. When this tactic is followed, provisional applications can constitute hundreds of pages. Previously, the filing fee for a provisional application was $80 irrespective of the number of pages. Now, however, the provisional costs $100 plus an additional $125 for every 50 pages more than 100.

In one recent case of mine, the cost of a provisional for a large company went up from $160 to over $950. Keeping the provisional shorter may have saved some money, but it would have been at the risk of a later patent being held invalid.

In summary, provisionals have their place and time—just keep in mind that there are no real shortcuts to patent protection.

The Good Shepherd:
Patent Prosecution and Management

Hurry Up and Wait 182

Dealing With Rejection 184

How Much Should You Say During Prosecution? 185

How Costs Mount Up During Prosecution 187

Post-Prosecution Activity 190

Management and Tracking 192

P atent prosecution is the process of shepherding a patent application through the Patent Office. The process is bureaucratic. At times, it may have an adversarial quality (your company versus the Patent Office) but in general, it's a matter of communicating and interacting with the Patent Office in an attempt to convince them to issue your patent. The good news is that most— somewhere between 50 and 60 percent—of all patent applications turn into patents. The bad news is that patent prosecution costs money and takes time: $3,000-8,000 and three years on average.

The goal, of course, is not simply to obtain the patent, but to most efficiently use company resources to obtain the patent with the best possible claims. You may determine during the prosecution process, for example, that the best course of action is to abandon the patent. In this chapter I'll discuss the basics of patent prosecution and how to keep track of patents after prosecution.

Hurry Up and Wait

What happens once the patent is filed? Not much.

It will take about a year before a Patent Office examiner even gets around to reviewing your patent application. The examiner then will spend probably less than a day on it conducting a search, reviewing the prior art (that is, the current state of the relevant technology), and rendering an opinion regarding the patentability of the invention. In all likelihood, the examiner will reject the application in a written "Office Action."

RULE: *Expect a negative first opinion.*

Because the first opinion by the examiner is more often than not negative, a cynical person might even believe Patent Office examiners, to guarantee job security, always find at least one fault with every patent application. So, don't despair when your attorney reports that the examiner has "rejected" the claims. It's not as bad as getting turned down at an eighth-grade dance. Instead, the rejection begins the process wherein the patent attorney provides a hybrid technical and legal analysis in an attempt to change the examiner's mind.

Who are Patent Examiners, and Why Are They So Unhappy?

George Washington and Thomas Jefferson did it. So did Clara Barton and Albert Einstein. They all worked as patent examiners, reviewing patent applications and determining patentability. In the U.S., patent examiners must be a United States citizen and hold a bachelor's degree in one of the physical sciences, life sciences, engineering disciplines, or computer science. Some also are pursuing or have a degree in law and use their experience at the Patent Office as a springboard for a career as a patent attorney. The examiners belong to an organization, the Patent Office Professional Association, that lobbies on their behalf.

Over the past few years, the Patent Office has been having an increasingly difficult time retaining patent examiners. A government study in 2005 confirmed that many examiners leave because of increasing tension between examiners and Patent Office management regarding workloads and production schedules. Consider, for example, that the Patent Office has approximately 4,500 patent examiners and there are approximately 100 applications per year per examiner. In addition to these working conditions, examiners have another incentive for leaving the Patent Office. The salary they receive is far less than they could make in the private sector.

To make matters worse, examiners in different countries can have different opinions—sometimes even conflicting opinions—so even if our government's Patent Office examiner deems the invention worthy of a patent, that position may not be adopted by examiners in other countries.

The examiner will conduct an independent search of prior art and, if the exact same thing claimed in your application is found in a prior art reference, the patent application claims will be rejected as not being novel. The examiner will say a claim is "anticipated." More typically, the exact same invention is *not* found but the examiner will combine two or more prior art references and conclude that, based on this combination, the claimed invention is obvious. The "not novel" rejection, also called "anticipation," is objective; the obviousness rejection is, at least somewhat, subjective.

We discussed obviousness in detail in Chapter 3. To understand this standard, I'd recommend reviewing the case involving the pet clippers—a company claims the right to use an electric Sunbeam clipper blade with a nonelectric pet grooming tool—and the Syscan case—in which a company claimed a patent on a combination of a scanner and a USB connection.

These examples, of course, don't prove the rule, but they do indicate that the Patent Office is willing to issue patents for technology developed by one company and put to use in another company's product. If you think that's a bad idea, you'd better be prepared. Many patents, maybe most of them, cover systems made up of subsystems and components engineered by others.

Dealing With Rejection

Patent attorneys know how to deal with all types of rejections. The attorney responds to the rejection via a written document aptly called a "response." This rejection (Office Action)/response cycle can repeat numerous times; also, there are many other kinds of rejections or objections possible in an Office Action and many different ways to respond. The patent claims can be amended, and/or the patent attorney can respond with technical and legal arguments as to why the invention is worthy of a patent. You can even appeal an examiner's rejection to higher authorities. The focus is always on the claims— don't forget the importance of the claims. A common beginner's mistake in prosecution is to tout deltas between the invention and the prior art cited by the Patent Office examiner that are not claimed in the patent application.

Project management during this "prosecution" phase of the patent application includes three important considerations:

- **Reevaluation.** After one or two rejections of the patent application, the patent committee should evaluate the likelihood of ever receiving a patent having the desired scope, as well as the cost of further prosecution. Without a monitoring effort, it can be relatively easy to rack up prosecution costs equal to or higher than the cost of filing the original patent application. Was that budgeted in this specific project? Is the patent still going to be worth it?

- **Be careful about "patenting around the prior art."** If it was thought that value lay in a specific inventive idea and that idea turns out not to be all that new, it's almost always possible to still get a patent by adding further constraints or specificity to the patent claims. These additional constraints represent other subsidiary ideas (provided these ideas were sufficiently disclosed in the specification of the originally filed application) and eventually, if you follow this approach, the Patent Office examiner will no longer find that combination in the prior art, and you have a patent. Problem is, that patent is not what the committee approved, it may not cover competitive products, and all too often I've run into situations where the resulting patent claims didn't even describe the company's own commercial product.

- **Know when to fold.** Sometimes you have to know when to give up, especially when the scope of any resulting patent will not offset the cost of the patent or the patent scope will not adequately protect against competition. We don't make new investments based on sunk costs, and patent prosecution is no different. If the resulting patent claims have been amended to the point that they no longer correspond to your value proposition, it might be time to give up.

How Much Should You Say During Prosecution?

CAVEAT: *The more said during patent prosecution, the better the chance of winning a patent … but the more said, the better the chance something said can be later used against the patent owner.*

What is said during the prosecution of a patent application in "Written Responses" to Office Actions can be reviewed by anyone. That applies to the prosecution of foreign patent applications as well—remember

Schick, which unfortunately opined in a European counterpart patent application to Gillette's U.S. patent that a "plurality of blades" could be more than three.

As I noted previously, Patent Office examiners in different countries can uncover different prior art and take different positions. Just because a U.S. Patent Office examiner holds your invention patentable doesn't mean a Patent Office examiner in Japan will. What you say in response to *any* examiner will be evaluated by a competitor in litigation (or by an investor or buyer during due diligence) and can be used against you.

Here lies another tension in patents: The more said during prosecution, the better the chance of winning a patent; but, the more said, the better the chance something said can be used against the patent owner. We are generally happy when a competitor's patent claims are long and include many requirements. We're also happy when the documentation between the competitor's patent attorney and the Patent Office is extensive. Amending the claims during patent prosecution can also severely impact patent scope, so all amendments need to be carefully reviewed by management.

Different patent attorneys have different ways of dealing with the tension involved in patent prosecution, but management must, at the least, know what is being said, what is being amended, how both affect the scope of the patent, and how the budget allocated for that patent will be impacted. If engineers receive incentives based on patent issuance, it is even more important for managers to stay on top of prosecution and ensure a patent isn't being pursued just for the sake of a patent. Some engineers and scientists like to write tomes they believe will convince the examiner he or she is wrong and/or just plain ignorant. You can expect that the patent attorney will pare down any long-winded responses. For example, imagine the hope is a patent with a claim for a new LCD including elements or requirements A, B, C, and D. An examiner in an Office Action rejects the claim, opining that prior patent X "teaches" or includes elements A, B, C, and D. If that's not true, if for example prior patent X says nothing about element D, the response to the examiner's rejection need make only two salient points:

- The applicant claims the combination A, B, C, and D.
- Prior patent X fails to teach element D.

The response will then conclude that prior patent X cannot be used as the basis for a not-novel or anticipation-type rejection.

The best approach is to keep it short and sweet, like an executive summary instead of a scientific paper.

How Costs Mount Up During Prosecution

The cost of patent application prosecution can get out of hand in a number of different ways. Typically, the Patent Office examiner will issue a first Office Action and the patent attorney will respond in a written Response. The claims might be amended. If the Patent Office examiner is not convinced the invention as claimed is worthy of a patent, the next Office Action will probably be deemed "Final." That, however, is not really the end of the game. Here are some of the post-endgame possibilities:

- **File a "Request for Continued Examination" (RCE) or a "Continuation" application.** An RCE or a Continuation application is really just the same patent application continued or refiled but keeping the original filing date. That application can be rejected in one or more Office Actions, Responses can be filed, and another RCE or continuation application filed, and so on potentially forever. Along the way, interviews either in person or via the telephone can be had with the Patent Office examiner. Any of the examiner's "Final" decisions can be appealed to a Patent Office Board. If the applicant loses there, he can appeal again to the Federal Circuit. Lose there and you can even try an appeal to the U.S. Supreme Court. By now, the cost of prosecution will easily exceed the cost of patent application preparation. Each RCE or continuation filing will cost between $1,000-3,000, and each response between $2,000-4,000. Two continuation applications maturing into patents have the same specifications; only the claims will differ. Suppose the first application has claims 1-10. The examiner may allow claims 1-5 but not 6-10. So, the applicant may allow claims 1-5 to issue in Patent No. 1, file a continuation application for claims 6-10, suffer a rejection or two, amend claims 6-10, and then be granted Patent No. 2 containing those claims.

Run Silent, Run Deep

In the past, patent "submariners" (notably inventor Jerome Lemelson) would play this patent continuation application contest on purpose and to their advantage by allowing a patent to issue only many years (20 or more in some cases) after the original application was filed, when the patented technology by now had been adopted by many businesses. Claims in these applications were even amended to specifically cover products recently introduced to the marketplace. Sellers and even users of those products were then sued.

Today, submariners are thwarted at least in part because now a patent is good only for 20 years from the date of the *original* filing. If the continuation contest is played over the course of fifteen years, for example, when the patent does issue, it's good for only five more years—not seventeen like in the glory days of submariners. So, not only does the continuation contest cost money, it eats up patent life.

- **File a divisional.** Divisional applications are similar to continuations. The difference is that at some point someone —usually the Patent Office examiner—decided there were two inventions in a single patent application. The rule is one invention per application. So, sometimes, when a given patent application has claims 1-5 covering a system and claims 6-10 covering a corresponding method, the Patent Office might assert that that's two different inventions. System claims 1-5 are then retained in the original application, and method claims 6-10 are placed in a divisional application. The original application is split in two but again, the only difference between the two is the claims.

- **File a continuation-in-part.** Continuation-in-part patent applications are used to reflect an advancement in technology. Suppose this year a patent application is filed for aerogel used in deep sea oil well piping. A year later that patent application is still pending and engineers at the aerogel company invent a new substance, call it "advancegel," different from aerogel, but just as good and less expensive to manufacture. A continuation-in-part application might be filed, where the original application is modified to disclose and claim the new "advancegel" substance for use in deep sea oil well piping. Why not just amend the original application to include "advancegel"? That would be nice for a variety of reasons, but it's prohibited. The claims of a patent application can be amended, as we already know, but only in so far as the specification of the *original* application provides support for the amendment to the claims. You simply cannot add new ideas to the specification of a given patent application once it's filed. The "in-part" of a continuation-in-part application means some of this application is the same as the original application, but part of it isn't. Since companies are continuously reengineering their products to add new functionality and the like, you often see more than one continuation-in-part patent application for a given product.

Let's consider a made-up course of patent filings for a product. It all starts with a provisional patent application. Suppose the provisional covers the use of aerogel in deep sea oil well pipes. Within a year after the provisional is filed, the real patent application, called a "utility" application, is filed. That patent application issues as a patent. But before that, some technological advancement was made to the technology and a continuation-in-part application was filed covering the use of "advancegel" in oil well pipes. Then, the Patent Office examiner believed this application really covered two different inventions (for example, "advancegel" in the pipes and the method of making the "advancegel" substance), and so one of the inventions became the subject matter of the claims of a divisional application. The divisional application was twice rejected by the Patent Office, so the company filed a continuation application.

There are an almost infinite number of different scenarios possible for any one "parent" or initial application, and you can see how a patent map with, say, three initial patent applications for a product, each with numerous continuations, divisionals, and continuation-in-parts, can get messy. Gillette's patent litigated against Schick spawned three related patent applications: a continuation, a divisional off that continuation, and a continuation off the divisional.

BOTTOM LINE: *You can't always assume that when you budget for one patent, the result of one patent application will really be just one patent.*

CAVEAT: *When a competitor's patent is being reviewed to see if you might be charged with infringement, don't assume there is only one patent at issue. The "related applications" field of that patent should list all related patent applications that precede it (parents and grandparents of the patent), but* not *patent applications that follow it (children of the patent). In Chapter 9, we'll explore the BlackBerry litigation, where the patentee held nine patents with a combined total of 2,000 claims!*

Post-Prosecution Activity

Congratulations! You've made it through the prosecution process, hopefully with a patent that contains valuable claims. Beware, though, there are several post-prosecution activities (not including litigation) that can still affect your patent. It's unlikely that your company's patents will be subject to any of these, but here is a snapshot explanation of some post-prosecution possibilities:

- **Interferences.** An interference is a costly, complex Patent Office (PTO) proceeding to determine who will get a patent when two or more applicants are claiming the same invention. In other words, it is a method of sorting out priority of inventorship. During an interference, the PTO determines which inventor first reduced the invention to practice.

- **Reissue applications.** A reissue application is an attempt to correct information in an issued patent. It is usually filed when a patent owner believes the claims are not broad enough, the claims are too broad (the applicant discovered a new prior art reference), or there are significant errors in the specification. In these cases, an attempt is made to correct the patent by filing an application to have the original patent reissued at any time during its term. The reissue patent will take the place of the original patent and expire the same time as the original patent would have expired. If the purpose is to broaden the claims of the patent through a reissue application, the applicant must do so within two years from the date the original patent issued. There is a risk in filing a reissue application, because all of the claims of the original patent will be examined and can be rejected.

- **Double Patenting.** If a patent is issued and the patent owner files a second application containing the same invention ("double patenting"), the second application will be rejected or, if the second application resulted in a patent, that patent will be invalidated. What does it mean when two applications contain the same invention? It means either that the two inventions are literally the same or that the second invention is an obvious modification of the first invention. For example, an inventor applied for a patent on polymer dispersants used in motor oil to keep engines clean. A patent issued in 1989. A continuation application was filed incorporating similar, but slightly broader, claims. The Court of Appeals for the Federal Circuit ruled that the continuation application was invalid for double patenting because it was an obvious modification of the first application.

- **Reexamination.** The Patent Office may hold a formal proceeding in which it reexamines an in-force patent to determine whether newly cited prior art references adversely affect the validity of the patent. A patent may be reexamined any time while it is in force. The patent owner or anyone else may initiate the reexamination. The patent reexamination process can be useful to patent owners as well as alleged (or would-be) infringers.

Management and Tracking

Throughout the prosecution process, it's essential that all of the activity discussed above is tracked and documented. Managers track things and design reports to suit their individual needs. There are many possible ways to track patents. Below I've provided one useful spreadsheet, for a fictitious device known as "Wally Robot," a service robot prototype. The spreadsheet is different from a status report from your patent attorney, and with good reason: Attorneys think in terms of files and "matters"; managers think in terms of assets, projects, products, and services.

The "Title" is typically the patent application or patent title, and the attorney docket No. is the name of the attorney's file. These two fields are not all that helpful—the title of a patent for a new robot motor might be "linear actuator with low current actuation" and the attorney docket number might be "21714US.02"—but these fields are necessary in order to communicate effectively with the patent attorney regarding this particular patent subproject.

The next three fields are tailored to provide the manager with a quick reference regarding what a particular patent is really about. If the patent is for a particular product or project that has a name and/or number, the product or project code name might be "motor for the Wally Robot"; the Division might be "Consumer Robotics"; and the internal control number might be the project number, the P.O. number for the P.O. that authorized the attorney's work, your in-house attorney's reference number, or all of these. Keep the status block simple and meaningful: "pending," "issued on 10/21/97," "expires 8/16/2009," "live," "dead," and the like. Cost to date includes all the patenting costs in order to track the costs versus benefit of the patenting effort. The goal here is to be able to sort the spreadsheet and to provide meaningful reports for various projects.

Suppose the Wally Robot project report has four entries: the motor patent application was filed six years ago, it has still not issued, and the cost to date is $18,000. The other three entries reflect issued patents covering:

- the machine vision subsystem

Title	Attorney Docket No.	Product/ Project Code Name	Internal Control No(s).	Division	Status	Cost to date	Foreign Protection	Action Items	Notes
Optical Switch	AB64-US	Wally Robot IBX Switch	06-14	Optics	Filed 7/20/2006 issued	$16,325	-	-	
Linear Actuator	21714US.02	Wally Robot Track Motor	P07481	Mechanical	Filed 8/20/2001	$18,000	Filed in CA, JP, GE		
Robot Control Algorithm	WR82.1	Control Software	CS204	Computer Science	Filed 8/20/2005	$22,410	Foreign filing decision by 8/20/2006		
New Robot With Enhanced Functionality	XHB76	Wally Robot Functionality	WR6RS	System Integration/ Engineering	Filed	$64,210	Filed CA, JP, GE, FR		

Patent Tracking Worksheet

- the software that controls the robot, and
- the robot's overall functionality.

Robot sales are fair but not as well as expected. With this report, the patent application for the motor might be viewed as serving a rather minor role, given the other three already-issued patents covering much more important technologies. In such a case, the motor patent application might be dropped before additional costs are incurred.

The "Foreign Protection" field can include just a listing of countries where patent applications have been filed or a more comprehensive listing by country of costs, status, action items, deadlines, and the like. If the robot motor patent application has been filed in Japan and Europe, and the costs of those filings already exceed the $18,000 U.S. cost, the appropriate management decision might be to drop all the foreign filings as well.

The "Action Items" block lists those tasks management is responsible for: "decide by 10/21/2008 if foreign protection is desirable," "have engineering review the draft patent application," maintenance fees due 1/26/2008 and 1/26/2012. The "Notes" section is just that and can be filled in to serve management's needs as necessary: "Dropped due to minor coverage, lack of sufficient sales, and high costs"; "Important key patent for this project"; or "Licensed to XYZ company after lawsuit settlement."

As the patent portfolio grows, reports can be generated for each project or product.

Other fields of interest to individual managers can be added at will, but again the idea is to keep it simple—when a report like this gets longer than a page, it typically has too much data. The idea is to be able to quickly ascertain the state of patent protection for any given project or product, the costs, and the protection afforded.

Suppose the Wally Robot project is a complete failure. Management can quickly kill all the patents and patent applications for this project by calling the patent attorney and having in hand the Wally Robot project report. Or, suppose instead the Wally Robot project is an unqualified success. The project report shows there are only four patent filings. Should additional patent applications be filed? Should protection be sought in additional foreign countries? Is it too late? Is engineering just now working on an enhancement to the drive motor?

Keep it simple and tailor your reporting based on previous experiences, reviews of existing reports, and what management above and below you finds useful. Gillette reportedly filed 70 different patent applications for the Mach3 razor. The main patent litigated against Schick spawned 20 foreign patent applications. Can a report for this patent project be limited to a page? Probably not, unless the font used is extremely small. If I were a manager at Gillette, though, I'd want an easy way to periodically review how the patent project has progressed and what it is costing. Here's a made-up example of a report, which might help:

Mach3 Patent Project

Subject	US Patents	Foreign Patents	Cost to Date
Overall Razor	6	6	$ 384,000
Blade Configuration	8	2	220,000
Blade Materials	12	3	260,000
Blade Coatings	4	4	110,000
Handle	8	8	512,000
Guard	10	4	216,000
Cap	12	6	240,000
Lube Strip	8	1	415,000
Miscellaneous	2	2	102,000
TOTAL	70	36	$ 2,459,000

Irrespective of the reporting format you find most helpful, remember our objectives: obtaining patents of value and maximizing the budget. To accomplish that, you have to ensure the patent attorney's time is spent primarily on securing broad patent claims with a reasonable chance of being blessed by the Patent Office. You also have to be aware of the time constraints in patent land. You have to police any continuation contests. You have to wisely choose when and where to foreign file. And you have to track it all.

Sound daunting? It can be. Don't despair, though. After the completion of a few patent projects, most managers I know get it and then improve their skills while at the same time reducing the time "these damn patents" take up in their workweek.

The Worldwide Patent Party

The One-Year Rule: How It Affects Foreign Patent Filing.............................198

How Do You File Outside the U.S.?...199

Where and When Should You File? 201

Foreign Patent Budgeting: The Robot 206

    The Cheapest Route: No Foreign Filing...209

    The Most Flexible (and Potentially Economical) Route:
       The PCT Application...209

    The Less-Expensive Course: Direct Filing..210

The *Running Tab*: What a Typical U.S. and Foreign
    Filing Might Cost...211

RULE: *A patent is only enforceable within the nation in which it was issued.*

With some minor exceptions, if you own a U.S. patent, you can stop others from making, using, selling, importing, or offering your claimed invention for sale *only* within U.S. borders. The same is true if you have a patent in another country. If you have a patent for a product in the U.S. and Japan, for example, anyone can make and sell it anywhere *but* the U.S. and Japan. Again, we're talking generalities here, and your patent attorney will be happy to tell you about the exceptions.

> *"80% of patent value comes from 20% of a company's patents."*
>
> —PARETO'S LAW (RECAST)

Knowing this, you may think that broad international protection is a prerequisite for hot technology. That may be true for large multinational enterprises like Gillette, which sought patent protection in a lot of different countries for their Mach3 razor. But that approach won't work for every company. When you do a cost-benefit analysis for foreign patent protection, you may find that the cost of acquiring a foreign patent is not justified by the product's market potential. It's cost-prohibitive.

The One-Year Rule: How It Affects Foreign Patent Filing

(THE ONE YEAR) RULE: *In the U.S., you can file for a patent within one year of the first sale or public disclosure.*

RULE: *Outside the U.S., you can't file for a patent if there has been any public sale or disclosure … unless you file a PCT application at the right time.*

RULE: *Still, you can file a PCT application only if you filed a U.S. patent application before a public sale or disclosure.*

One rule I've discussed throughout this book is that you can't patent a product if it's been offered for sale, actually sold, or publicly disclosed ("in person," at a trade show, for example, or via a published paper or article) more than one year before a patent application is filed for the product. Stated another way, you have one year to file a patent application after a sale or disclosure event.

Unfortunately, this one year rule (or "one-year grace period" as it is sometimes called) doesn't apply if you want patent protection in foreign countries. The one-year grace period exists only in the U.S., as a favor to small businesses who often can't afford to run to the Patent Office for every new idea.

So, if you sell a product, you cannot later apply for foreign patent protection, with one important exception: You can file an application in the United States *before* the invention is sold or made public and then begin selling it. You then have one year to make use of the Patent Cooperation Treaty (PCT). With a PCT filing, your U.S. filing date will count as your date for foreign filings under that system. In other words, even though technically you have sold your product before filing for a patent in a foreign country, you will not be penalized, because under the PCT, your filing date in that country will be your U.S. filing date. The PCT is not mandatory; you can file in foreign countries without it. But it can be useful, as we'll see below.

How Do You File Outside the U.S.?

You can always file an individual patent application directly in any foreign nation's patent office by retaining a patent agent or patent attorney in that country. The primary rule, as stated above, is that you must do so before public disclosure or sale.

Alternatively, you can take the PCT route. The U.S. is a signatory nation to several international patent treaties, including the Paris Convention and the Patent Cooperation Treaty (PCT). (Most industrialized nations in the world are members of both.)

As an alternative to filing directly in foreign countries, you can file a PCT application within one year of the U.S. patent's filing date.

That entitles you to subsequently seek patent protection in any Paris Convention country (known as "Convention Countries"), and your company's application in the Convention country will be entitled to the filing date of the inventor's earliest U.S. application.

The PCT application:

- allows you to sell or disclose the product immediately after the U.S. patent is filed without losing foreign patent rights
- permits you to obtain an early filing date that is good in every member country in which you are seeking patent protection
- provides an initial international patent search by a government entity, usually by the U.S. Patent Office or the European Patent Office—and some PCT member countries will rely heavily on this search, and
- is initially prosecuted in one patent office (typically the U.S. Patent Office); foreign countries often give credence to that patent office's findings, which can lower the foreign prosecution costs when the PCT is filed in foreign countries.

But don't get the impression that the PCT is a "worldwide" patent application. It isn't. In fact, there is no such thing. Think of a PCT as accepting an invitation to a worldwide patent party at which you haven't yet arrived.

After filing the PCT application, your company must eventually attend the party and file separate "national" applications in each country (or group of countries) where you want coverage. This means retaining a foreign patent agent in that country and usually involves translation of the patent application into the member nation's language.

If your company is interested in filing for a patent in European countries, it's a good idea to use the European Patent Office (EPO). The EPO grants "Europatents" that are good in all member countries. A company can make one patent filing in the EPO, and if a Europatent is issued, the patent is automatically valid in each member country of the EPC that is designated in the inventor's application, provided that the inventor registers, files translations, appoints an agent in each country, and pays the necessary registration fees in each country.

There is an additional advantage for filing at the EPO. The European Patent Convention is considered the same as a single country (a jurisdiction) under the Paris Convention and the PCT. Therefore, a U.S. inventor can file at the EPO, and the effective filing date will be the same as the inventor's original U.S. filing date.

Filing in the EPO is very expensive and requires payment of an annuity or tax to the EPO each year the inventor's application is on file there, until the Europatent issues. If the inventor registers the patent in any EPC member country, the inventor must then pay annuities in that country for the life of the patent.

Keep in mind, though, just as the PCT doesn't equal a worldwide patent, an EPO filing isn't really a "European Patent." There's a European patent *application,* but it costs money to register that application, once granted, in each of the Western European countries.

First to File/First to Invent

One other factor to keep in mind about foreign filing is that in other nations, the patent office gives priority to the first person to file for an invention. In the U.S., priority is given to the first to invent—not the first to file.

Again, that's why we keep good records of the invention events in the U.S. But, don't be led to believe that, in foreign countries, someone can patent someone else's idea. For example, if you have a product you sell in Japan but don't have the budget to obtain a patent there, no Japanese-based company could "patent your product."

Where and When Should You File?

CAVEAT: *Consider the implications on foreign filing before your company makes any public sale or disclosure.*

The decision when and where to file for foreign patents requires that you guess the potential income from the patented products in different countries, and it also requires considering a lot of other factors, listed below. One thing is clear: Don't procrastinate. And before your company makes any public sale or disclosure, consider the implications for foreign filings.

Few, if any, companies file for both U.S. and foreign patents for *all* inventions. In some cases, patents are filed all over the world; for other inventions, only U.S. patent protection is sought; and for still other products, a U.S. patent application is filed as are patents in Japan and Western Europe. As but one example, the Gillette three-bladed razor patent was filed in 20 countries, but the Toro soil aerator patent was filed only in eight countries.

Some companies have standing marching orders regarding where to always foreign file. A common scenario is filing in Canada, the EPO countries, and Japan. Such marching orders make it easy to manage the where to file decision, but it's always a good idea to question the marching orders from time to time, especially in situations where they don't make sense. Good patent management includes not necessarily following the lemming in front of you off a cliff.

When making a marketability-per-nation analysis, your patent committee needs to ask the questions listed below. Although these questions require some degree of speculation, it is possible to acquire sufficient economic data about the trade potential, business climate, and demographics in foreign countries to make an educated guess about filing for a patent.

The discussion about foreign patents often starts with questions in areas such as:

- **Current sales potential.** In which countries will there be the greatest immediate market share? Would you be able to sell your invention in the target nation today? Without sales potential, there may be no reason to seek patent protection.
- **Future market.** Do you expect a possible future market for the invention within the next 10 to 15 years? Even if the current market is weak, it may be worth pursuing a patent if a future market is expected.
- **Local partner.** Are there possibilities of finding a partner to license to or create a joint venture with in order to market the

invention in the nation? The chances for successfully exploiting an invention usually increase when a local partner is involved.

- **Competition.** Do you have competitors in a foreign country, and do you need a patent to prevent them from copying your product? What is the status of competitors in this nation? The presence of competitors can be interpreted in different ways. It may indicate a healthy, substantial market with room for more competition. On the other hand, lack of competitors, particularly in an emerging technology, may prove to be a positive sign. On yet another hand, a major competitor, particularly one that has dominated the market for five to ten years, could prove difficult to challenge. Are there countries in which the product is most likely to be manufactured by a competitor but primarily exported elsewhere?

- **Production costs.** Can the invention be cost-efficiently produced in this nation? Although inventions can always be imported, it may be more cost-efficient (or even necessary in some cases) to produce an invention within the nation.

- **Day-to-day operations.** Do you have the means to observe and administer the market in this country? If you must control day-to-day operations from a distance, you will have a more difficult time making a success of the market, especially if your resources are limited.

- **Ability to sue patent infringers.** How difficult is it to sue an infringer in this country? Having a patent doesn't automatically stop an infringer; you must go after the infringer in the nation where the patent was granted. This is one of the drawbacks of foreign patent protection: There is no international method to stop patent infringers. You must sue in each country where an infringement has occurred.

- **Sales and distribution.** What channels exist for getting the invention to market? Even if an invention has sales potential, you will need a way to distribute the product to buyers. The lack of strong distribution channels is a disincentive to seeking a foreign patent.

- **Marketing.** How hard will it be to gain exposure to the market? Will it be possible to reach a substantial numbers of buyers through advertising, direct marketing, or other means? The more difficult it is to reach buyers, the lower your chances for success.
- **Obstacles to sales.** Are there any impediments to selling in this market? You may need to determine if there are regulatory rules (for example, safety standards for medical devices) or trade or union rules that will affect your ability to sell in a nation.
- **Licensee.** Do you have a licensee who would be willing to pay the cost of foreign filing in exchange for royalties abroad?
- **The claim game (again).** Do the claims of a particular patent really roadblock potential competitors? Is this a low value patent? If so, perhaps it shouldn't be filed in every country possible.

Research Resources for Assessing Foreign Patent Potential

To help you research commercial potential in foreign markets, consult the following resources:

- **EUBusiness** (www.eubusiness.com). EUBusiness is a reliable source of information for facts and statistics on EU economy and specific industries.
- **European Patent Office** (www.european-patent-office.org/online). The EPO provides links to patent licensing exchanges, mailing lists, patent information providers, registered European patent agents, law offices, and patent offices for member states.
- **National Trade Data Bank** (http://iserve.wtca.org/portal/index.jsp). This data bank is a fee-based site (you must pay to use it) that provides detailed statistical information on trade in specific products. Print copies of the National Trade Data Bank are sometimes available in large urban public libraries and university libraries.
- **The Federation of International Trade Associations** (FITA) (www.fita.org/ webindex/index.html). FITA has many international business and trade links, leads, statistics, and other helpful information.
- **The U.S. Commercial Service** (www.ita.doc.gov/cs). This service offers free online Country Commercial Guides that analyze categories of industry and trade for each nation. The site also provides Customized Market Analysis Reports— one of the most thorough means of determining the market for your product within a nation. Although expensive (ranging from $2,000 to $4,000 per country), these reports answer a wide range of questions about the likelihood of commercial success. (For a listing of the questions answered by each report and the cost per nation, access the site.)
- **The U.S. Department of Commerce** (DOC) (www.doc.gov) and the **U.S. Small Business Administration** (SBA) (www.sbaonline.sba.gov). Both of these government resources are interested in helping the sales of U.S. goods overseas. If an inventor has a good track record and the possibility of actually placing a product in the market (or already has a product and is seeking to market it overseas), the DOC and SBA offer assistance.
- **The World Trade Centers Association** (http://iserve.wtca.org/portal/index.jsp). The WTCA provides an international trade data bank online.
- **VIBES** (Virtual International Business and Economic Sources) (http://library. uncc.edu/vibes/). VIBES provides over 1,600 links to international business and economic sources, including statistical tables and research articles.

Foreign Patent Budgeting: The Robot

Suppose your company is preparing to market a new robot. Since we now know about the rules for patenting both in the U.S and abroad, let's explore the budgetary considerations. Assume the timeline shown below for the patent project.

Before the first robot was sold or offered for sale, a U.S. patent application was filed. Good. That's a necessity if foreign patents are desired. Then, within a year after that, a Patent Cooperation Treaty (PCT) patent application was filed designating numerous foreign countries. Eighteen months after that, a European Union (EPO) patent application was filed for patents in the U.K., France, and Germany; a Japanese patent application was filed; and a Canadian patent application was filed.

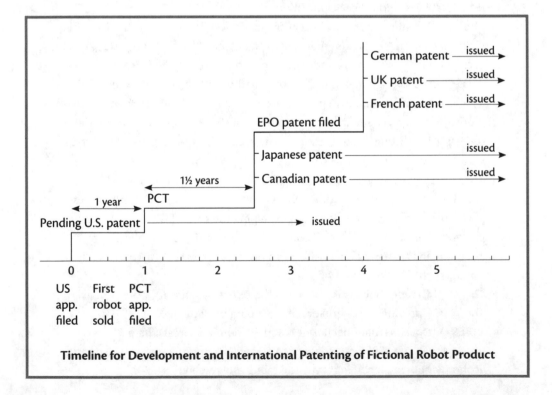

Timeline for Development and International Patenting of Fictional Robot Product

All these separate patent applications are prosecuted in their respective countries' Patent Offices. At the end of the day, we have six patents protecting the robot in six different countries. Managers need to know not only the total cost but also how to budget for these costs. Here is a table which provides examples of patenting costs.

Activity	Event	Expense	When Incurred
US patenting effort	filing	$10,000–20,000	upon US filing
	prosecution	$5,000–10,000	within years 2–3 after US filing
	issuance	$1,000–2,000	within years 3–4 after US filing
PCT	filing	$3,000–5,000	one year after US filing
	prosecution	$5,000–10,000	within 1–1½ years after PCT filing
Japan	filing	$8,000–10,000	1½ years after PCT filing
	prosecution	$5,000–10,000	within 2–3 years after Japan filing
	issuance	$1,500–2,500	3–4 years after Japan filing
Canada	filing	$2,000–3,000	1½ years after PCT filing
	prosecution	$3,000–5,000	within 2–3 years after Canada filing
	issuance	$600–1,000	3–4 years after Canada filing
EPO	filing	$8,000–10,000	1½ years after PCT filing
	prosecution	$5,000–8,000	within 3–4 years after EPO filing
	grant	$2,000–4,000	within 4 or more years after EPO filing
UK	filing (registration)	$1,000–2,000	soon after EPO grant
Germany	filing (registration)	$3,000–5,000	soon after EPO grant
France	filing (registration)	$3,000–5,000	soon after EPO grant
	Total	$66,000–113,000	

You can see the bad news: U.S. patents are expensive; foreign patents are outrageously expensive.

Surprisingly, a new patent application is not actually prepared for filing in Japan, Europe, or Canada. Instead, the U.S. patent application is just refiled, after a translation if required. So, what you are paying for here? It's everyone's cut in the foreign patenting effort:

- the U.S. patent attorney who takes charge of the foreign filing effort (5-10% or less of the total)
- the foreign patent attorneys who charge for the work they have to do in order to obtain patent pending status in their respective countries, including a translation if necessary (25-30%)
- the foreign patent office's fees, which are usually quite higher than the those of the U.S. (15-25%), and
- the separate prosecution effort in each foreign country (35-40%).

We can now lay to rest the myth that there is some kind of "worldwide" patent. There is no such thing, as the above chart and cost table make clear. Globalization has rendered some of the laws and rules concerning patents more harmonious, but it has yet to produce a patent system that extends across national borders.

Now for some good news. Although foreign patents are expensive, a lot of the expense is not incurred for some time. Hopefully, before the real heavy costs are incurred, you will have ascertained whether it's beneficial to incur them. Using the above table, let's look more closely at the budget now on a timeline.

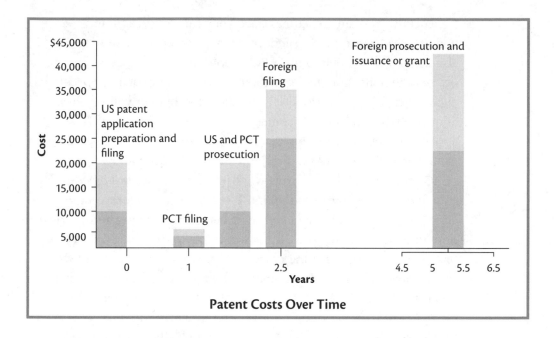

Patent Costs Over Time

Here are three routes to take for foreign filing.

The Cheapest Route: No Foreign Filing

Let's assume the budget for a given patent project is limited. One default decision might be to forgo foreign filing altogether. And, as you now know, if the invention was made public before a U.S. application was filed or it's now more than a year after the U.S. application was filed, the decision has been made for us: There can be no foreign filing. That's not very good patent management, however.

The Most Flexible (and Potentially Economical) Route: The PCT Application

The worst possible scenario is it's now a few years after the U.S. application was filed, it looks like the U.S. patent will have high value (many broad claims have been allowed by the Patent Office examiner), the product protected by the patent is selling well, and the overseas market looks good—but it's now impossible to file foreign patent applications. *Now the budget would support foreign filings*, but it's too late.

Luckily, you can sometimes have your cake and eat it, too. At the end of Year 1 after a U.S. patent filing, it costs somewhere between about $3,000 to $5,000 to file a PCT application and preserve the right, but not the obligation, to file the expensive foreign patent applications eighteen months later. Hopefully, by then, the budget will be easier to analyze. In other words, sometimes it's worth filing the PCT application and then waiting the 18 months to determine whether you should actually embark on filings in various foreign nations.

Of course, it doesn't always work out this nicely. Start-ups, for example, may be forced to file in the United States before venture capitalists or other investors will fund them. Engineering and product development then takes a year or two. By now, the PCT application has been filed and it's at the point in time where we're only a few months away from the deadline for filing the expensive foreign patent applications. Money is running out, a second round of financing hasn't been secured, the product is not yet on the market, and the U.S. Patent Office has yet to rule on the viability of the claims in our U.S. patent application. At that point the decision becomes much harder, and more of a gamble.

The Less-Expensive Course: Direct Filing

I said that it was relatively flexible and economical to file a PCT patent application. As you can see from the discussion above, that's true. But a PCT patent application doesn't really save you any money. In fact, it ultimately costs *more* to file a PCT application than if your company had filed individual foreign patent applications and bypassed the PCT. But those initial filings are expensive ($3,000 to $10,000 depending on the country). So, if you are confident of your need for foreign patent rights and your company is financially prepared for the initial costs, the direct route would be the least expensive.

The *Running Tab*: What a Typical U.S. and Foreign Filing Might Cost

Let's say you have reviewed the data and determine that your company will file patents in Japan, Canada, and Australia one year after the U.S. application. You would rather take the PCT route because you can spread expenses and decision making over a longer period of time. The projected cots at the one-year mark as shown in the following tables:

PCT Route		
	Activity	**Expense**
Now	PCT Filing	$3,000 to $5,000
Within 18 months	PCT Prosecution	$5,000 to $10,000
At 18 months	Japanese patent filing	$8,000 to $10,000
At 18 months	Canadian patent filing	$2,000 to $3,000
At 18 months	Australian patent filing	$3,000 to $5,000
	Total	$21,000 to $33,000

Non-PCT (Direct) Route		
	Activity	**Expense**
Now	Japanese filing	$8,000 to $10,000
	Canadian filing	$3,000 to $5,000
	Australian filing	$3,000 to $5,000
	Total	$14,000 to $20,000

As you can see, the non-PCT route or direct route is less expensive, but you incur $14,000–20,000 in costs *now,* at one year after filing the U.S. patent application, instead of only $3,000–5,000 via the PCT route. That, combined with the benefit (sometimes) of PCT prosecution, leads many companies to choose the PCT route. But at least now you know that PCT does not equal a patent—or even less expensive patent protection.

Live and Let Die: The Exhausting Effects of Patent Litigation

The Battle Over the BlackBerry 216

The Claim Game: Part Three 218

The BlackBerry: From Application to Trial 220

The BlackBerry: Judgment and Reexamination 222

Post-Trial: The Never-ending Story 223

    First Appeal and a Bogus Settlement 225

    Final Appeal and Settlement..226

    Unfair Results?..227

What Did NTP Do Right? 230

What Did RIM Do Wrong? 231

Common Lessons for All Litigation 231

What to Expect in Patent Litigation......................................232

Before We Begin ...

In this chapter I discuss a famous case involving well-heeled opponents fighting over a world-famous technology. But don't assume that the complexity of this case is unique to high profile patent cases. As I write this chapter, I'm involved in a new patent infringement case that involves at least the following initial questions:

- Does a provisional patent application adequately disclose the invention claimed in the utility patent in the lawsuit?
- What is the effective date of a patent filing, because the patent in this lawsuit is the result of a "continuation-in-part application"?
- Is a theory of "joint infringement" of a method claim viable?
- Is the patent obvious based on prior patents?
- Did the allegedly infringing activity occur more than one year before the patent application was filed?
- Is a reexamination by the Patent Office possible, and will the result help my client?
- Is a stay of the litigation pending reexamination possible? And advantageous?
- Is the patent infringed?
- Do previous opinions provided to my client protect my client from treble damages? Do they protect my client from an award requiring my client to pay the other side's attorney fees?
- Is it less expensive to take a license than to litigate?
- Does it make business sense to just stop the alleged infringing activity rather than incur the high cost of litigation?
- Does the patent owner have the resources to take the case all the way through to a trial and appeal?
- Does my client have the resources to take the case to a trial and appeal?

This patent lawsuit was just filed, and already these numerous issues require extensive research. Some of the legal issues raised have yet to be decided by a court.

I expect the number of issues to at least triple. And as you can see, it doesn't take long before patent litigation becomes very, very expensive.

As a general rule, if your patents are *never* litigated, they probably aren't serving their purpose. In other words, if no one dares to copy your patented technology, chances are that it has little value. In the business world, imitation of your patents is the greatest form of flattery—at least economic flattery. Infringement means that you have something worth stealing.

There are some exceptions to this rule. Sometimes there is no need to litigate, because competitors simply stay away from a patent-protected product. And some patents are held just so a company has trading cards to play in case *the company* is sued for patent infringement. The basic deal goes something like this: Company A with patent X sues company B for infringing patent X. Company B then offers up its patent Y to company A. If a deal is struck, the settlement results in company A receiving rights to company B's patent Y and company B receiving rights to company's A's patent X. Other times, investors simply demand patents, any patents. In the dotcom era, the mantra was "Get some IP!" ("IP" meaning intellectual property, that is, patents, copyrights, trademarks, or trade secrets). The resulting "IP" was often worthless, especially when the company filed a "napkin provisional" (slang for a hastily prepared provisional patent application). And we know what happened to most dotcom companies.

> *"I knew that a country without a Patent Office and good patent laws was just a crab, and couldn't travel any way but sideways and backways."*
>
> —MARK TWAIN, "A CONNECTICUT YANKEE IN KING ARTHUR'S COURT"

Inevitably, though, there will likely be litigation. If it is your company doing the suing, the value proposition should be: Is it worth the cost and uncertainty of the suit just to make our competitor stop selling its infringing product? Your goal is an injunction. You can analyze whether you can realistically hope for a large royalty, increased damages (due to willful infringement), and a court order requiring that the infringer pay your attorneys fees, but in very few cases should you bank on such rewards.

The cost-benefit analysis is often difficult, because it's hard to find any predictability in patent litigation. As one court put it, "Patent cases turn peculiarly on a conceptually dense dynamic between physical objects, words in claims, and principles of law."

You already know a little about patent litigation from the cases peppered throughout the previous chapters. You know, for example, that the primary focus of patent litigation is the claims, of course, which can be construed in ways that favor the patent owner (Gillette) or the alleged infringer (Toro). The claims, once construed, can be subjected to a validity attack, like in the Amazon case. Some patents, because of low value claims, aren't litigated when a competitor enters the market with a competing product, as discussed with reference to the X-it case study. Some claims, if litigated, don't survive because of missed patent deadlines, as outlined in the New Railhead case.

But what really happens in patent litigation? Why does it cost millions? Let's review the particulars of a case that received widespread media attention.

The Battle Over the BlackBerry

The public rarely gets worked up about an intellectual property lawsuit, unless that lawsuit may deprive people of something they hold dear. For example, when movie studios threatened to take away their Betamax VCRs in the 1970s, the public outcry resulted in Congressional hearings and a change in the way copyright law is interpreted.

The public became equally incensed several years ago, when a patent lawsuit was filed by NTP, a company that owned wireless communication patents, against RIM, the makers of the BlackBerry device. As the litigation proceeded over the next few years, the public—a sizeable portion of which had become addicted to BlackBerry devices (hence their nickname "CrackBerry")—decried the court rulings that seemed to foreshadow the disappearance of their precious handheld devices.

At one point it even became a matter of national security: The Department of Justice intervened to warn the court that disabling the BlackBerry service would be detrimental to the public, because federal employees and even members of Congress regularly use the BlackBerry service, especially in times of public emergencies.

BlackBerry

National safety fears aside—the country and the BlackBerry managed to survive this patent imbroglio—the BlackBerry case illustrated many of the typical twists and turns of typical patent litigation. As with many highprofile cases, there had been several false reports of settlement. The Patent Office, as often happens in high stakes patent litigation, took a second look at the underlying patents. That second look prompted more rulings as courts adjudicated as to whether the Patent Office reevaluations should have an effect on the pending litigation.

Some novel issues also arose. Was there, for example, any way that certain activities conducted outside of the United States could be subject to the litigation? In another twist, a court issued an important decision regarding a distinguishing difference between method or process and apparatus or system patents. Eventually, the case offered a hard and painful lesson for the BlackBerry manufacturer, and it provided a general lesson for all companies: There are serious consequences for not adequately investigating a patent threat.

Let's take a closer look at what really happened in the BlackBerry patent infringement litigation. We'll focus on two potential worst-case scenarios that existed when the case was filed:

- The BlackBerry system could have been permanently shut down.
- The patents at issue could have been rendered invalid by the Patent Office.

The Claim Game: Part Three

Before looking into the history of the BlackBerry infringement, let's digress for a moment to consider patent claims. As you now know, technically, patents are not really infringed; it's the patent claims that are infringed. These final words in the patent—the claims are literally the "last words" in every patent—define the invention in hybrid legal and technical language. If an accused infringer's product meets the requirements in a set of patent claims, patent infringement has been established. Conversely, if all the requirements in a claim can be shown to be met by a previous idea—something that existed before the patent was filed—the claim is invalid.

I've talked about playing the claim game in two instances: when you review a patent (Chapter 4), and when you prosecute a patent (Chapter 6). In patent litigation, the game is played once more, this time by a judge and jury.

A judge must construe the words of the claim to determine what they mean and cover. Claim construction is an arduous task. Federal judges at the trial court level get it wrong, at least in the view of the appellate court, 50% of the time.

When viewed from a judge or jury's perspective, the factors discussed earlier—clarity of claim language, broad versus narrow wording, claim prosecution history (the give-and-take at the Patent Office between the applicant and patent examiner), choice of method versus system claims, and relationship between independent and dependent claims—all come into play.

Typically, the claim game is played in two parts in a trial for patent litigation. First, the judge construes the language of the claims. That is, the judge reviews and interprets any ambiguous language or terminology that could have multiple meanings. For example, based on the claim below, the judge in the BlackBerry case construed the following terms: "electronic mail system," "gateway switch," "originating processor," and "originated information."

Sometimes, if the parties have so elected, the judge also determines whether infringement has occurred. Normally, however, one or both of the parties elect to have a jury trial. (Yes, to the chagrin of many businesspeople, juries normally decide whether a patent is infringed.)

Here is a claim from one NTP patent. (Note, "RF" refers to radio frequency.)

> 1. A system for transmitting originated information from one of a plurality of originating processors in an electronic mail system to at least one of a plurality of destination processors in the electronic mail system comprising:
>> at least one gateway switch in the electronic mail system, one of the
>>> at least one gateway switch receiving the originated information and storing the originated information prior to transmission of the originated information to the at least one of the plurality of destination processors;
>> a RF information transmission network for transmitting the originated
>>> information to at least one RF receiver which transfers the originated information to the at least one of the plurality of destination processors;
>> at least one interface switch, one of the at least one interface switch
>>> connecting at least one of the at least one gateway switch to the RF information transmission network and transmitting the originated information received from the gateway switch to the RF information transmission network; and wherein
>> the originated information is transmitted to the one interface switch by
>>> the one gateway switch in response to an address of the one interface switch added to the originated information at the one of the plurality of originating processors or by the electronic mail system and the originated information is transmitted from the one interface switch to the RF information transmission network with an address of the at least one of the plurality of destination processors to receive the originated information added at the originating processor, or by either the electronic mail system or the one interface switch; and
>> the electronic mail system transmits other originated information from
>>> one of the plurality of originating processors in the electronic mail

system to at least one of the plurality of destination processors in the electronic mail system through a wireline without transmission using the RF information transmission network.

One challenge in playing the claim game with the BlackBerry litigation was that some of NTP's patent claims are phrased as "system" type claims, like the claim above covering the various components of a wireless email system (components such as a gateway switch and a radio frequency transmission network), while other patent claims are of the "method" type, covering the various steps associated with running a wireless email system. We'll see that this distinction added some complexity to the decision and resulted in a partial reversal. And it became even more complicated when an appeals court played the claim game and sent the case back to trial a second time because of the initial judge's incorrect interpretation of three claims.

Much of the expense, as we'll see, might have been avoided had the owners of the BlackBerry played the claim game themselves before disregarding a cease-and-desist letter from the patent owner.

The BlackBerry: From Application to Trial

In 1991, 164,306 patent applications were filed with the United States Patent and Trademark office. One of these applications—filed on May 20, 1991—was by Thomas Campana, Jr., who filed a patent application for his idea to merge existing email systems with radio frequency wireless communication networks. That way, he noted in his application, you could receive emails when out of the office and without the necessity of a computer connected to a telephone line.

The Patent Office granted Mr. Campana's first patent on July 25, 1995, and ultimately that one patent spawned eight more. (If you're not aware of how that happens, it's done by playing the "continuation contest," which is explained in Chapter 7.)

In 1999, four years after his patent issued, the Canadian company Research in Motion (RIM) released a wireless handheld product known as the BlackBerry. Previously, RIM had primarily been a pager company, but that all changed with the introduction of their new product line. The BlackBerry had the usual bells and whistles associated with a combined mobile phone and personal digital assistant (PDA)—for example, address book, calendar, to-do lists—but it also had a unique email feature that allowed users to access email over wireless networks.

The BlackBerry became one of those disruptive technologies that changed the marketplace. As its subscriber base increased from two million users in 2004 to six million in 2006, obsessive use of the device's keyboard even gave birth to a new type of repetitive stress injury nicknamed "BlackBerry Thumb." RIM quickly became a market leader in handheld wireless email devices via its BlackBerry line of products and the successful deals it struck with various wireless carriers.

Thomas Campana, Jr., was an electrical engineer inventor and entrepreneur. Coincidentally, the first company he founded, ESA Telecon Systems, Inc., was a contract engineering business supplying gear to pager companies. In 1992, he and his patent attorney formed NTP, Inc. to patent and license Campana's inventions. Campana's patents were put in NTP's name and investors were brought in to cover the costs of any potential litigation expenses.

NTP knew what it had. As you now know, a company needs to infringe only a single patent claim in order to lose a patent lawsuit. Campana's combined patents had over 2,000 such claims! On January 27, 2000, in a letter by NTP, RIM was placed on notice regarding six of the Campana patents and offered a license. Charles Meyer, RIM's in-house attorney, discussed the NTP patents with his staff and quickly (perhaps too quickly, it later turned out) concluded there was no infringement.

When RIM then refused to take a license, NTP filed suit in Richmond, Virginia's federal district court. On this court's "rocket docket"—the fast track for patent lawsuits—things moved quickly: The suit was filed in November of 2001 and, despite numerous motions filed by RIM (most of which failed), a jury was impaneled within a year.

After a 13-day trial, RIM was found liable for infringing 14 claims represented in five NTP patents. The presiding judge, James Spencer, said the case was "not even close." Even before the jury verdict, Judge Spencer had summarily ruled that RIM infringed four patent claims spread across three NTP patents.

The BlackBerry: Judgment and Reexamination

A patent owner who wins at trial can obtain several legal remedies for infringement. The owner can:
- recover compensatory damages
- obtain a court order preventing further infringing activity
- halt importation of infringing devices, and
- in exceptional cases, recover triple damages and attorney fees.

NTP was awarded compensatory damages totaling $34.4 million. Surprisingly, that amount was not the worst possible outcome. What RIM feared was a court-ordered injunction that would essentially shut down RIM's BlackBerry system. An injunction did issue, was held in abeyance, but was then dissolved—but not for the reason you might think.

To stave off the possibility of an injunction, RIM filed requests for reexamination of NTP's patents with the Patent Office. Reexamination basically means the Patent Office, after once granting the patent (subsequent to the inevitable Office Action/response cycle), reviews its earlier decision and determines if granting the patent was the wrong result.

In other words, just having a patent is not the end game: The patent can always be challenged in litigation and also at the Patent Office.

At the same time, RIM also moved for a new trial, filed an appeal, and moved to stay all of these proceedings pending the Patent Office's second look at the NTP patents during the reexamination process. In other words, RIM wanted to put all the decision making on hold until the Patent Office completed its reexamination of the patents. The Patent Office will take a second look at most patents (the Patent Office reviews 90% of the patents proposed for reexamination) but rarely strikes down all of the patent claims (the Patent Office only does so in 12% of reexaminations). So the odds were not in RIM's favor at the reexamination.

If the $34.4 million awarded to NTP was for compensatory damages, you may be wondering what exactly was NTP being compensated for?

The answer: lost profits.

A patent owner can recover money from the defendant for lost profits. When determining lost profits as damages in a patent infringement case, two questions are asked:

- How many of the infringer's historical sales would not have been made absent the infringing feature or invention?
- How many of those sales would have been made by the patent owner if the infringer had not been competing in the marketplace?

Of course, as you know, NTP did not sell any products. So how could it have lost so many millions in sales? A patent owner can also recover damages for infringement as a royalty based on what the patent owner would have obtained from a licensed sale of the defendant's device. For example, a court might examine what royalties the patent owner would have received if it had licensed the defendant's sale of the infringing device. That was the case in the BlackBerry litigation.

(Note: A patent owner is not entitled to the defendant's profits resulting from infringement (although the owner of a design patent can recover the defendant's profits).)

Post-Trial: The Never-ending Story

NTP's motion for a new trial was unsuccessful, as was its request to stay an injunction pending reexamination, but, luckily for RIM, the appeal was reason enough to hold off on implementing the injunction until Judge Spencer's rulings and the jury verdict could be reviewed by the Federal Circuit. That wouldn't be decided for some time. So, meanwhile, RIM went to work on damage control. The company was especially concerned that the judge, in a subsequent ruling, would find willful infringement. If so, the $34.4 million judgment could be tripled and RIM could also be required to pay NTP's attorney fees.

RIM would have committed willful infringement if it knew of NTP's patents and deliberately infringed them. Often, when a company obtains a noninfringement and/or invalidity opinion by a lawyer before proceeding with product sales, the resulting activity is not considered willful infringement. (Conversely, the Federal Circuit has ruled that the *absence* of an opinion of counsel is not, by itself, determinative of willful infringement.)

So, RIM first attempted to convince Judge Spencer that it had a good faith belief it didn't infringe the NTP patents. Based on the non-infringement conclusions of RIM's in-house attorney, Charles Meyer, RIM argued the infringement couldn't be willful and thus enhanced damages were not proper.

Unfortunately for RIM, Judge Spencer found Mr. Meyer's opinions incompetent as they were conclusory, based on insufficient information, and lacking in objectivity given the fact he worked for RIM. Judge Spencer also found RIM's behavior during litigation to be egregious. Despite these rulings, Judge Spencer did not award treble damages, because RIM didn't know about NTP's patents when it developed the BlackBerry system. Instead, Judge Spencer "enhanced" the damages—that is, he increased them to a total award of $47 million. He also awarded attorney fees, making RIM's total bill from the court approximately $53 million.

Before awarding the attorney fees ($5.25 million), Judge Spencer had to find that the fees were reasonable, and he also had to find the case "exceptional." The case was exceptional, according to the judge, given RIM's limited investigation after receiving NTP's notice letter and RIM's litigation behavior. But, since NTP filed suit initially claiming infringement of eight patents having a combined total of over 2,400 claims and then later asserted only five of those patents and sixteen claims against RIM at trial, the judge cut 20% of NTP's legal bill, for a total of $4.2 million. The Judge ruled that NTP's legal fees were reasonable when he showed that RIM's attorney fees in *a single quarter* of the litigation amounted to $4.9 million. The total award? Over $51 million. Still, the biggest threat to RIM was an injunction halting use of the BlackBerry system.

First Appeal and a Bogus Settlement

Now all that was left were RIM's appeal and perhaps settlement. The injunction issued against RIM was held in abeyance pending the appeal. Unless the judgment was reversed on appeal (or the parties settled), RIM could face the odd possibility that the patents would be invalidated but that RIM still couldn't sell the BlackBerry. This could be the result if the injunction was instituted first and then, later, the Patent Office's reexamination of NTP's patents resulted in the patent claims being held invalid. The best RIM could then hope for would be a new trial, but courts are very reluctant to grant new trials.

RIM filed its appeal on August 29, 2003, and on December 14, 2004, the Federal Circuit issued its first decision. A three-judge panel of the Federal Circuit sided with NTP.

RIM then moved for a rehearing and also pursued settlement negotiations with NTP via mediation in front of a magistrate judge. In March of 2005, RIM boldly announced a settlement whereby RIM would pay NTP $450 million. As a result of this announcement, RIM's stock purportedly jumped $14 per share.

NTP, however, declared there was in fact no settlement. In response, RIM asked the Federal Circuit to stay the appeal and to have Judge Spencer decide this latest dispute regarding whether there really had been a settlement. In briefing on that issue, NTP asserted that RIM, once again, was simply attempting to avoid facing the consequences of infringing NTP's patents. The Federal Circuit refused RIM's request and ultimately, in November of 2005, Judge Spencer ruled there was in fact no settlement between NTP and RIM. The injunction was now still very much a threat—much more important than the damages RIM would have to pay NTP.

Final Appeal and Settlement

In a further twist, the Federal Circuit agreed to a rehearing of its earlier decision and issued a second decision in August of 2005. The result was a fairly complex decision that reflected the effect of U.S. patents and international law. The issue was the fact that although BlackBerry devices are sold in the United States, RIM and its relay station for sending email wirelessly are both located in Canada. U.S. patents like NTP's do not reach most activities conducted outside of the United States (see Chapter 8 for more on the boundaries of international patent law) and, moreover, NTP's patents only covered complete systems and methods for wireless email, not the BlackBerry device itself, which is only a component of the system.

The problem was made more complex because some of NTP's patent claims are phrased as "system" type claims, covering the various components of a wireless email system (components such as a gateway switch and a radio frequency transmission network), while other patent claims are of the "method" type, covering the various steps associated with running a wireless email system.

Instead of listing components, method claims list steps, reciting action verbs like "transmitting." Many patents have both method and system claims—the Amazon "one-click" patent discussed in Chapter 4 is a good example.

The Federal Circuit held that RIM put NTP's patented *system* into use in the United States even though its relay is located in Canada, but RIM did not use NTP's patented *method*, because utilization of the relay does not occur in the United States.

Because patent infringement occurs when an infringing product is imported into the United States or sold in the United States, what happens if the invention is a method? How do you import or sell a method? Difficult question. Also, when the method is carried out beyond the borders of the United States and delivered to a product shipped into the United States, can there be patent infringement? Does moving data and information across the borders constitute the importation of a product under the patent laws?

The end result was that RIM didn't infringe NTP's six *method* type claims but did infringe seven NTP *system* type patent claims. The Federal Circuit also remanded the case back to Judge Spencer to determine if three other NTP system-type claims were infringed by RIM, given Judge Spencer's incorrect interpretation of them.

No bonus points if you can guess what RIM did next: It appealed this decision to the United States Supreme Court. Although the Supreme Court turns down most patent cases, RIM again moved to place the litigation on hold. By now, the Patent Office had initially rejected some of NTP's patent claims in the early stages of the re-examination process. At this point, the Justice Department was on RIM's side: It asked Judge Spencer to hold off on a final ruling, because an injunction against the BlackBerry service could adversely impact public safely. These final motions for a stay were again denied and then, on January 23, 2006, the Supreme Court turned down RIM's appeal.

In March 2006, RIM and NTP settled. RIM would pay NTP $612.5 million.

Unfair Results?

Why did RIM pay NTP over 10 times more than the final judgment? The payment was for the future rights to license the technology and thereby avoid a permanent injunction (an action that would have put the company out of business). In the next chapter I'll discuss how these licenses work.

Even at this point after settlement, there was still the possibility that the Patent Office could strike down all of NTP's patent claims and that decision could be upheld after the inevitable appeals by NTP. Or, if NTP sued someone else, say one of RIM's competitors, that party could successfully invalidate NTP's patent claims.

The last two results would produce an interesting outcome which, on first blush, might not seem too fair. RIM tried to invalidate NTP's patents and failed. As a result, RIM was forced to pay NTP $612.5 million to avoid an injunction.

Suppose NTP's patents are later eradicated, either in court or by the Patent Office, and NTP loses all appeals regarding those decisions. Even then, it's highly unlikely RIM would get its money back.

How can that be: that a company's product can be found to infringe a patent, sales of the product prohibited, and the company ordered to pay damages, and then, later, the patent is cancelled?

The answer lies in a quirk, not really in patent law so much, but in civil law in general: Trial courts do not determine if a patent claim is really valid. Instead, the challenger in court must prove by clear and convincing evidence that the claim, presumed by law to be valid, is in fact invalid. If the challenger cannot meet that evidentiary standard, the court then finds simply that the challenger failed to meet its burden.

The patent claim is not found "valid"; it's found "not invalid."

And that is what happened to RIM. RIM attempted to convince both Judge Spencer and the Federal Circuit that NTP's patent claims were invalid and failed in its efforts. That was their only shot.

Later, someone else can challenge a patent previously found "not invalid" in another court, and the result might be different. Or a company can challenge the worrisome patent at the Patent Office (as did RIM) via the reexamination procedure. At the Patent Office, there is no presumption the patent is valid and the Patent Office either allows a patent claim to stand as is, allows a claim after some modification, or refuses to allow one or more claims.

In a case where a patent is reexamined out of existence by the Patent Office (a fairly rare occurrence), a company previously found to have infringed that patent would have to go back to court and ask for a new trial in order to determine if the infringing product—previously enjoined—could now be sold. But courts have fairly wide latitude in deciding whether or not to grant a new trial on that basis.

So, to continue to be able to market RIM's BlackBerry system, RIM had to pay. If NTP's patent claims were all later stricken, then, anyone *but RIM* could offer a BlackBerry-type service without fear of infringing NTP's patents or having to pay.

Fair? Probably not.

5/20/1991	Thomas Campana files his first patent application for a wireless email system
1992	NTP formed
7/25/1995	Campana's first patent issues
1/27/2001	NTP notifies RIM regarding infringement of six NTP patents
11/2001	NTP sues RIM
8/2002	Judge Spenser construes NTP's patent claims
	Judge Spencer summarily rules RIM infringes four of NTP's patent claims
11/14/2002	The jury rules in favor of NTP
1/2003	The Patent Office announces it will reexamine the NTP patents
5/23/2003	RIM moves for a new trial—denied by Judge Spencer, who then enhances the damages the jury awarded NTP
6/23/2003	Judge Spencer rules regarding NTP's attorneys' fees, which must be paid by RIM
8/5/2003	The injunction issued against RIM is stayed pending appeal
8/29/2003	RIM files its appeal
12/14/2004	The Federal Appeals court issues its first decision, largely in favor of NTP
3/16/2005	RIM announces a $612.5M settlement with NTP
6/2005	Campana dies of cancer
8/2/2005	The Appeals Court issues its second decision, again largely in favor of NTP

A Timeline of the Blackberry Litigation

It is also probably a little unfair that Mr. Campana was deemed a "patent troll"—a derogatory term indicating someone who sues for patent infringement but who does not make or sell any products using the patented technology. Even worse, Mr. Campana never saw the fruits of his efforts, because he died of cancer two months before the first appeal was filed.

In the litigation, millions were spent on attorneys and probably more than a few trees destroyed in the numerous motions filed by both parties. Judge Spencer keeps a "docket report" in his court and, in the BlackBerry litigation, there were 426 separate entries. In late 2005, Judge Spencer reportedly said, "I intend to move swiftly on this [case]. I've spent enough of my life and my time on NTP and RIM." In a word, patent infringement battles can be exhausting. Even for a judge.

What Did NTP Do Right?

Let's start by looking at what NTP, the victor in this battle, did right:

- **NTP had lots of patents and lots of patent claims.** That provided NTP with numerous fallback positions in the face of RIM's challenges to NTP's patents both on the infringement and invalidity fronts.
- **NTP had both system- and method-type claims.** When, on appeal, the method claims failed NTP, the system claims picked up the slack.
- **NTP picked a court that moved things along quickly.** Small companies can generally react better and faster under tighter deadlines than a large company.

NTP also had a little luck: Just after RIM settled with NTP, the U.S. Supreme Court ruled in a different case that injunctions were no longer automatic in cases where patent infringement is found. Had that ruling occurred earlier, RIM may have been in a better position to assert that the BlackBerry product could stay on the market despite the fact that it infringed NTP's patents.

What Did RIM Do Wrong?

Let's consider three things that RIM did incorrectly:

- **RIM didn't take NTP's patents seriously.** As I mentioned earlier, a knee-jerk reaction that a patent is "crazy" or "ludicrous" doesn't make the problem go away.
- **RIM asked for reexamination too late in the game.** As you can see, the timing for reexamination is crucial to the litigation, and RIM waited too long before seeking reexamination of NTP's patents.
- **RIM should have attempted serious settlement earlier.** Waiting so long to settle, and announcing settlement when there wasn't one, set back RIM's bargaining position.

Common Lessons for All Litigation

This case highlights certain aspects common to all patent infringement lawsuits. These general truisms are as follows:

- **Litigation is expensive.** NTP spent over $5 million and RIM spent a lot more than that in a case which only lasted a year.
- **Patent infringement lawsuits are risky for both sides.** The patent owner's patent, for example, can be subjected to invalidity defenses both in court and at the Patent Office.
- **It's not over till it's over.** The losing side can appeal and appeal again. Indeed, since the Federal Circuit reviews a trial judge's claim construction without according the trial judge any deference, there is almost no reason (except for the cost) not to appeal a loss, irrespective of which side you're on. The appellate court, by some reports, reverses the trial judge almost 50% of the time when claim construction is at issue.
- **The heart of a patent infringement case is claim construction—an inexact science.** Predicting the outcome of many lawsuits is very difficult when you consider the inexactitude associated with judicial claims construction and then couple that with the other internal conflicts in patent law. Exactly how the claims of the patent will be construed cannot always be predicted with great accuracy.

- **Litigation exacts a powerful emotional toll.** Consider the 426 docket entries in the BlackBerry case. Even if only half of those docket entries involved briefing by the parties, that means each side filed over 100 briefs in a single year. Numerous hearings were held. If you were the manager overseeing this lawsuit, your workload would have been severe and the emotional toll heavy. Some personalities simply aren't built for adversarial litigation. If one of your key witnesses, an inventor listed on the patent, for example, is introverted, has trouble conversing, or is just plain wishy-washy, expect trouble at the trial when your opponent's attorney subjects this witness to cross-examination. I once had a case involving the president of a small business who, although a very nice man, came across like a used car salesman whenever he was asked a direct question. He wasn't really shifty, but he *looked* shifty—and that definitely hurt our case.

Obviously, if a competitor is infringing one of your patents, there may be no other way to protect your market share and investment absent litigation. If you are willing to litigate, as least make sure the potential return is worth the effort and uncertainty.

What to Expect in Patent Litigation

Based on history, you should not bank on a large judgment or an early settlement. It's true that, like all litigation, the vast majority of patent cases settle before trial. But it would be unwise to budget for an early settlement. Sometimes when you grab a tiger by the tail, it will not let go.

What you should expect is a large expense and a lot of time. Here's just a short list of options available to a defendant in a patent infringement lawsuit aside from asserting the patent isn't infringed. The defendant can:

- Try and transfer the case to a different court.
- Reexamine the patent.
- Allege that the patent is invalid for numerous reasons.
- File motions regarding numerous aspects of discovery, no matter how remotely relevant to the core issues in the dispute.
- Seek protective orders.

- Move for summary judgment.
- Ask for reconsideration of each of the court's rulings.
- File counterclaims.
- Assert jurisdictional defenses.
- Move to exclude your evidence.

The list goes on and on, and each time the defendant exercises one of these options, that's a distinct battle in the war, usually involving briefing for the court by both sides and court hearings on the briefing. Patent litigators even argue in court about the other side's briefing. There can be a motion, a reply to the motion, a reply to the reply, and so on. In a single year, the BlackBerry litigation involved over 400 docket entries—that's 400 different documents prepared by the attorneys and filed with the court.

The result for management is twofold: large time and money expenditures (expect to pay a few million in attorney fees, according to one survey). Keep in mind that there will be many instances where you or your employees will be asked to devote significant time to a particular aspect of the case.

Also, action items in patent litigation must often be rushed because of strict deadlines. Patent litigation heats up, cools down, and then heats up again in a seemingly never-ending cycle. Worse, *you* will have strict deadlines, but the judge will not. Some judges, like Judge Spencer, will move a case along fairly quickly; others don't.

It is not uncommon, for instance, for a court to delay ruling on a key issue on a case for months or more. I've had cases where a court waited over a year to rule on a key issue once it was briefed by the parties. Appeals can be terribly slow: Although the trial judge in the BlackBerry case moved everything along pretty fast, the Federal Circuit took over a year to issue its first ruling.

If it is your company that is being sued, the options are to fight, settle, or change. If you fight, you can choose a full-scale war with many battles, or simply pick a single battle and roll the dice. If you settle, that might mean your product being taken off the market (and perhaps a payment of damages), or the payment of a royalty for each product sold via a license deal. If you change, that typically means playing the claim game with the competitor's patent and removing some feature or component your product claimed in the patent.

In the main, patent litigation, and even the threat of patent litigation, should be taken very seriously. It's all too easy to simply say, "Let's sue them" or, conversely, "Ignore them—their patent is invalid." The claim game has to be played, the likelihood of success determined, the budget laid out, and the contingencies accounted for. Document what you hope to achieve, and make sure the litigation attorneys agree that goal is indeed achievable. Also, strive to keep the goal in mind during the various battles throughout the course of the war.

In-house and outside counsel typically manage the litigation itself but the engineering manager, at the least, needs to be aware of the big picture, set the goals to be achieved, and track the progress of the case to see if management's objectives are being served.

In the next chapter on licensing, I'll talk about how licenses and patent settlements work together.

Caveat Emptor: Buying and Licensing Patents

Determining Patent Value...237

Do You *Really* Need the Patent?...239

Is This a Blocking Patent?..241

Getting Around the Blocking Patent: Buying the
Patented Product Instead of Acquiring a License....................................242

Will You Get Sued?...243

Assignment or License?...244

Licensing a Patent...247

Exclusivity...249

Royalties...249

Option to License...250

License Terms...250

What Happens If Problems Develop With a Licensed Patent?..............255

Buying a Patent..256

I n the last chapter, I explained that RIM, the maker of the BlackBerry, was ordered by a court to pay $53 million to NTP, the patent owner. Yet the case eventually settled for $612.5 million.

The additional $559.5 million payment was for a license that permitted RIM to continue using the patented technology in BlackBerry devices. The license fee headed off a court-ordered injunction—a situation that could have doomed the BlackBerry device.

> *"The only thing that keeps us alive is our brilliance. The only way to protect our brilliance is patents."*
>
> —DR. EDWIN LAND, INVENTOR OF THE POLAROID INSTANT CAMERA

When a company, without relinquishing ownership, permits someone to use patented technology, it's referred to as a license. In return for granting the license, the owner of the patent receives compensation, usually in the form of periodic payments known as royalties.

Most patent licenses are made without any litigation; they're voluntary—for example, Company A negotiates with Company B (or a university or government lab) for the right to use a patented technology. But some licenses, like that in the BlackBerry case, are spurred on by the intimidating prospect of litigation or an injunction. These "coerced" arrangements enable the parties to "legitimize" behavior that had previously been illegal.

In a license, the patent holder (the "licensor") retains ownership, while another company (the "licensee") rents the patent rights for a period of time. Some companies prefer not to rent, but to sell the patent outright. This is accomplished by executing a document known as an assignment, and in that case, the buyer stands in the shoes of the previous patent owner and can exercise all of the same rights. The buyer now owns the patent.

Whether by license or assignment, patent transfers raise questions within a company. For example, how does your company decide if a license is *really* needed? And when should you buy a patent outright versus license it? Generally, management's responsibility in any patent transfer is to decide four things:

- **What's being transferred?** The management team must play the claim game in order to determine what patent (or patents) are needed and whether there is any additional technology—for example, a patent application filing or know-how—also required. Know-how is knowledge that may not be patentable (or protectible as a trade secret) but that enables the accomplishment of a task.
- **The type of transfer.** Will your company seek an assignment, exclusive license, or nonexclusive license?
- **How much is it worth?** Both sides in the transfer must sift through numerous financial choices—for example, will your company pay a lump sum for all rights or an ongoing royalty for a license? If it's a royalty, will it include a guaranteed minimum annual payment, and will the royalty be based on sales per unit or based on a revenue marker?
- **How long?** If you're licensing the technology, how long should the license last? You don't want to pay for too long a period, and you don't want to have to renegotiate after a short period if the product is a hit.

There's no reason for a manager to deal with all of the legal and financial terms—much of the decision making is generally left to attorneys and CFOs—but the manager plays an essential part in assisting the decision makers. This chapter will help familiarize you with the terms and principles of patent transfers.

Determining Patent Value

RULE: *The key aspect of any patent license is valuation of the patent being licensed.*

At the heart of the patent acquisition equation is patent value. How much do you pay for a patent? When do you pay it? And what are you paying for?

Unfortunately, determining a patent's value is the subject of a separate book. In fact, several books have been written on the subject of patent value, and several patent analytics—methods for valuating intellectual property—have even been patented. Patent value is also a subject of interest for investment funds that choose to invest in companies whose patent portfolios may be undervalued.

Most experts agree, though, that determining patent value isn't something you can measure objectively. One patent analytic, for example, examines how many later patents reference the patent being valued. Such an analytic may uncover a blocking patent, described later in this chapter, but it also—since the strength of the claims are not analyzed—might not.

Like picking stocks or race horses, the ability to value patents is part science and part wishful thinking. Although there are no surefire methods of predicting patent value, there are some factors that can help you ballpark the worth of a patent. The key factors are:

- **How broad are the claims?** The claim game is played to make sure an assignment or license is really needed, that the patent covers the product you expect to sell, and that the patent covers predictable competitive products.

- **Does this patent decrease our R&D expenditures?** No patent will eliminate your total R&D costs, but sometimes buying or licensing someone else's patent rights is akin to buying their R&D, which might be less expensive than incurring your own R&D costs. Understand, though, that rarely do patents provide sufficient detail to enable you to manufacture a product.

- **Fame of the patent and/or patent owner.** Sometimes there is a marketing or sales value connected with the "bragging rights" in a given patent.

- **How much life is left on the patent?** As you know, patents expire. A patent with 12 years more life is generally more valuable than a patent with only two years left.

- **Is there a blocking patent?** A blocking patent prevents the manufacture of a product even if a license is taken for other patents covering the product. (I discuss blocking patents later in this chapter.) If you are licensing an improvement patent and there is a blocking patent, you might need to license the blocking patent as well. That would lower the value of the improvement patent. Remember the ladder example when we played the claim game? The first basic ladder patent was a blocking patent to the second step-ladder patent. Conversely, if you are licensing the blocking patent, there could be improvement patents that might prevent you from optimizing the product.

- **Is there more than one patent?** A 2005 study by University of Pennsylvania Law School professors found that individual patents, on average, are worth nothing. "The real value of patents lies not in their individual significance, but instead in their aggregation into a patent portfolio." The rights to a "family" of patents—perhaps due to continuations, divisionals, and continuations-in-part (see Chapter 7)—could be more valuable than the rights to just one patent.

- **Are their foreign patents?** As explained in Chapter 8, a U.S. patent cannot be used to thwart competitors in foreign countries. An acquisition involving patents in many foreign countries may be more valuable than a single U.S. patent.

- **Does anyone else already have a license?** Depending on the length and breadth of any existing licenses, that may lower (or in some cases, raise) the value of the patent to your company.

- **When is your product expected to generate a profit?** If a patent has only a few years left, or if a patent owner is seeking large upfront licensing fees, then the timing of your product's profitability will affect the patent's value. For example, if your product doesn't sell well, you essentially paid a royalty for products that were never sold.

Do You *Really* Need the Patent?

Imagine that you've come across a patent "of interest" either because a competitor sent it to your company, it was discovered in a patent search, it is generally known in the industry, it's listed on a competitor's product, or it was discussed at an industry conference or in a paper. Should you try to buy the patent? Do you need a license?

We'll see below that these questions are sometimes answered by playing the claim game.

Understand also that there are numerous reasons for taking a license to a patent even though the patent is not infringed (or you believe it is invalid)—including of course, cases where the license fees cost less than litigation. Patent trolls have this down to a science, and even sophisticated companies regularly take licenses rather than incur the costs and uncertainty associated with litigation. Sometimes, the royalty *isn't even tied to the allegedly infringing products*. Instead, the royalty is some small fraction (.01%) of a company's total revenue each year. In other instances, a license for a patent is paid for just to prevent a competing product from entering the market.

Here's an example of how the claim game comes into play when determining whether you need a patent license. Suppose you sell a well regarded product with components A, B, and C but hold no patent. Now suppose someone else patents the combination A, B, C, and D. It might be worth quite a lot to ensure that the patent doesn't come into the hands of a competitor, even if you have no plans to modify your product to include component D. Still, proper management involves at least knowing whether there is a case for infringement before purchasing or signing up for a license. If the patent claim requires elements A, B, C, and D, can we still sell a viable product if we just leave out component D?

Always start with the principle that if your product won't infringe the claims, there is no need to pay for the rights to the patent. Then, ask whether there is an easy design-around of the patent claims that was not explored. Is there a "second best alternative" for the product that doesn't infringe but is still commercially viable?

The worst scenario imaginable would be that your company pays for patent rights and none of your competitors incur that cost because selling a competing product doesn't infringe the claims of the patent licensed.

A value proposition for the potential license should be documented and discussed—for example, if we license this patent, we too can use aerogel in our deep sea oil well piping without fear of a lawsuit by the patent owner.

Is This a Blocking Patent?

Another factor in determining whether or not to acquire patent rights is whether the patent at issue is a "blocking" patent. A blocking patent is a patent that would block the manufacture of a product even if a license is taken for other patents covering the product. For example, let's say you had a patent for a bicycle. Somebody else had the patent for the wheel. You could not manufacture the wheel as part of your bicycle. The wheel is a blocking patent. (You can however, buy wheels manufactured by the patent owner, as discussed below).

Here's another example: Suppose you want to sell a product made up of components A, B, C, and D. You license a patent with a claim reciting A, B, C, and D. A blocking patent with a claim reciting just A, B, and C, however, would prevent you from selling your product.

Here's a made-up case where a so-called "blocking patent" turned out to be a good thing. An inventor comes up with a nifty idea for a simple disposable device that aids nurses during the placement of a catheter in a patient—a procedure performed many times a day in most major hospitals. A patent search is conducted and lo and behold, the concept is disclosed and claimed in two patents, both listing the same woman as the sole inventor. That seemed weird to the inventor, because he knew the industry fairly well and had never seen such a product in the marketplace. From the cover page of the patents, a search is made to see if the patents had ever been licensed or assigned. The answer was no. A check is made to see if the patents had ever been litigated. Again, no. The inventor? Nothing could be found in public searches.

The decision was then made to take a chance and call her.

Turns out she was a nurse in a distant state. She conceived of the product six years ago but didn't have the time, energy, or wherewithal to move beyond patenting to either have the product manufactured herself or to seek out licensees of the patents. The patents just sat there. And now, ten years later, she is more than willing to entertain the notion of selling the patents to recoup her patenting and maintenance fee costs. For less than the cost of procuring two patents on his own, the inventor purchased the two patents broadly covering his idea and more—and yes, the inventor played the claim game.

Getting Around the Blocking Patent: Buying the Patented Product Instead of Acquiring a License

As a response to a blocking patent, it's sometimes more appropriate to buy the patented *product* from the patent owner or one of her licensees and receive the implied license (see "Putting the Wheels On, The Implied License Solution," below), rather than manufacture the product yourself and incur the license fees.

Putting the Wheels On: The Implied License Solution

I mentioned how the owner of a bicycle patent was stymied, unable to manufacture wheels for his bike because the wheel patent is held by another company. Let's assume you own the bicycle patent. Although you can't manufacture the wheel without permission, you *can* buy the wheels directly from the patent owner (or someone licensed by the patent owner). That's because under patent law, when you purchase a product from a patent owner, you have an implied license to use or sell that product. So if you buy wheels, you can use them as a component for your bicycle without asking for permission.

As you can imagine, if that rule of implied licenses were not true, the high tech world would indeed be messy. Consider a popular electronic device like the iPod. In the iPod, the Apple Computer Company includes a processor likely protected by numerous patents and also other various individual electronic chips protected by patents owned by a variety of different firms. Because Apple purchases the microprocessor and the chips either from the patent owners or their authorized licensees, Apple need not license all of those patents.

Apple, in turn, has patents for the iPod covering inventive methods of combining all those electronic circuits in new ways. If you were to purchase iPods and incorporate them in your patented sound amplification systems, you would not need to license the iPod patents from Apple.

Sometimes your company won't have the ability to buy a patented product and incorporate it. That's the case with "patent trolls": companies that hold patents but do not make products or provide services. Instead, patent trolls always demand licenses.

Assuming the potential buyer has the capability of manufacturing the product, the calculation is: Does the cost of their product exceed our cost to make and sell their product plus the license fees? If you can manufacture and sell the product for the same amount as it would cost to buy their product or more, then the decision is to buy. If you can make and sell the product for *less* than it would cost to buy theirs by an amount less than the license fees, then the decision is to license. Don't forget, though, that the patent owner understands this calculation as well and can jockey around the license fees to get a result the patent owner desires.

Other times, companies decide to buy patented products rather than license, or license rather than buy patented products, because they are embroiled in litigation and seeking a settlement that will keep the business operating efficiently.

Another factor involved in the decision is the viability of the supply source in the case where the decision is to buy the product instead of license. A company I knew once decided to enter a new field in the medical arena involving x-ray equipment. A patent search revealed fundamental dominant patents concerning a key component of the equipment. The patent owner sold the key component and had licensed two other companies the right to manufacture and sell it. Analysts were called in to run the computations concerning the license or buy decision. The key consideration? It was not what you might think. This company was in it for the long haul and worried that the sellers of the key component might not be able to supply it in sufficient quantity for a sufficient length of time. Still, the key is knowing that a decision may be required in some situations.

Will You Get Sued?

Another factor in deciding whether to acquire patent rights is a pragmatic one. If someone demands a license, claiming that you are infringing, do you need a license if you know that the owner is bluffing? What if you feel that your company can outspend the other party if a lawsuit is filed? This sometimes-dangerous approach generally breaks down into predicting these factors:

- **Does the patent owner really have the resources to sue you if you do not take a license?** Has the patent owner sued before? The patent owner's history of suing others might help—but be careful here, as the patent owner could assign or license the patent to someone who could have the resources to sue you.
- **What's the cost of litigation?** If your company is embroiled in a court battle—that is, you are actually in a courtroom arguing over the patent—you should budget a minimum of one to three million dollars.
- **Who will prevail in litigation?** The claim game gives us guidance and provides us with the best-guess estimate. But remember that claim construction is an inexact science. If the decision is *not* to take a license, it's probably best to engage outside counsel to document the noninfringement and/or invalidity opinion.

This examination isn't academic. We learned in the previous chapter how the manufacturers of the BlackBerry wireless email transmitters incurred over $5 million in extra damages by failing to have outside counsel render an opinion regarding the allegedly infringing patents.

Sometimes, the decision involves issues of relative power. If a company is facing a possible injunction, for example, and has customer orders that must be filled, there is no choice but to take a license. Often, it doesn't really matter who is right and who is wrong. A small business that simply cannot incur the cost of litigation may have to take a license from a large company that has the resources to litigate, even though the patent or patents in question aren't infringed by the small business and/or are invalid.

Assignment or License?

CAVEAT: *The conditions and obligations of an agreement, not the title, determine whether it is an assignment or a license.*

I've discussed some factors that affect patent transfers and acquisitions—for example, how to assess patent value and patent worth. Now, let's examine the relative values and strengths of patent assignments and licenses.

Keep in mind that even though they have different legal meanings, the terms "assignment," and "license," are sometimes used interchangeably. In fact, these two types of agreements can sometimes have the exact same effect. This is true in the case of an unlimited exclusive license, in which a licensee obtains the sole right to market the invention for an unlimited period of time. Since in this situation the licensor is not retaining any rights that could be made the subject of another license, the license really has the same effect as an assignment.

In other cases, a patent owner may enter into an "assignment" stating that all rights revert to the seller if the buyer stops exploiting the patented technology. And some assignments, like licenses, provide for periodic royalty payments. Both of these provisions in an assignment—reversion and royalties—are more commonly associated with a license and demonstrate the overlap between the two transfers. For that reason, it's important to examine the specific conditions and obligations of each agreement rather than simply to rely on terms such as assignment and license.

In general, an assignment will cost your company more than an exclusive license which, in turn, will cost you more than a non-exclusive license. The reason an assignment costs more is that the patent owner is giving it all up at this point. Usually, the owner gets a lump sum payment at the time the agreement is made and nothing after that.

The exclusive license generally costs less than the assignment because the patent owner retains various ways to get the patent back: at the end of the exclusive term, for example, or if the licensee fails to pay the royalties due. The exclusive typically costs more than the nonexclusive because it gives the licensee "exclusive" rights to the technology and therefore prohibits any use by competitors. Sometimes there is no choice—for example, when it turns out the patent owner has already licensed the technology to someone else on a nonexclusive basis. At that point your only choice is a nonexclusive arrangement.

Sometimes, though, the decision is out of your hands. The patent owner may refuse to grant a license. In that case, the "buy or license" decision is simple: You'll have to buy.

One remaining consideration is money. An assignment requires a large upfront payment, or large periodic annual payments. A license generally requires periodic payments tied to sales. Here are some factors taken into account regarding whether to pay all at once or instead periodically via royalty payments:

- **Do you have a choice?** Sometimes, you simply are not offered a choice.
- **What are your probabilities of success?** In Chapter 3, we discussed the probabilities of successfully manufacturing a successful product and exploiting a given market. If these probabilities are high and based on well-reasoned assumptions, then if the price is right you may want to acquire all rights and pay it all at once up front.
- **What are the tax and accounting consequences?** There are different tax treatments between fully paid-up licenses or an assignment and yearly royalty payments.
- **Are there any administrative headaches and costs?** It takes time and money to monitor and work a license where periodic royalty payments are required. Also, one advantage of a fixed upfront price is that you don't have to report to the licensor or assignor your revenue and sales figures.
- **Do you want to avoid controversies?** If a royalty-based deal will be for, say, 10% of the profit of each product sold that infringes the patent, controversies could arise as to what the profit is and whether a product infringes. An upfront, fully paid-up license eliminates such controversies.
- **What is the basis for the royalty?** In the case of a license, is the patent owner seeking a royalty for our whole product or only for the relative value of a patented component in our product?

One final issue is, how much should the upfront payment be? The old saw that it's seven times the average yearly royalty income is about as reliable as the "standard" royalty of 12%. For the licensor, the upfront payment should be a high as possible; for the licensee, the upfront payment should be as low as possible. It's all a matter of bargaining position and patent value.

Licensing a Patent

A license is an agreement that allows someone else to use or sell patented technology for a limited period of time. In return, the patent owner receives either a one-time payment or continuing payments called royalties. These royalties can be based on revenue or units sold.

I've used the analogy that a license is like a lease, and the royalties are rental payments. A patent assignment, in contrast, is like buying the house outright. And, just as the owner of a rental property can reclaim possession if the tenant fails to pay, so can a patent owner reclaim possession of the rights under a license if the licensee fails to make royalty payments (or otherwise breaches the license agreement). In addition, some licenses are tied to milestones that the licensee must achieve (minimum yearly sales, for example), or else the license ends.

The great thing about licenses is their flexibility. A license agreement can be drafted according to the specific needs of the licensor or licensee. For example, the patent owner can exclusively license a patent to one company or grant several different companies nonexclusive licenses. It's possible to limit the license to only several claims of a patent, limit the license to only one or two defined products or a specific market, and/or grant a license for the full life of the patent or for only a few years of that life. Often multiple patents are included in a license—for example, as was done in the BlackBerry litigation.

The flowchart below illustrates the steps in the licensing process from the perspective of the patent owner. (This chart is from the Nolo book *Profit From Your Idea: How to Make Smart Licensing Decisions*, by Richard Stim.)

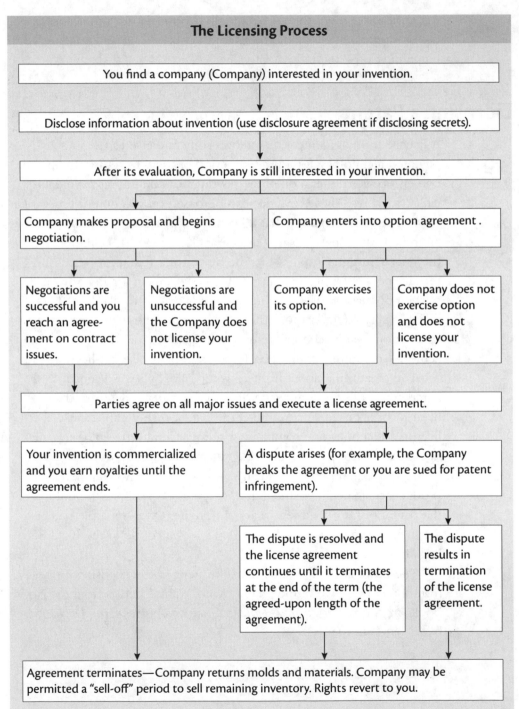

The Licensing Process

You find a company (Company) interested in your invention.

Disclose information about invention (use disclosure agreement if disclosing secrets).

After its evaluation, Company is still interested in your invention.

Company makes proposal and begins negotiation.

Company enters into option agreement .

Negotiations are successful and you reach an agreement on contract issues.

Negotiations are unsuccessful and the Company does not license your invention.

Company exercises its option.

Company does not exercise option and does not license your invention.

Parties agree on all major issues and execute a license agreement.

Your invention is commercialized and you earn royalties until the agreement ends.

A dispute arises (for example, the Company breaks the agreement or you are sued for patent infringement).

The dispute is resolved and the license agreement continues until it terminates at the end of the term (the agreed-upon length of the agreement).

The dispute results in termination of the license agreement.

Agreement terminates—Company returns molds and materials. Company may be permitted a "sell-off" period to sell remaining inventory. Rights revert to you.

Exclusivity

An exclusive license means that only the licensee has rights to the patent. For that reason, an exclusive license is favored by the licensee, who may have to pay more for the right to be the only authorized manufacturer and seller of a patented product protected by the patent claims. A nonexclusive license, on the other hand, means that multiple licenses may be granted to the same technology, and therefore any one licensee may have to compete with other licensees.

Royalties

I often get asked, "What is a reasonable royalty?" There are rough guidelines within each industry, but the final calculation depends on market forces and bargaining power. Keep in mind that the royalty percentage is only one factor in calculation of what is paid. For example, is the royalty based on gross sales revenue, retail price, per unit manufacture, and so on? What types of deductions can be made against the royalty? If, for example, your company negotiates the right to deduct marketing costs (rare) from revenue before determining royalties, that may be worth far more than a higher royalty number. The truth is, courts have awarded reasonable royalties ranging from less than 1% of the product's selling price to 20% of gross sales.

Another reason there is no such thing as a "standard" reasonable royalty is because no two licensing situations and no two patents are the same. Imaging Patent No. 1 claims the primary functionality of a new digital handheld device, and Patent No. 2 claims the specific configuration of the user interface for that device. If you seek to manufacture the device, you might pay a high royalty based on the selling price for Patent No. 1, but I bet you wouldn't want to pay a high royalty based on the selling price of the *complete* device for Patent No. 2.

Conversely, if you seek to manufacture only the user interface and sell that to a device manufacturer, you'd probably see no need at all for Patent No. 1 but might pay a fairly high royalty based on the selling price of the user interface for Patent No. 2.

Option to License

Sometimes a company is wary of entering directly into a license agreement and wants to investigate the technology and its marketing potential first. In this case, a company may take a more cautious route, signing an option agreement that grants the company an evaluation period—usually several months—after which the license must be signed or abandoned. Commonly, a nonrefundable fee is paid for the option rights.

License Terms

There is no need for you to familiarize yourself with the lingo and legalese found in most licensing agreements, but you should be aware of the basic terms that are negotiated. As a manager, your expertise may be required when evaluating offers or in the midst of negotiations. Although there is no standard form for a patent license— each license deal is distinct—it helps to use a standardized worksheet when compiling licensing deal points. To give you an idea of what a worksheet may look like, I've included one (also from *Profit From Your Idea: How to Make Smart Licensing Decisions)* that can be used to identify most of the major factors in a licensing agreement.

License Agreement Worksheet

Licensed Property

Patent No. _____

Patent Application Serial No. _____

Trade Secrets _____

_____

Trademarks _____

_____

Trademark Registration No(s). _____

_____

Licensed Products Definition

Industry (Have you limited the license to a particular industry?) _____

_____

Product (Have you limited the license to a particular product or products?)

_____

Territory

☐ Worldwide

☐ Countries _____

☐ Other _____

Exclusivity

☐ Exclusive

☐ Exclusive only as to these rights: _____

☐ Nonexclusive

License Agreement Worksheet

Rights Granted (check those rights granted to licensee)

☐ Sell

☐ Make or manufacture

☐ Distribute

☐ Use

☐ Revise

☐ Import

☐ Lease

☐ Right to improvements

☐ Advertise

☐ Promote

☐ Other rights _____

☐ Other rights _____

☐ Other rights _____

Rights Reserved

☐ All rights reserved (except those granted in license)

☐ No rights reserved

☐ Specific rights reserved

Have you signed any other licenses?   ☐ Yes   ☐ No

If so, do you need to reserve specific rights? ☐ Yes   ☐ No

Term

Have you agreed upon:

☐ A fixed term (How long? _____)

☐ A term limited by patent length

☐ Unlimited term until one party terminates

License Agreement Worksheet (continued)

☐ An initial term with renewals (see below)

☐ Other _____

Renewals

If you have agreed upon an initial term with renewals:

How many renewal periods? _____

How long is each renewal period? _____

What Triggers Renewal?

☐ Licensee must notify of intent to renew.

☐ Licensor must notify of intent to renew.

☐ Agreement renews automatically unless Licensee indicates it does not
want to renew.

Net Sales Deductions

What is the licensee permitted to deduct when calculating net sales?

☐ Quantity discounts

☐ Debts and uncollectibles

☐ Sales commissions

☐ Promotion and marketing costs

☐ Fees

☐ Freight and shipping

☐ Credits and returns

☐ Other _____

Is there a cap on the total amount of the deductions?   ☐ Yes   ☐ No

If so, how much? _____

License Agreement Worksheet (continued)

Royalty Rates

☐ Licensed products   _____%

☐ Combination products _____%

☐ Accessory products   _____%

☐ Per-use royalty _____%   or Usage standard _____

☐ Other products _____   _____%

☐ Other products _____   _____%

Do you have any sliding royalty rates? _____

Advances and Lump Sum Payments

☐ Advance $_____   Date due _____

☐ Lump sum payment(s) $_____   Date due _____

Guaranteed Minimum Annual Royalty (GMAR)

☐ GMAR $_____   Date due _____

☐ Does the GMAR carry forward credits?

☐ Does the GMAR carry forward deficiencies?

Audit Rights

No. of audits permitted per year _____

No. of days' notice _____

License Agreement Worksheet (continued)

> ### Things Change: Licensing in a World of Changing Technology
>
> Even if a license is taken, don't forget that technology evolves. An existing license may not be needed as the technology changes. The claim game must be played periodically during the life of a given license and during a product's lifecycle. Suppose that a patent claim covers elements A, B, C, and D and initially your product includes all these elements. Later in time, however, suppose the product evolved and now includes elements A, B, C, and E. That is, component D has been replaced with component E. The license may not be required anymore and no more royalty payments need be paid, because there is now no patent infringement. Be careful, though, to ensure that no one else has a patent with a claim for elements A, B, C, and E. Hopefully, it's your company if the technological evolution was managed correctly. Also, understand that a lot of litigation occurs after a license deal is made and surrounds the question of whether royalty payments are due for sales regarding a certain product. It's best, then, that a patent license clearly spell out what triggers a royalty payment.

What Happens If Problems Develop With a Licensed Patent?

What happens when the licensed patent faces trouble? Typically, the patent owner will guarantee payment of the required maintenance fees but not guarantee that the patent will adequately protect the licensee or be free from challenges.

Usually, if the patent is invalidated or limited by a court to no longer cover the licensee's product, the licensee need not make any further royalty payments. Previously paid royalties, however, are typically not returned or paid back.

Also, although many licensors would like to prevent their licensees from challenging the licensed patent, that is typically difficult to accomplish. In a recent case, a licensee challenged the very patent licensed and yet continued to make the royalty payments so the licensee wouldn't be subject to an injunction. The Supreme Court said that's okay. So now licensees can have their cake and eat it, too—if the licensee loses the challenge, there is no real downside. The licensee can challenge the patent, keep on selling the patented product while paying royalties, and either win (in which case no further royalties would be due) or lose (in which case the licensee just keeps on selling the product and paying royalties like before).

Finally, a typical licensor would not want to have to pick up the tab if the licensor or licensee is sued for infringing someone else's patent.

In a license, some of these considerations can be negotiated to lower the risks on the part of either the licensor or licensee. It's all a matter of bargaining power. If you desperately need a hot new patented technology offered by a university's technology licensing office, expect a license that greatly favors the university, not you.

Buying a Patent

RULE: *Buying a patent doesn't necessarily mean that you can sell the patented technology or a product incorporating it.*

There are two things to keep in mind regarding the purchase of patents:

- **The seller of the patent retains no rights to the patent.** In fact, the selling company would usually be considered an infringer if that company were to then sell a product covered by the patent claims.
- **The buyer of a patent is not really receiving the right to sell anything.** A patent only permits its owner to sue others for infringement. For example, suppose you invent the wheel and I invent the bicycle. If you patented your wheel, I can't manufacture your wheel to use on my bicycle without your permission ... even though I have a patent for my bicycle. You have what is known as a "blocking patent." And if I were to sell my bicycle patent, the new owner would have the same problem. The new owner

won't receive the right to manufacture the wheels for the bicycle—at least not until he licenses or buys the rights to use the wheel patent or any other patented technologies used in my bicycle. (Note: there is an exception to this rule; see "Putting the Wheels On: The Implied License Solution," above).

When purchasing a patent, your patent management team must research and analyze any other outstanding patents that affect your ability to sell your products based on the purchased patent. In the due diligence surrounding a patent transfer deal, then, any potential blocking patents are reviewed to properly place a value on the rights being acquired.

In summary, an implied license means that when you purchase a patented product, you can do with it what you will, within certain limitations. Repairing a product protected by a patent is generally allowed, for example, but refurbishing it may not be legal. The business of reselling and refurbishing products also drifts into trademark law. You should seek advice from your general counsel before advertising another company's name or logo in connection with the sale of your products.

When a patent is sold, the owner assigns his rights to the purchaser. An assignment, normally only a page or two in length, is the document executed between the parties to document the transaction. Usually, a patent assignment is very simple to accomplish once the price has been negotiated.

An assignment is usually "as is" unless the parties negotiate and document otherwise. This being the case, you must check to make sure the patent owner can really sell the patent and that it has a value commensurate with the selling price. And now that you own the patent, if you litigate it and a court or the Patent Office limits the scope of the claims or determines they are not valid, you will typically have no recourse against the seller (assignor). So you really need to do your homework regarding a patent to be assigned.

Too many companies spend too much time negotiating a patent assignment price tag and too little time evaluating the scope of what is being purchased. I once represented a buyer of a university-owned patent. The buyer and the university had agreed on a fairly high price. The buyer had not yet read the patent! It then turned out:

- The patent didn't really cover what the buyer wanted to manufacture
- Contrary to what the buyer thought, the patent didn't provide enough detail to manufacture a product
- The patent could not be asserted against U.S. Government contractors (the government had a royalty-free license to the university patent because the government funded the invention), and the government was my client's primary customer!

That meant my client's competitors could supply the product to the government without paying for the patent rights! Not really a very valuable patent, at least to my client.

Once the assignment is complete, it's a good idea to record the assignment with the Patent Office, and that's simple, too. Patent assignments are recorded, like real estate transactions, to protect you (the assignee) against later (improper) transfers by the patent owner.

Patent Glossary

abstract A concise, one-paragraph summary of the patent. It details the structure, nature, and purpose of the invention. The abstract is used by the Patent and Trademark Office and the public to quickly determine the gist of what is being disclosed.

actual damages (also known as compensatory damages) In a lawsuit, money awarded to one party to cover actual injury or economic loss. Actual damages are intended to put the injured party in the position he was in prior to the injury.

answer A written response to a complaint (the opening papers in a lawsuit) in which the defendant admits or denies the allegations and may provide a list of defenses.

best mode The inventor's principal and preferred method of embodying the invention.

Board of Appeals and Patent Interferences (BAPI) A tribunal of judges at the Patent and Trademark Office that hears appeals from final Office Actions.

complaint Papers filed with a court clerk by the plaintiff to initiate a lawsuit by setting out facts and legal claims (usually called causes of action).

compositions of matter Items such as chemical compositions, conglomerates, aggregates, or other chemically significant substances that are usually supplied in bulk (solid or particulate), liquid, or gaseous form.

conception The mental part of inventing, including how an invention is formulated or how a problem is solved.

confidentiality agreement (also known as a nondisclosure agreement or NDA) A contract in which one or both parties agree not to disclose certain information.

continuation application A new patent application that allows the applicant to re-present an invention and get a second or third bite at the apple. The applicant can file a new application (known as a "continuation") while the original (or "parent") application is still pending. A continuation application consists of the same invention, cross-referenced to the parent application and a set of claims. The applicant retains the filing date of the parent application for purposes of determining the relevancy of prior art.

Continuation-In-Part (CIP) This form of extension application is used when a portion or all of an earlier patent application is continued and new matter (not disclosed in the earlier application) is included. CIP applications are used when an applicant wants to present an improvement but is prevented from adding a pending application to it because of the prohibition against adding "new matter."

contributory infringement Occurs when a material component of a patented invention is sold with knowledge that the component is designed for an unauthorized use. This type of infringement cannot occur unless there is a direct infringement. In other words, it is not enough to sell infringing parts; those parts must be used in an infringing invention.

copyright The legal right to exclude others, for a limited time, from copying, selling, performing, displaying, or making derivative versions of a work of authorship such as a writing, music, or artwork.

counterclaim A legal claim usually asserted by the defendant against an opposing party, usually the plaintiff.

Court of Appeals for the Federal Circuit (CAFC) or the "Federal Circuit" The federal appeals court that specializes in patent appeals. If the Board of Appeals and Patent Interferences rejects an application appeal, an applicant can further appeal to the CAFC within 60 days of the decision. If the CAFC upholds the Patent and Trademark Office, the applicant can request the United States Supreme Court hear the case (although the Supreme Court rarely hears patent appeals).

date of invention The earliest of the following dates: (a) the date an inventor filed the patent application (provisional or regular); (b) the date an inventor can prove that the invention was built and tested in the U.S. or a country that is a member of North American Free Trade Association (NAFTA) or the World Trade Organization (WTO); or

(c) the date an inventor can prove that the invention was conceived in a NAFTA or WTO country, provided the inventor can also prove diligence in building and testing it or filing a patent application on it.

declaratory relief A request that the court sort out the rights and legal obligations of the parties in the midst of an actual controversy.

deposit date The date the Patent and Trademark Office receives a patent application.

deposition Oral or written testimony of a party or witness and given under oath.

design patent Covers the unique, ornamental, or visible shape or design of a nonnatural object.

divisional application A patent application used when an applicant wants to protect several inventions claimed in the original application. The official definition is "a later application for a distinct or independent invention, carved out of a pending application and disclosing and claiming only subject matter disclosed in the earlier or parent application" (MPEP 201.06). A divisional application is entitled to the filing date of the parent case for purposes of overcoming prior art. The divisional application must be filed while the parent is pending. A divisional application can be filed as a CPA.

Doctrine of Equivalents (DoE) A form of patent infringement that occurs when an invention performs substantially the same function in substantially the same manner and obtains the same result as the patented invention. A court analyzes each element of the patented invention separately. As a result of a Supreme Court decision, the DoE must be applied on an element-by-element basis to the claims.

double patenting When an applicant has obtained a patent and has filed a second application containing the same invention, the second application will be rejected. If the second application resulted in a patent, that patent will be invalidated. Two applications contain the same invention when the two inventions are literally the same or the second invention is an obvious modification of the first invention.

enhanced damages (treble damages) In exceptional infringement cases, financial damages may be increased, at the discretion of the court, up to triple the award for actual damages (known as "enhanced damages").

experimental use doctrine A rule excusing an inventor from the one-year bar provided that the alleged sale or public use was primarily for the purpose of perfecting or testing the invention.

file wrapper estoppel (or prosecution history estoppel) Affirmative defense used in patent infringement litigation that precludes the patent owner from asserting rights that were disclaimed during the patent application process. The term is derived from the fact that the official file in which a patent is contained at the Patent and Trademark Office is known as a "file wrapper." All statements, admissions, correspondence, or documentation relating to the invention are placed in the file wrapper. Estoppel means that a party is prevented from acting contrary to a former statement or action when someone else has relied to his detriment on the prior statement or action.

final Office Action The examiner's response to the applicant's first amendment, The final Office Action is supposed to end the prosecution stage, but a "final action" is rarely final.

first Office Action (sometimes called an "official letter" or "OA") Response from the patent examiner after the initial examination of the application. It is very rare that an application is allowed in the first Office Action. More often, the examiner rejects some or all of the claims.

first sale doctrine (also known as the exhaustion doctrine) Once a patented product (or product resulting from a patented process) is sold or licensed, the patent owner's rights are exhausted and the owner has no further rights as to the resale of that particular article.

indirect infringement Occurs either when someone is persuaded to make, use, or sell a patented invention without authorization (inducing infringement), or when a material component of a patented invention is sold with knowledge that the component is designed for an unauthorized use (contributory infringement). An indirect infringement cannot occur unless there is a direct infringement. In other words, it is not enough to sell infringing parts; those parts must be used in an infringing invention.

infringement An invention is infringing if it is a literal copy of a patented invention or if it performs substantially the same function in substantially the same manner and obtains the same result as the patented invention (see "Doctrine of Equivalents").

injunction A court order requiring that a party halt a particular activity. In the case of patent infringement, a court can order all infringing activity be halted at the end of a trial (a permanent injunction), or the patent owner can attempt to halt the infringing activity immediately, rather than wait for a trial (a preliminary injunction). A court uses two factors to determine whether to grant a preliminary injunction: (1) Is the plaintiff likely to succeed in the lawsuit? and (2) Will the plaintiff suffer irreparable harm if the injunction is not granted? The patent owner may seek relief for a very short injunction known as a temporary restraining order, or TRO, which usually lasts only a few days or weeks. A temporary restraining order may be granted without notice to the infringer if it appears that immediate damage will result—for example, that evidence will be destroyed.

interference A costly, complex Patent and Trademark Office proceeding that determines who will get a patent when two or more applicants are claiming the same invention. It is basically a method of sorting out priority of inventorship. Occasionally an interference may involve a patent that has been in force for less than one year.

invention Any new article, machine, composition, or process or new use developed by a human.

lab notebook A system of documenting an invention that usually includes descriptions of the invention and novel features; procedures used in the building and testing of the invention; drawings, photos, or sketches of the invention; test results and conclusions; discussions of any known prior art references; and additional documentation such as correspondence and purchase receipts.

literal infringement Occurs if a defendant makes, sells, or uses the invention defined in the plaintiff's patent claim. In other words, the infringing product includes each and every component, part, or step in the patented invention. It is a literal infringement because the defendant's device is actually the same invention in the patent claim.

machine A device or things used for accomplishing a task; usually involves some activity or motion performed by working parts.

magistrate An officer of the court, who may exercise some of the authority of a federal district court judge, including the authority to conduct a jury or nonjury trial.

manufactures (sometimes termed "articles of manufacture") Items that have been made by human hands or by machines; may have working or moving parts as prime features.

means-plus-function clause (or means for clause) A provision in a patent claim in which the applicant does not specifically describe the structure of one of the items in the patent and instead describes the function of the item. Term is derived from the fact that the clause usually starts with the word "means."

new matter Any technical information, including dimensions, materials, and so on, that was not present in the patent application as originally filed. An applicant can never add new matter to an application (PTO Rule 118).

new-use invention A new and unobvious process or method for using an old and known invention.

nonobviousness A standard of patentability. In 1966, the U.S. Supreme Court established the steps for determining unobviousness in the case of *Graham v. John Deere*, 383 US 1 (1966).

Notice of Allowance A document issued when the examiner is convinced that the application meets the requirements of patentability. An issue fee is due within three months.

objects and advantages A phrase used to explain "what the invention accomplishes." Usually, the objects are also the invention's advantages, since those aspects are intended to be superior over prior art.

Office Action (OA, also known as Official Letter or Examiner's Action) Correspondence (usually including forms and a letter) from a patent examiner that describes what is wrong with the application and why it cannot be allowed. Generally, an OA will reject claims, list defects in the specifications or drawings, raise objections, or cite and enclose copies of relevant prior art demonstrating a lack of novelty or nonobviousness.

on-sale bar Prevents an inventor from acquiring patent protection if the application is filed more than one year from the date of sale, use, or offer of sale of the invention in the United States.

one-year rule A rule that requires an inventor to file a patent application within one year after selling, offering for sale, or commercially or publicly using or describing an invention. If an inventor fails to file within one year of such occurrence, the inventor is barred from obtaining a patent.

patent A grant from a government that confers upon an inventor the right to exclude others from making, using, selling, importing, or offering an invention for sale for a fixed period of time.

patent application A set of papers that describe an invention and that are suitable for filing in a patent office in order to apply for a patent on the invention.

Patent Application Declaration (PAD) A declaration that identifies the inventor or joint inventors and provides an attestation by the applicant that the inventor understands the contents of the claims and specification and has fully disclosed all material information. The Patent and Trademark Office provides a form for the PAD.

patent misuse A defense in patent infringement that prevents a patent owner who has abused patent law from enforcing patent rights. Common examples of misuse are violation of the antitrust laws or unethical business practices.

patent pending (also known as the "pendency period") Time between filing a patent application (or Provisional Patent Application) and issuance of the patent. The inventor has no patent rights during this period. However, when and if the patent later issues, the inventor will obtain the right to prevent the continuation of any infringing activity that started during the pendency period. If the application has been published by the Patent and Trademark Office during the pendency period and the infringer had notice, the applicant may later seek royalties for these infringements during the pendency period. It's a criminal offense to use the words "patent applied for" or "patent pending" (they mean the same thing) in any advertising if there's no active, applicable regular or provisional patent application on file.

patent prosecution The process of shepherding a patent application through the Patent Office.

Patent Rules of Practice Administrative regulations located in Volume 37 of the Code of Federal Regulations (37 CFR § 1).

pendency period (see "patent pending").

permanent injunction A durable injunction issued after a final judgment on the merits of the case; permanently restrains the defendant from engaging in the infringing activity.

Petition to Make Special An applicant can, under certain circumstances, have an application examined sooner than the normal course of Patent and Trademark Office examination (one to three years). This is accomplished by filing a "Petition to Make Special" (PTMS), together with a Supporting Declaration.

plant patent Covers plants that can be reproduced through the use of grafts and cuttings (asexual reproduction).

power of attorney A document that gives another person legal authority to act on your behalf. If an attorney is preparing an application on behalf of an inventor, a power of attorney should be executed to authorize the patent attorney or agent to act on behalf of the inventor. The power of attorney form may be combined with the Patent Application Declaration.

prior art The state of knowledge existing or publicly available either before the date of an invention or more than one year prior to the patent application date.

process (sometimes referred to as a "method") A way of doing or making things that involves more than purely mental manipulations.

Provisional Patent Application (PPA) An interim document that clearly explains how to make and use the invention. The PPA is equivalent to a reduction to practice (see below). If a regular patent application is filed within one year of filing the PPA, the inventor can use the PPA's filing date for the purpose of deciding whether a reference is prior art. In addition to an early filing date, an inventor may claim patent pending status for the one-year period following the filing of the PPA.

reduction to practice The point at which the inventor can demonstrate that the invention works for its intended purpose. Reduction to practice can be accomplished by building and testing the invention (actual reduction to practice) or by preparing a patent application or provisional patent application that shows how to make and use the invention and that it works (constructive reduction practice). In the event of a dispute or a challenge at the Patent and Trademark Office, invention documentation is essential in order to prove the "how and when" of conception and reduction to practice.

reissue application An application used to correct information in a patent. It is usually filed when a patent owner believes the claims are not broad enough, the claims are too broad (the applicant discovered a new reference), or there are significant errors in the specification. In these cases, the applicant seeks to correct the patent by filing an application to get the applicant's original patent reissued at any time during its term. The reissue patent will take the place of the applicant's original patent and expire the same time as the original patent would have expired. If the applicant wants to broaden the claims of the patent through a reissue application, the applicant must do so within two years from the date the original patent issued. There is a risk in filing a reissue application, because all of the claims of the original patent will be examined and can be rejected.

repair doctrine Affirmative defense based on the right of an authorized licensor of a patented device to repair and replace unpatented components. It also includes the right to sell materials used to repair or replace a patented invention. The defense does not apply for completely rebuilt inventions, unauthorized inventions, or items that are made or sold without authorization of the patent owner.

request for admission Request for a party to the lawsuit to admit the truthfulness of a statement.

Request for Continued Examination (RCE) A paper filed when a patent applicant wishes to continue prosecuting an application that has received a final Office Action. Filing the RCE with another filing fee effectively removes the final action so that the applicant can submit further amendments, for example, new claims, new arguments, a new declaration, or new references.

request for production of documents The way a party to a lawsuit obtains documents or other physical evidence from the other side.

sequence listing An attachment to a patent application used if a biotech invention includes a sequence listing of a nucleotide or amino acid sequence. The applicant attaches this information on separate sheets of paper and refers to the sequence listing in the application (see PTO Rule 77). If there is no sequence listing, the applicant states "Non applicable."

Small Entity Status A status that enables small entities to pay a reduced application fee. There are three types of small entities: (1) independent inventors, (2) nonprofit companies, and (3) small businesses. To qualify, an independent inventor must either own all rights or have transferred—or be obligated to transfer—rights to a small business or nonprofit organization. Nonprofit organizations are defined and listed in the Code of Federal Regulations and usually are educational institutions or charitable organizations. A small entity business is one with fewer than 500 employees. The number of employees is computed by averaging the number of full- and part-time employees during a fiscal year.

specification A patent application disclosure made by the inventor and drafted so that an individual skilled in the art to which the invention pertains could, when reading the patent, make and use the invention without needing further experiment. A specification is constructed of several sections. Collectively, these sections form a narrative that describes and distinguishes the invention. If it can later be proved that the inventor knew of a better way (or "best mode") and failed to disclose it, that failure could result in the loss of patent rights.

statute of limitations The legally prescribed time limit in which a lawsuit must be filed. In patent law there is no time limit (statute of limitations) for filing a patent infringement lawsuit, but monetary damages can be recovered only for infringements committed during the six years prior to the filing the lawsuit. For example if a patent owner sues after ten years of infringement, the owner cannot recover monetary damages for the first four years of infringement. Despite the fact that there is no law setting a time limit, courts will not permit a patent owner to sue for infringement if the owner has waited an unreasonable time to file the lawsuit ("laches").

statutory subject matter An invention that falls into one of the five statutory classes: process (method), machine, article of manufacture, composition, or "new use" of one of the first four.

successor liability Responsibility for infringement that is borne by a company that has purchased another company that is liable for infringements. In order for successor liability to occur, there must be an agreement between the companies to assume liability or a merger between the companies, or the purchaser must be a "continuation" of the purchased business. If the sale is made to escape liability and lacks any of the foregoing characteristics, liability will still attach.

tying A form of patent misuse in which, as a condition of a transaction, the buyer of a patented device must also purchase an additional product. For example, in one case a company had a patent on a machine that deposited salt tablets in canned food. Purchasers of the machine were also required to buy salt tablets from the patent owner. A party that commits patent misuse may have its patent invalidated, may have to pay monetary damages, or both.

utility patent The main type of patent, which covers inventions that function in a unique manner to produce a utilitarian result.

Index

A

Abstract, on patent title page, 89
Additions to patented device
    improvement patents, 64–65
    infringement and, 27–28
    new technologies in old products,
      65–67
Aerator patent litigation, 31–37
Aerogel, 66–67, 74–75
Amazon.com, company history, 40
Amazon.com v. Barnes & Noble, 37–43
Appeals
    Blackberry litigation, 225–27
    federal court of appeals, 29
Application
    drafting of, 12, 14, 172–74
    filing of, 14, 175
    provisional patent application,
      177–80
Application fees
    full patent, 176
    provisional patent, 180
Application Number, on patent title
    page, 88
Armstrong, Edwin, 76
Assignee, on patent title page, 88
Assignment
    buying a patent, 256–58
    of innovations to employer, 133–35
    license compared to, 244–47
    recording with the Patent Office, 258
Attorney-inventor meeting
    goals of, 172–74
    preparing for, 169–72

B

Background section, 96–98
Barnes & Noble, company history, 40
Barnes & Noble, Amazon.com v., 37–43
Best mode embodiment, 100
Bezos, Jeff, 1-click patent, 37–43
Blackberry litigation, 216–31
    appeals, 225–27
    bogus settlement, 225
    claim construction, 218–20
    damages awarded to NTP, 222, 223
    NTP offers a license, 221
    overview, 216–18
    post-trial activities, 223–25
    reexamination of NTP's patents,
      222–23
    RIM liable for infringement, 222
    settlement, 227
    timeline for, 229
Blocking patent, 238–39, 241
Broad scope patents, 74–76
Buying a patent. *See* Assignment

C

Chief financial officer, patent committee and, 151

Chief technology officer, patent committee and, 150

Claim chart, 119

Claims, 105–25
    analyzing for patentability, 155–57
    common terms, 123
    defined, 106
    fiber optic switch claims, 116–19
    importance of, 105–6
    independent and dependent, 108–9, 119–21
    infringement, 109, 119
    ladder claims, 109–15
    means plus function language, 123–25
    words used to describe, 121–23

Classification of patents
    Patent Office references for, 161
    on title page, 88

Clearance search warning, 165

Combining components, obviousness of, 58–60

Competitors, and patent worth, 72–73

Confidentiality
    employee and nonemployee, 138–39
    Patent Office and applications, 137

Continuation application, 187–88

Continuation-in-part patent application, 189

Convention Countries, 200

Copyrights, 81

Corporate counsel, patent committee and, 150

Cost-benefit analysis
    average expenses, 71–72
    competitors and, 72–73
    formula for, 78
    scope of the patent, 73–77
    of searches, 158–59
    value as defense or deterrent, 77

Costs of litigation
    challenging a patent, 42–43
    infringers' costs, 47
    See also Litigation

Cost tracking, 176–77
    foreign patents, 209–12

Cross References to Related Applications section, 94

Cubic zirconium, 51

D

Databases for patent searches, 162

Date of Patent
    filing date compared to, 90–91
    on patent title page, 89

Deceptive devices, 51

Deere & Co., history, 32

Defensive patents, 77

Delphion, 162

Dembiczak, Anita, 60–62

Dependent claims, 108, 119–21

Description of the Drawings section, 100–101

Design patents, 82

Detailed Description section, 102–4

Disclosure clause, employer ownership of innovations and, 134

Disclosure forms for inventions, 143–46

Disruptive technologies
Blackberry as, 221
scope of patents and, 76–77
Divisional applications, 188
Documentation policies, 139–47
failure to document, 146–47
importance of, 139
invention disclosure forms, 143–46
inventor's notebooks, 140–43
Dog chew patent litigation, 43–47
Double patenting, 191
Drawings
Description of the Drawings section,
100–101
on patent title page, 89
standards for, 92–94
Duty of trust, trade secrets and, 138

E

Embodiment, 100
Detailed Description section, 102–4
Employer ownership of innovations, 134
Engineering manager, patent committee
and, 150
EPO. *See* European Patent Office
Escape ladder example, 68–69
EUBusiness, 205
Europatents, 200
European Patent Office
filing with, 200–201
information resources, 205
searching databases of, 162
Examiners
obviousness and, 39
on patent title page, 89
prior art found by, 127

qualifications of, 183
rejection of application by, 182
work load of, 183
See also Office Action
Exclusivity, 249
Expiration, 14
failure to pay maintenance fees, 125
Eye surgery system litigation, 79–80

F

Federal Circuit, 29
Federation of International Trade
Associations, 205
Fees. *See* Application fees; Maintenance
fees
Fiber optic switch claims, 116–19
Fiduciary duty, trade secrets and, 138
Field of Invention section, 94, 95
Field of Search, on patent title page, 88
File wrappers, 126
Filing Date
issue date compared to, 90–91
on patent title page, 88
Foreign markets, resources for assessing,
205
Foreign patents
cost for individual country filings,
206–8
cost for PCT filing, 209–10
costs summarized, 211–12
how to file, 199–201
marketability-per-nation analysis,
202–4
one-year rule and, 198–99
Forged notebooks, 142–43
FreshPatents.com, 86

Furminator pet-grooming tool patent, 55–56

G

Gillette
    company history, 24
    Mach3 patent drawing, 25
Gillette v. Schick, 21–31
Glossary of terns, 259–69
Google, patent search engine, 86, 162

H

"Hired to invent," 135–36

I

ICO Suite, 162
Implied license, 242
Imprecision in language, 36, 45–46
Improvement patents, 64–65
    adding new technology to older
        devices, 65–67
    new use for old product, 67
Independent claims, 119–21
    infringing, 109
Independent contractors, ownership of
    innovations and, 136
Information asymmetry, 1
Infringement
    additions to patented device, 27–28
    costs of litigation, 42–43
    independent claims, 109, 119
Interferences, 190
Intl. Cl., on patent title page, 88
Invention, 12
Invention capture, 12, 140–46
Invention disclosure forms, 143–46

Inventors, on patent title page, 88
Inventor's notebooks, 140–43
Issue date. *See* Date of Patent

J

John Deere v. Toro, 31–37
Juicy Whip, 51, 54

L

Ladder claims, 109–15
Language. *See* Nature of language
    problem
Lasik eye surgery system litigation,
    79–80
Lawn aerator patent litigation, 31–37
Lemelson, Jerome, 188
LexPat, 162
Licensee, 236
Licensing patents, 247–56
    assignment compared to, 244–47
    exclusivity, 249
    flowchart of steps, 248
    implied license, 242
    option rights, 250
    problems with licensed patent,
        255–56
    royalties, 249
    technology evolution and, 255
    valuation of a patent, 237–39
    worksheet for agreement, 251–54
Licensor, 236
Lifecycle of a patent, 11–14
Litigation
    Blackberry case, 216–31
    common aspects of, 231–32
    defendant's options, 232–34

overview, 215–16
See also Costs of litigation

M

Maintenance fees, 14, 176
   failure to pay, 125
Marketability-per-nation analysis, 202–4
Marketing representative, patent
   committee and, 150–51
Means plus function claim language,
   123–25
Method and system patents, 64
   See also Blackberry litigation
Micropatent, 162
Microwave patent, 130–31
Mohsen, Amr, 142–43
Multiple patents, 62–63

N

National Trade Data Bank, 205
Nature of language problem
   Gillette razor description, 26, 27, 28
   imprecision in language, 36, 45–46
   and patent descriptions, 20–21
   unintelligible language, 44–46
   words used to describe claims,
      121–23
NDA (nondisclosure agreement), 137–38
Newness standard, 52–55
New use for old product, 67
Nondisclosure agreement (NDA), 137–38
Nonpublication Request, patent
   application, 137
Notebooks, 140–43
Novelty. *See* Newness standard
NTP. *See* Blackberry litigation

Numbers in patent drawings, 92–94

O

Obviousness
   combining components, 58–60
   description of, 39
   John Deere patent infringement case
      and, 32
   See also Unobviousness standard
Office Action, 182
   Written Responses to, 184, 185–87
1-click patent, 37–43
One-year rule, 53
   foreign patent filing and, 198–99
Option rights, 250
Ordinary innovation, 58

P

Paris Convention, 199–201
PatBase, 162
Patentability decisions
   improvement patents, 64–67
   manager's role, 50
   standards for, 52–64
   what is patentable, 50–52
Patentability study, components of,
   165–67, 168
Patent committees, 148–52
   marketability-per-nation analysis,
      202–4
Patent Cooperation Treaty (PCT),
   199–201
   cost of filing with, 209–10
Patent examiners *See* Examiners
Patent management, 16–17
   claims analysis, 155–57

documentation policies, 139–47
foreign filings, 201–4
invention disclosure forms, 143–46
limits on Written Responses, 185–87
minimum requirements, 132
patent committees, 148–52
patent transfer issues, 236–37
policies and ownership, 132–36
prosecution process management, 192–96
rejection and continuing the prosecution, 184–85
review process, 174–75
trade secret issues, 136–39
PatentMax, 162
Patent myths, 10–11
Patent Number, on patent title page, 89
Patent Office
application fees, 176
classification system of, 161
confidentiality of applications, 137
file wrappers, 126
problems retaining examiners, 183
provision application fees, 180
searching databases of, 86, 162
See also Examiners
"Patent pending"
defined, 154
provisional patent application, 177–80
stopping competitors with, 73
Patent principles, 7–10
Patent prosecution, 14
cost of, 182, 187–90
initial rejection by examiner, 182–84

management and tracking during, 192–96
post-prosecution activities, 190–91
worksheet for tracking, 93
Patent trolls, 46
PCT. See Patent Cooperation Treaty
Pet-grooming tool patent, 55–56
Plant patents, 82
Plastic leaf bag patent, 60–62
Post-prosecution activities, 190–91
Power of attorney clause, employer ownership of innovations and, 134
Preliminary injunction, 25
Prior art, 52–55
Background section of patent, 96–98
not all is included, 127–28
See also Searching patents
Product development lifecycle, 13, 14–16
Prosecution. See Patent prosecution
Provisional patent application, 177–80
Pumpkin leaf bag patent, 60–62

R
Raytheon, microwave patent, 130–31
Razor patent litigation, 21–31
RCE (Request for Continued Examination), 187–88
Reading a patent
applications, 84
Background section, 96–98
claims, 105–25
Description of the Drawings section, 100–101
Detailed Description section, 102–4
drawings, 91–94
Field of Invention section, 94, 95

Related Applications section, 94
Summary section, 98–100
title page, 86–89
Reexamination, 126, 191
Reference number in patent drawings, 92, 94
References Cited
on patent title page, 88
See also Prior art
Reissued patents, 126, 196
Rejection of application
initial rejection, 182–84
managing the prosecution, 184–85
Related Applications section, 94
Request for Continued Examination (RCE), 187–88
Research in Motion. *See* Blackberry litigation
RIM. *See* Blackberry litigation
Royalties, 249

S

Scanner patents, 56–57
Schick, company history, 24
Schick, Gillette v., 21–31
Scope of the patent, 73–77
Searching patents
clearance search warning, 165
computer search problems, 160–61
cost-benefit analysis of doing, 158–59
disclosure of results required, 164–65
online sources, 86
resources for, 162
undiscovered information, 163
Shop right, 133
Signatures for notebooks, 140–41

Specification
importance of, 115–16
Patent Office definition, 104
Spencer, Percy, 130–31
Star Trek transporter example, 62–63
State laws, limits on employer ownership of innovations, 135
"Submarine patents," 90, 188
Substitution inventions, and improvement patents, 64–65
Summary of the Invention section, 98–100
Sunbeam clipper blade, 55–56
Supreme Court, patent cases and, 29
Syscan scanner patents, 56–57
System and method patents, 64
See also Blackberry litigation

T

Telefex gas pedal patent, 58–60
3M, violation of one-year rule by, 53
Time for filing, 53
See also One-year rule
Title page, 86–89
Toro Company
aerator patent drawing, 33
cam-based system drawing, 35
history, 32
Toro, John Deere v., 31–37
Trademarks, 81
Trade secrets, 70
patent management system and, 136–39
Transfers of patents
assignment or license, 244–47
buying a patent, 256–58

buying the product instead of a license, 242–43
licensing a patent, 247–56
management issues, 236–37
needs analysis, 239–40
possibility of lawsuit, 243–44
valuation of patent, 237–39

U

Unintelligible language, 44–46
Unobviousness standard
    determining, 55–62
    See also Obviousness
U.S. Cl., on patent title page, 88
U.S. Commercial Service, 205
U.S. Dept. of Commerce, 205
U.S. economy and patents, 6–7
Usefulness, 51–52
USPTO. *See* Patent Office

U.S. Small Business Administration, 205
Utility patents, rules for, 51–52

V

Valuation of patent, 237–39
VIBES, 205

W

Witnesses, for inventor's notebooks,
    140–41
Worksheet for prosecution tracking, 193
World Trade Centers Association, 205
Worldwide patent myth, 208
Written agreements
    costs of continuation responses, 187
    for patent ownership, 133–35
Written Responses, to Office Actions,
    184, 185–87

CATALOG
...more from Nolo

BUSINESS	PRICE	CODE
Business Buyout Agreements (Book w/CD)	$49.99	BSAG
The California Nonprofit Corporation Kit (Binder w/CD)	$69.99	CNP
California Workers' Comp: How to Take Charge When You're Injured on the Job	$34.99	WORK
The Complete Guide to Buying a Business (Book w/CD)	$24.99	BUYBU
The Complete Guide to Selling a Business (Book w/CD)	$34.99	SELBU
Consultant & Independent Contractor Agreements (Book w/CD)	$29.99	CICA
The Corporate Records Handbook (Book w/CD)	$69.99	CORMI
Create Your Own Employee Handbook (Book w/CD)	$49.99	EMHA
Dealing With Problem Employees	$44.99	PROBM
Deduct It! Lower Your Small Business Taxes	$34.99	DEDU
Effective Fundraising for Nonprofits	$24.99	EFFN
The Employer's Legal Handbook	$39.99	EMPL
The Essential Guide to Family and Medical Leave (Book w/CD)	$39.99	FMLA
The Essential Guide to Federal Employment Laws	$39.99	FEMP
The Essential Guide to Workplace Investigations (Book w/CD)	$39.99	NVST
Every Nonprofit's Guide to Publishing (Book w/CD)	$29.99	EPNO
Form a Partnership (Book w/CD)	$39.99	PART
Form Your Own Limited Liability Company (Book w/CD)	$44.99	LIAB
Home Business Tax Deductions: Keep What You Earn	$34.99	DEHB
How to Form a Nonprofit Corporation (Book w/CD)—National Edition	$49.99	NNP
How to Form a Nonprofit Corporation in California (Book w/CD)	$49.99	NON
How to Form Your Own California Corporation (Binder w/CD)	$59.99	CACI
How to Form Your Own California Corporation (Book w/CD)	$39.99	CCOR
How to Write a Business Plan (Book w/CD)	$34.99	SBS
Incorporate Your Business (Book w/CD)	$49.99	NIBS
Investors in Your Backyard (Book w/CD)	$24.99	FINBUS
The Job Description Handbook (Book w/CD)	$29.99	JOB
Legal Guide for Starting & Running a Small Business	$34.99	RUNS
Legal Forms for Starting & Running a Small Business (Book w/CD)	$29.99	RUNSF
LLC or Corporation?	$24.99	CHENT
The Manager's Legal Handbook	$39.99	ELBA
Marketing Without Advertising	$20.00	MWAD
Music Law: How to Run Your Band's Business (Book w/CD)	$39.99	ML
Negotiate the Best Lease for Your Business	$24.99	LESP
Nolo's Quick LLC	$29.99	LLCQ
Patent Savvy for Managers: Spot and Protect Valuable Innovations in Your Company	$29.99	PATM
The Performance Appraisal Handbook (Book w/CD)	$29.99	PERF
The Progressive Discipline Handbook (Book w/CD)	$34.99	SDBH
Small Business in Paradise: Working for Yourself in a Place You Love	$19.99	SPAR
The Small Business Start-up Kit (Book w/CD)	$24.99	SMBU
The Small Business Start-up Kit for California (Book w/CD)	$24.99	OPEN
Starting & Building a Nonprofit: A Practical Guide (Book w/CD)	$29.99	SNON
Starting & Running a Successful Newsletter or Magazine	$29.99	MAG
Tax Deductions for Professionals	$34.99	DEPO
Tax Savvy for Small Business	$36.99	SAVVY
Whoops! I'm in Business	$19.99	WHOO
Working for Yourself: Law & Taxes for Independent Contractors, Freelancers & Consultants	$39.99	WAGE
Working With Independent Contractors (Book w/CD)	$29.99	HICI
Your Limited Liability Company: An Operating Manual (Book w/CD)	$49.99	LOP
Your Rights in the Workplace	$29.99	YRW

Prices subject to change.

ORDER 24 HOURS A DAY @ www.nolo.com
Call 800-728-3555 • Mail or fax the order form in this book

CONSUMER	PRICE	CODE
How to Win Your Personal Injury Claim	$29.99	PICL
Nolo's Encyclopedia of Everyday Law	$29.99	EVL
Nolo's Guide to California Law	$24.99	CLAW
Your Little Legal Companion (Hardcover)	$9.95	ANNI

ESTATE PLANNING & PROBATE

	PRICE	CODE
8 Ways to Avoid Probate	$19.99	PRAV
The Busy Family's Guide to Estate Planning (Book w/CD)	$24.99	FAM
Estate Planning Basics	$21.99	ESPN
The Executor's Guide: Settling a Loved One's Estate or Trust	$34.99	EXEC
Get It Together: Organize Your Records so Your Family Won't Have To (Book w/CD)	$21.99	GET
How to Probate an Estate in California	$49.99	PAE
Make Your Own Living Trust (Book w/CD)	$39.99	LITR
Nolo's Simple Will Book (Book w/CD)	$36.99	SWIL
Plan Your Estate	$44.99	NEST
Quick & Legal Will Book (Book w/CD)	$19.99	QUIC
Special Needs Trust: Protect Your Child's Financial Future (Book w/CD)	$34.99	SPNT

FAMILY MATTERS

	PRICE	CODE
Always Dad: Being a Great Father During & After a Divorce	$16.99	DIFA
Building a Parenting Agreement That Works	$24.99	CUST
The Complete IEP Guide	$34.99	IEP
Divorce & Money: How to Make the Best Financial Decisions During Divorce	$34.99	DIMO
Divorce Without Court: A Guide to Mediation & Collaborative Divorce	$29.99	DWCT
Do Your Own California Adoption (Book w/CD)	$34.99	ADOP
Every Dog's Legal Guide: A Must-Have for Your Owner	$19.99	DOG
Get a Life: You Don't Need a Million to Retire Well	$24.99	LIFE
The Guardianship Book for California	$34.99	GB
A Judge's Guide to Divorce (Book w/CD)	$24.99	JDIV
A Legal Guide for Lesbian and Gay Couples (Book w/CD)	$34.99	LG
Living Together: A Legal Guide for Unmarried Couples (Book w/CD)	$34.99	LTK
Nolo's Essential Guide to Divorce	$24.99	NODV
Nolo's IEP Guide: Learning Disabilities	$29.99	IELD
Parent Savvy	$19.99	PRNT
Prenuptial Agreements: How to Write a Fair & Lasting Contract (Book w/CD)	$34.99	PNUP
Work Less, Live More	$17.99	RECL
The Work Less, Live More Workbook: Get Ready for Semi-Retirement (Book w/CD)	$19.99	RECW

GOING TO COURT

	PRICE	CODE
Beat Your Ticket: Go To Court & Win—National Edition	$21.99	BEYT
The Criminal Law Handbook: Know Your Rights, Survive the System	$39.99	KYR
Everybody's Guide to Small Claims Court—National Edition	$29.99	NSCC
Everybody's Guide to Small Claims Court in California	$29.99	CSCC
Fight Your Ticket & Win in California	$29.99	FYT
How to Change Your Name in California	$34.99	NAME
Legal Research: How to Find & Understand the Law	$39.99	LRES
Nolo's Deposition Handbook	$34.99	DEP
Represent Yourself in Court: How to Prepare & Try a Winning Case	$39.99	RYC
Win Your Lawsuit: A Judge's Guide to Representing Yourself in California Superior Court	$39.99	SLWY

HOMEOWNERS, LANDLORDS & TENANTS

	PRICE	CODE
Buying a Second Home (Book w/CD)	$24.99	SCND
The California Landlord's Law Book: Rights & Responsibilities (Book w/CD)	$44.99	LBRT
The California Landlord's Law Book: Evictions (Book w/CD)	$44.99	LBEV
California Tenants' Rights	$29.99	CTEN
Deeds for California Real Estate	$27.99	DEED
Every Landlord's Legal Guide (Book w/CD)	$44.99	ELLI
Every Landlord's Guide to Finding Great Tenants (Book w/CD)	$19.99	FIND
Every Landlord's Tax Deduction Guide	$34.99	DELL
Every Tenant's Legal Guide	$29.99	EVTEN

ORDER 24 HOURS A DAY @ www.nolo.com
Call 800-728-3555 • Mail or fax the order form in this book

	PRICE	CODE
For Sale by Owner in California (Book w/CD)	$29.99	FSBO
How to Buy a House in California	$34.99	BHCA
Leases & Rental Agreements (Book w/CD)	$29.99	LEAR
Neighbor Law: Fences, Trees, Boundaries & Noise	$26.99	NEI
Nolo's Essential Guide to Buying Your First Home (Book w/CD)	$24.99	HTBH
Renters' Rights: the Basics	$24.99	RENT

IMMIGRATION

	PRICE	CODE
Becoming A U.S. Citizen: A Guide to the Law, Exam and Interview	$24.99	USCIT
Fiancé & Marriage Visas	$34.99	IMAR
How to Get a Green Card	$29.99	GRN
U.S. Immigration Made Easy	$39.99	IMEZ

MONEY MATTERS

	PRICE	CODE
101 Law Forms for Personal Use (Book w/CD)	$29.99	SPOT
Chapter 13 Bankruptcy: Repay Your Debts	$39.99	CHB
Credit Repair (Book w/CD)	$24.99	CREP
How to File for Chapter 7 Bankruptcy	$29.99	HFB
IRAs, 401(k)s & Other Retirement Plans: Taking Your Money Out	$34.99	RET
Lower Taxes in Seven Easy Steps	$16.99	LTES
The New Bankruptcy: Will It Work for You?	$21.99	FIBA
Nolo's Guide to Social Security Disability (Book w/CD)	$29.99	QSS
Solve Your Money Troubles	$19.99	MT
Stand Up to the IRS	$29.99	SIRS
Surviving An IRS Tax Audit	$24.95	SAUD

PATENTS AND COPYRIGHTS

	PRICE	CODE
All I Need is Money: How to Finance Your Invention	$19.99	FINA
The Copyright Handbook: What Every Writer Needs to Know (Book w/CD)	$39.99	COHA
Getting Permission: How to License & Clear Copyrighted Materials Online & Off (Book w/CD)	$34.99	RIPER
How to Make Patent Drawings	$29.99	DRAW
The Inventor's Notebook	$24.99	INOT
Legal Guide to Web & Software Development (Book w/CD)	$44.99	SFT
Nolo's Patents for Beginners	$24.99	QPAT
Patent, Copyright & Trademark: An Intellectual Property Desk Reference	$39.99	PCTM
Patent It Yourself	$49.99	PAT
Patent Pending in 24 Hours	$34.99	PEND
Patent Savvy For Managers: Spot & Protect Valuable Innovations in Your Company	$29.99	PATM
Patenting Art & Entertainment: New Strategies for Protecting Creative Ideas	$39.99	PATAE
Profit from Your Idea (Book w/CD)	$34.99	LICE
The Public Domain	$34.99	PUBL
Trademark: Legal Care for Your Business and Product Name	$39.99	TRD
What Every Inventor Needs to Know About Business & Taxes (Book w/CD)	$21.99	ILAX

SENIORS

	PRICE	CODE
Long-Term Care: How to Plan & Pay for It	$19.99	ELD
Social Security, Medicare & Goverment Pensions	$29.99	SOA

SOFTWARE Call or check our website at www.nolo.com for special discounts on Software!

	PRICE	CODE
Incorporator Pro	89.99	STNC1
LLC Maker—Windows	$89.95	LLP1
Patent Pending Now!	$119.99	PP1
PatentEase—Windows	$349.00	PEAS
Personal RecordKeeper 5.0 CD—Windows	$59.95	RKD5

Special Upgrade Offer

Save 35% on the latest edition of your Nolo book

Because laws and legal procedures change often, we update our books regularly. To help keep you up-to-date, we are extending this special upgrade offer. Cut out and mail the title portion of the cover of your old Nolo book and we'll give you 35% off the retail price of the New Edition of that book when you purchase directly from Nolo. This offer is to individuals only. Prices and offer subject to change without notice.

Order Form

Name

Address

City

State, Zip

Daytime Phone

E-mail

Our "No-Hassle" Guarantee

Return anything you buy directly from Nolo for any reason and we'll cheerfully refund your purchase price. No ifs, ands or buts.

☐ Check here if you do not wish to receive mailings from other companies

Item Code	Quantity	Item	Unit Price	Total Price

Method of payment

☐ Check   ☐ VISA

☐ American Express

☐ MasterCard

☐ Discover Card

Subtotal	
Add your local sales tax (California only)	
Shipping: RUSH $12, Basic $6 (See below)	
"I bought 2, ship it to me FREE!"(Ground shipping only)	
TOTAL	

Account Number

Expiration Date

Signature

Shipping and Handling

Rush Delivery—Only $12

We'll ship any order to any street address in the U.S. by UPS 2nd Day Air* for only $12!

* Order by 9:30 AM Pacific Time and get your order in 2 business days. Orders placed after 9:30 AM Pacific Time will arrive in 3 business days. P.O. boxes and S.F. Bay Area use basic shipping. Alaska and Hawaii use 2nd Day Air or Priority Mail.

Basic Shipping—$6

Use for P.O. Boxes, Northern California and Ground Service.

Allow 1-2 weeks for delivery.

U.S. addresses only.

For faster service, use your credit card and our toll-free numbers

Call our customer service group Monday thru Friday 7am to 6pm PST

Phone
1-800-728-3555

Fax
1-800-645-0895

Mail
Nolo
950 Parker St.
Berkeley, CA 94710

NOLO

Get the Latest in the Law

 Nolo's Legal Updater
We'll send you an email whenever a new edition of your book is published!
Sign up at **www.nolo.com/legalupdater**.

 Updates at Nolo.com
Check **www.nolo.com/update** to find recent changes in the law that
affect the current edition of your book.

 Nolo Customer Service
To make sure that this edition of the book is the most recent one, call us at
800-728-3555 and ask one of our friendly customer service representatives
(7:00 am to 6:00 pm PST, weekdays only). Or find out at **www.nolo.com**.

Complete the Registration & Comment Card ...
... and we'll do the work for you! Just indicate your preferences below:

Registration & Comment Card

NAME _____ DATE _____

ADDRESS _____

CITY _____ STATE _____ ZIP _____

PHONE _____ EMAIL _____

COMMENTS _____

WAS THIS BOOK EASY TO USE?   (VERY EASY)   5   4   3   2   1   (VERY DIFFICULT)

☐ Yes, you can quote me in future Nolo promotional materials. *Please include phone number above.*

☐ Yes, send me **Nolo's Legal Updater** via email when a new edition of this book is available.

Yes, I want to sign up for the following email newsletters:

   ☐ **NoloBriefs** (monthly)
   ☐ **Nolo's Special Offer** (monthly)
   ☐ **Nolo's BizBriefs** (monthly)
   ☐ **Every Landlord's Quarterly** (four times a year)

☐ Yes, you can give my contact info to carefully selected
partners whose products may be of interest to me.

PATM1

Nolo
950 Parker Street
Berkeley, CA 94710-9867
www.nolo.com

YOUR LEGAL COMPANION